W9-CTZ-429

WELCOME
TO THE
MONKEY
HOUSE

KURT VONNEGUT, JR.

A DELL BOOK

Published by
DELL PUBLISHING CO., INC., 750 Third Avenue
New York, New York 10017

Printed in the U.S.A.
First Dell printing—January 1970
Fifth Dell printing—January 1971
Tenth Dell printing—February 1972
Fifteenth Dell printing—January 1973

*Acknowledgment is made to the following magazines and publishers
in whose pages these stories first appeared:*
The Atlantic Monthly: "Der Arme Dolmetscher"
(originally published under the title "Das
Ganz Arm Dolmetscher").
Collier's Magazine: "The Foster Portfolio,"
"All the King's Horses," "Tom Edison's Shaggy
Dog," "More Stately Mansions," "Report on the
Barnhouse Effect," "Epicac," and "The Euphio Question."
Cosmopolitan: "Next Door,"
"The Manned Missiles," and "Adam."
Esquire: "Deer in the Works."
Fantasy and Science Fiction Magazine:
"Harrison Bergeron."
Galaxy Publishing Corporation: "Unready To
Wear" and "Tomorrow and Tomorrow and
Tomorrow" (originally published under the
title "The Big Trip Up Yonder").
Ladies Home Journal: "Long Walk to Forever,"
"D.P.," and "Go Back to Your Precious Wife and Son."
The New York Times: "New Dictionary" (originally
published under the title "The Random House Dictionary").
Playboy: "Welcome to the Monkey House."
Saturday Evening Post: "Who Am I This Time?,"
"Miss Temptation," "The Lie," and
"The Kid Nobody Could Handle."
Venure: "Where I Live" (originally published
under the title "So You've Never Been to Barnstable").

FOR
KNOX BURGER
TEN DAYS OLDER THAN I AM.
HE HAS BEEN A VERY GOOD
FATHER TO ME.

"Beware of all enterprises
that require new clothes."

THOREAU

CONTENTS

PREFACE

HERE IT IS, a retrospective exhibition of the shorter works of Kurt Vonnegut, Jr.—and Vonnegut is still very much with us, and I am still very much Vonnegut. Somewhere in Germany is a stream called the Vonne. That is the source of my curious name.

I have been a writer since 1949. I am self-taught. I have no theories about writing that might help others. When I write I simply become what I seemingly must become. I am six feet two and weigh nearly two hundred pounds and am badly coordinated, except when I swim. All that borrowed meat does the writing.

In the water I am beautiful.

My father and paternal grandfather were architects in Indianapolis, Indiana, where I was born. My maternal grandfather owned a brewery there. He won a Gold Medal at the Paris Exposition with his beer, which was Lieber Lager. The secret ingredient was coffee.

My only brother, eight years older than I, is a successful scientist. His special field is physics as it relates to clouds. His name is Bernard, and he is funnier than I am. I remember a letter he wrote after his first child, Peter, was born and brought home. "Here I am," that letter began, "cleaning shit off of practically everything."

My only sister, five years older than I, died when she was forty. She was over six feet tall, too, by an angstrom unit or so. She was heavenly to look at, and graceful, both in and out of water. She was a sculptress. She was christened "Alice," but she used to deny that she was really an Alice. I agreed. Everybody agreed. Sometime in a dream maybe I will find out what her real name was.

Her dying words were, "No pain." Those are good dying words. It was cancer that killed her.

And I realize now that the two main themes of my novels were stated by my siblings: "Here I am cleaning shit off of practically everything" and "No pain." The contents of this book are samples of work I sold in order to finance the writing of the novels. Here one finds the fruits of Free Enterprise.

I used to be a public relations man for General Electric, and then I became a free-lance writer of so-called "slick fiction," a lot of it science fiction. Whether I improved myself morally by making that change I am not prepared to say. That is one of the questions I mean to ask God on Judgment Day—along with the one about what my sister's name really was.

That could easily be next Wednesday.

I have already put the question to a college professor, who, climbing down into his Mercedes-Benz 300SL *gran turismo,* assured me that public relations men and slick writers were equally vile, in that they both buggered truth for money.

I asked him what the very lowest grade of fiction was, and he told me, "Science fiction." I asked where he was bound in such a rush, and learned that he had to catch a Fan-Jet. He was to speak at a meeting of the Modern Language Association in Honolulu the next morning. Honolulu was three thousand miles away.

My sister smoked too much. My father smoked too much. My mother smoked too much. I smoke too much. My brother used to smoke too much, and then he gave it up, which was a miracle on the order of the loaves and fishes.

And one time a pretty girl came up to me at a cocktail party, and she asked me, "What are you doing these days?"

"I am committing suicide by cigarette," I replied.

She thought that was reasonably funny. I didn't. I thought it was hideous that I should scorn life that much, sucking away on cancer sticks. My brand is Pall Mall. The authentic suicides ask for Pall Malls. The dilettantes ask for Pell Mells.

I have a relative who is secretly writing a history of parts of my family. He has showed me some of it, and he told me this about my grandfather, the architect: "He died in his forties—and I think he was just as glad to be out of it." By "it," of course, he meant life in Indianapolis—and there is that yellow streak about life in me, too.

The public health authorities never mention the main reason many Americans have for smoking heavily, which is that smoking is a fairly sure, fairly honorable form of suicide.

It is disgraceful that I should ever have wanted out of "it," and I don't want out any more. I have six children, three of my own and three of my sister's. They've turned out gloriously. My first marriage worked, and continues to work. My wife is still beautiful.

I never knew a writer's wife who wasn't beautiful.

In honor of the marriage that worked, I include in this collection a sickeningly slick love story from *The Ladies Home Journal*, God help us, entitled by them "The Long Walk to Forever." The title I gave it, I think, was "Hell to Get Along With."

It describes an afternoon I spent with my wife-to-be. Shame, shame, to have lived scenes from a woman's magazine.

The New Yorker once said that a book of mine, *God Bless You, Mr. Rosewater*, was ". . . a series of narcissistic giggles." This may be another. Perhaps it would be helpful to the reader to imagine me as the White Rock girl, kneeling on a boulder in a nightgown, either looking for minnows or adoring her own reflection.

WHERE I LIVE

NOT VERY LONG AGO, an encylopedia salesman stopped by America's oldest library building, which is the lovely Sturgis Library in Barnstable Village, on Cape Cod's north shore. And he pointed out to the easily alarmed librarian that the library's most recent general reference work was a 1938 *Britannica,* backstopped by a 1910 *Americana.* He said many important things had happened since 1938, naming, among others, penicillin and Hitler's invasion of Poland.

He was advised to take his astonishment to some of the library's directors. He was given their names and addresses. There was a Cabot on the list—and a Lowell and a Kittredge, and some others. The librarian told him that he had a chance of catching several directors all at once, if he would go to the Barnstable Yacht Club. So he went down the narrow yacht club road, nearly broke his neck as he hit a series of terrific bumps put in the road to discourage speeders, to kill them, if possible.

He wanted a martini, wondered if a nonmember could get service at the bar. He was appalled to discover that the club was nothing but a shack fourteen feet wide and thirty feet long, a touch of the Ozarks in Massachusetts. It contained an hilariously warped ping-pong table, a wire lost-and-found basket with sandy, fragrant contents, and an upright piano that had been under a leak in the roof for years.

There wasn't any bar, any telephone, any electricity. There weren't any members there, either. To cap it all, there wasn't a drop of water in the harbor. The tide, which can be as great as fourteen feet, was utterly out.

And the so-called yachts, antique wooden Rhodes 18's, *Beetlecats,* and a couple of *Boston Whalers,* were resting on the bluish-brown glurp of the emptied harbor's floor. Clouds of gulls and terns were yelling about all that glurp, and about all the good things in it they were finding to eat.

A few men were out there, too, digging clams as fat as partridges from the rim of Sandy Neck, the ten-mile-long sand finger that separates the harbor from the ice-cold bay. And ducks and geese and herons and other waterfowl were out there, too, teemingly, in the great salt marsh that bounds the harbor on the west. And, near the harbor's narrow mouth, a yawl from Marblehead with a six-foot keel lay on her side, waiting for the water to come back in again. She should never have come to Barnstable Village, not with a keel like that.

The salesman, very depressed, insensitive to the barbarous beauty all around him, went to lunch. Since he was in the seat of the most booming county in New England, Barnstable County, and since the boom was a tourist boom, he had reason to expect something mildly voluptuous in the way of a place to eat. What he had to settle for, though, was a chromium stool at a formica counter in an aggressively un-cute, un-colonial institution called the Barnstable News Store, another Ozarks touch, an Ozarks department store. The motto of the place: "If it's any good, we've got it. If it's no good, we've sold it."

After lunch, he went trustee-hunting again, was told to try the village museum, which is in the old brick Customs House. The building itself is a memorial to long-gone days when the harbor was used by fair-sized ships, before it filled up with all that bluish-brown glurp. There was no trustee there, and the exhibits were excruciatingly boring. The salesman found himself strangling on apathy, an affliction epidemic among casual visitors to Barnstable Village.

He took the customary cure, which was to jump into his car and roar off toward the cocktail lounges, motor courts, bowling alleys, gift shoppes, and pizzerias of Hyannis, the commercial heart of Cape Cod. He there worked off his frustrations on a miniature golf course called Playland. At that time, that particular course had a pathetic, maddening feature typical of the random butchery of the Cape's south shore. The course was built on the lawn of what had once been an American Legion Post—and, right in the middle of the cunning little bridges and granulated cork fairways was a Sherman tank, set there in simpler and less enterprising days as a memorial to the veterans of World War Two.

The memorial has since been moved, but it is still on the south side, where it is bound to be engulfed by indignities again.

The dignity of the tank would be a lot safer in Barnstable Village, but the village would never accept it. It has a policy of never accepting anything. As a happy consequence, it changes about as fast as the rules of chess.

The biggest change in recent years has taken place at the polls. Until six years ago, the Democratic poll watchers and the Republican poll watchers were all Republicans. Now the Democratic poll watchers are Democrats. The consequences of this revolution have not been nearly as awful as expected—so far.

Another break with the past has to do with the treasury of the local amateur theatrical society, the Barnstable Comedy Club. The club had a treasurer who, once a month for thirty years, angrily refused to say what the balance was, for fear that the club would spend it foolishly. He resigned last year. The new treasurer announced a balance of four hundred dollars and some odd cents, and the membership blew it all on a new curtain the color of spoiled salmon. This ptomaine curtain, incidentally, made its debut during a production of *The Caine Mutiny Court Martial* in which Captain Queeg did *not* nervously rattle steel balls in his hand. The balls were eliminated on the theory that they were suggestive.

Another big change took place about sixty years ago, when it was discovered that tuna were good to eat. Barnstable fishermen used to call them "horse mackerel," and curse whenever they caught one. Still cursing, they would chop it up and throw it back into the bay as a warning to other horse mackerel. Out of courage or plain stupidity, the tuna did not go away, and now make possible

a post-Labor Day festival called the Barnstable Tuna
Derby. Sportsmen with reels as big as courthouse clocks
come from all over the Eastern seaboard for the event,
the villagers are always mystified as to what brought them.
And nobody ever catches anything.

Another discovery that still lies in the future for the
villagers to make and to learn to live with is that mussels
can be eaten without causing instant death. Barnstable
Harbor is in places clogged with them. They are never
disturbed. One reason for their being ignored, perhaps, is
that the harbor abounds in two other delicacies far
simpler to prepare—striped bass and clams. To get clams,
one can scratch almost anywhere when the tide is out. To
get bass, one follows the birds, looks for cone-shaped
formations of them, casts his lure to the place where the
cone points. Bass will be feeding there.

As for what else the future holds: Few Cape villages
have much chance of coming through the present greedy,
tasteless boom with their souls intact. H. L. Mencken once
said something to the effect that "Nobody ever went broke
overestimating the vulgarity of the American people," and
fortunes now being made out of the vulgarization of the
Cape surely bear this out. The soul of Barnstable Village
just might survive.

For one thing, it is not a hollow village, with everything
for rent, with half of the houses empty in the winter. Most
of the people live there all year round, and most of them
aren't old, and most of them work—as carpenters, sales-
men, masons, architects, teachers, writers, and what have
you. It is a classless society, a sometimes affectionate and
sentimental one.

And these full houses, often riddled by termites and dry
rot, but good, probably, for a few hundred years more,
have been built chockablock along Main Street since the
end of the Civil War. Developers find very little room in
which to work their pious depredations. There is a seeming vast green meadow to the west, but this is salt marsh,
the bluish-brown glurp capped by a mat of salt hay. It was
this natural hay, by the way, that tempted settlers down
from Plymouth in 1639. The marsh, laced by deep creeks

that can be explored by small boats, can never be built upon by anyone sane. It goes underwater at every moon tide, and is capable of supporting a man and his dog, and not much more.

Speculators and developers got very excited for a while about the possibility of improving Sandy Neck, the long, slender barrier of spectacular dunes that bounds the harbor on the north. There are grotesque forests of dead trees out there, trees suffocated by sand, then unburied again. And the outer beach, for all practical purposes infinite, puts the beach of Acapulco to shame. Surprisingly, too, fresh water can be had out there from quite shallow wells. But the local government, thank God, is buying up all of Sandy Neck but the tip, at the harbor mouth, and is making it a public park to be kept unimproved forever.

There is a tiny settlement on the tip of the neck, the tip that the government is not taking over. It is clustered around the abandoned lighthouse, a lighthouse that was once needed when there was water enough around to let big ships come and go. The bleached and tacky settlement can be reached only by boat or beach buggy. There is no electricity there, no telephone. It is a private resort. Less than a mile from Barnstable Village, the tip of the neck is where many villagers go when they need a vacation.

And all of the anachronistic, mildly xenophobic, charming queernesses of Barnstable Village might entitle it to the epithet, "Last Stronghold of the True Cape Codders," if it weren't for one thing: Hardly anyone in the village was born on Cape Cod. Just as petrified wood is formed by minerals slowly replacing organic materials, so has the present-day petrified Barnstable been formed by persons from Evanston and Louisville and Boston and Pittsburgh and God-only-knows-where-else, slowly replacing authentic rural Yankees.

If the real Cape Codders could rise from their churchyard graves, cast aside their beautifully lettered slate headstones, and attend a meeting of the Barnstable Village Civic Association, they would approve of the proceedings. Every proposal that has ever come before the organization has been hotly debated and voted down, except that a new siren be bought for the rescue truck. The siren goes *bweep-bweep-bweep* instead of *rowrrr,* and is guaranteed to be audible at a distance of three miles.

The library, incidentally, now has a new *Britannica,* and a new *Americana,* too, purchases it made effortlessly, since it has money coming out of its ears. But so far, the school marks of the children and the conversation of the adults have not conspicuously improved.

Since the village exists for itself, and not for passersby, and since it specializes in hastening tourists on to paradises elsewhere, visitors play hell finding anything to like about it. For a quick sample of how good it can be, a visitor might stop off at St. Mary's Church on Main Street, which has, unadvertised anywhere, the most enchanting church garden in America. The garden is the work of one man, Robert Nicholson, an Episcopalian minister, a good man who died young.

At a village cocktail party one time—and the villagers *do* drink a lot—Father Nicholson was talking to a Roman Catholic and a Jew, trying to find a word to describe the underlying spiritual unity of Barnstable. He found one. "We're Druids," he said.

(1964)

HARRISON BERGERON

THE YEAR WAS 2081, and everybody was finally equal. They weren't only equal before God and the law. They were equal every which way. Nobody was smarter than anybody else. Nobody was better looking than anybody else. Nobody was stronger or quicker than anybody else. All this equality was due to the 211th, 212th, and 213th Amendments to the Constitution, and to the unceasing vigilance of agents of the United States Handicapper General.

Some things about living still weren't quite right, though. April, for instance, still drove people crazy by not being springtime. And it was in that clammy month that the H-G men took George and Hazel Bergeron's fourteen-year-old son, Harrison, away.

It was tragic, all right, but George and Hazel couldn't think about it very hard. Hazel had a perfectly average intelligence, which meant she couldn't think about anything except in short bursts. And George, while his intelligence was way above normal, had a little mental handicap radio in his ear. He was required by law to wear it at all times. It was tuned to a government transmitter. Every twenty seconds or so, the transmitter would send out some sharp noise to keep people like George from taking unfair advantage of their brains.

George and Hazel were watching television. There were tears on Hazel's cheeks, but she'd forgotten for the moment what they were about.

On the television screen were ballerinas.

A buzzer sounded in George's head. His thoughts fled in panic, like bandits from a burglar alarm.

7

"That was a real pretty dance, that dance they just did," said Hazel.

"Huh?" said George.

"That dance—it was nice," said Hazel.

"Yup," said George. He tried to think a little about the ballerinas. They weren't really very good—no better than anybody else would have been, anyway. They were burdened with sashweights and bags of birdshot, and their faces were masked, so that no one, seeing a free and graceful gesture or a pretty face, would feel like something the cat drug in. George was toying with the vague notion that maybe dancers shouldn't be handicapped. But he didn't get very far with it before another noise in his ear radio scattered his thoughts.

George winced. So did two out of the eight ballerinas.

Hazel saw him wince. Having no mental handicap herself, she had to ask George what the latest sound had been.

"Sounded like somebody hitting a milk bottle with a ball peen hammer," said George.

"I'd think it would be real interesting, hearing all the different sounds," said Hazel, a little envious. "All the things they think up."

"Um," said George.

"Only, if I was Handicapper General, you know what I would do?" said Hazel. Hazel, as a matter of fact, bore a strong resemblance to the Handicapper General, a woman named Diana Moon Glampers. "If I was Diana Moon Glampers," said Hazel, "I'd have chimes on Sunday—just chimes. Kind of in honor of religion."

"I could think, if it was just chimes," said George.

"Well—maybe make 'em real loud," said Hazel. "I think I'd make a good Handicapper General."

"Good as anybody else," said George.

"Who knows better'n I do what normal is?" said Hazel.

"Right," said George. He began to think glimmeringly about his abnormal son who was now in jail, about Harrison, but a twenty-one-gun salute in his head stopped that.

"Boy!" said Hazel, "that was a doozy, wasn't it?"

It was such a doozy that George was white and trembling, and tears stood on the rims of his red eyes. Two of the eight ballerinas had collapsed to the studio floor, were holding their temples.

"All of a sudden you look so tired," said Hazel. "Why don't you stretch out on the sofa, so's you can rest your handicap bag on the pillows, honeybunch." She was referring to the forty-seven pounds of birdshot in a canvas bag, which was padlocked around George's neck. "Go on and rest the bag for a little while," she said. "I don't care if you're not equal to me for a while."

George weighed the bag with his hands. "I don't mind it," he said. "I don't notice it any more. It's just a part of me."

"You been so tired lately—kind of wore out," said Hazel. "If there was just some way we could make a little hole in the bottom of the bag, and just take out a few of them lead balls. Just a few."

"Two years in prison and two thousand dollars fine for every ball I took out," said George. "I don't call that a bargain."

"If you could just take a few out when you came home from work," said Hazel. "I mean—you don't compete with anybody around here. You just set around."

"If I tried to get away with it," said George, "then other people'd get away with it—and pretty soon we'd be right back to the dark ages again, with everybody competing against everybody else. You wouldn't like that, would you?"

"I'd hate it," said Hazel.

"There you are," said George. "The minute people start cheating on laws, what do you think happens to society?"

If Hazel hadn't been able to come up with an answer to this question, George couldn't have supplied one. A siren was going off in his head.

"Reckon it'd fall all apart," said Hazel.

"What would?" said George blankly.

"Society," said Hazel uncertainly. "Wasn't that what you just said?"

"Who knows?" said George.

The television program was suddenly interrupted for a

news bulletin. It wasn't clear at first as to what the bulletin was about, since the announcer, like all announcers, had a serious speech impediment. For about half a minute, and in a state of high excitement, the announcer tried to say, "Ladies and gentlemen—"

He finally gave up, handed the bulletin to a ballerina to read.

"That's all right—" Hazel said of the announcer, "he tried. That's the big thing. He tried to do the best he could with what God gave him. He should get a nice raise for trying so hard."

"Ladies and gentlemen—" said the ballerina, reading the bulletin. She must have been extraordinarily beautiful, because the mask she wore was hideous. And it was easy to see that she was the strongest and most graceful of all the dancers, for her handicap bags were as big as those worn by two-hundred-pound men.

And she had to apologize at once for her voice, which was a very unfair voice for a woman to use. Her voice was a warm, luminous, timeless melody. "Excuse me—" she said, and she began again, making her voice absolutely uncompetitive.

"Harrison Bergeron, age fourteen," she said in a grackle squawk, "has just escaped from jail, where he was held on suspicion of plotting to overthrow the government. He is a genius and an athlete, is under-handicapped, and should be regarded as extremely dangerous."

A police photograph of Harrison Bergeron was flashed on the screen-upside down, then sideways, upside down again, then right side up. The picture showed the full length of Harrison against a background calibrated in feet and inches. He was exactly seven feet tall.

The rest of Harrison's appearance was Halloween and hardware. Nobody had ever born heavier handicaps. He had outgrown hindrances faster than the H-G men could think them up. Instead of a little ear radio for a mental handicap, he wore a tremendous pair of earphones, and spectacles with thick wavy lenses. The spectacles were intended to make him not only half blind, but to give him whanging headaches besides.

Scrap metal was hung all over him. Ordinarily, there was a certain symmetry, a military neatness to the handicaps issued to strong people, but Harrison looked like a walking junkyard. In the race of life, Harrison carried three hundred pounds.

And to offset his good looks, the H-G men required that he wear at all times a red rubber ball for a nose, keep his eyebrows shaved off, and cover his even white teeth with black caps at snaggle-tooth random.

"If you see this boy," said the ballerina, "do not—I repeat, do not—try to reason with him."

There was the shriek of a door being torn from its hinges.

Screams and barking cries of consternation came from the television set. The photograph of Harrison Bergeron on the screen jumped again and again, as though dancing to the tune of an earthquake.

George Bergeron correctly identified the earthquake, and well he might have—for many was the time his own home had danced to the same crashing tune. "My God—" said George, "that must be Harrison!"

The realization was blasted from his mind instantly by the sound of an automobile collision in his head.

When George could open his eyes again, the photograph of Harrison was gone. A living, breathing Harrison filled the screen.

Clanking, clownish, and huge, Harrison stood in the center of the studio. The knob of the uprooted studio door was still in his hand. Ballerinas, technicians, musicians, and announcers cowered on their knees before him, expecting to die.

"I am the Emperor!" cried Harrison. "Do you hear? I am the Emperor! Everybody must do what I say at once!" He stamped his foot and the studio shook.

"Even as I stand here—" he bellowed, "crippled, hobbled, sickened—I am a greater ruler than any man who ever lived! Now watch me become what I *can* become!"

Harrison tore the straps of his handicap harness like wet tissue paper, tore straps guaranteed to support five thousand pounds.

Harrison's scrap-iron handicaps crashed to the floor.

Harrison thrust his thumbs under the bar of the padlock that secured his head harness. The bar snapped like celery. Harrison smashed his headphones and spectacles against the wall.

He flung away his rubber-ball nose, revealed a man that would have awed Thor, the god of thunder.

"I shall now select my Empress!" he said, looking down on the cowering people. "Let the first woman who dares rise to her feet claim her mate and her throne!"

A moment passed, and then a ballerina arose, swaying like a willow.

Harrison plucked the mental handicap from her ear, snapped off her physical handicaps with marvelous delicacy. Last of all, he removed her mask.

She was blindingly beautiful.

"Now—" said Harrison, taking her hand, "shall we show the people the meaning of the word dance? Music!" he commanded.

The musicians scrambled back into their chairs, and Harrison stripped them of their handicaps, too. "Play your best," he told them, "and I'll make you barons and dukes and earls."

The music began. It was normal at first—cheap, silly, false. But Harrison snatched two musicians from their chairs, waved them like batons as he sang the music as he wanted it played. He slammed them back into their chairs.

The music began again and was much improved.

Harrison and his Empress merely listened to the music for a while—listened gravely, as though synchronizing their heartbeats with it.

They shifted their weights to their toes.

Harrison placed his big hands on the girl's tiny waist, letting her sense the weightlessness that would soon be hers.

And then, in an explosion of joy and grace, into the air they sprang!

Not only were the laws of the land abandoned, but the law of gravity and the laws of motion as well.

They reeled, whirled, swiveled, flounced, capered, gam-boled, and spun.

They leaped like deer on the moon.

The studio ceiling was thirty feet high, but each leap brought the dancers nearer to it.

It became their obvious intention to kiss the ceiling.

They kissed it.

And then, neutralizing gravity with love and pure will, they remained suspended in air inches below the ceiling, and they kissed each other for a long, long time.

It was then that Diana Moon Glampers, the Handi-capper General, came into the studio with a double-bar-reled ten-gauge shotgun. She fired twice, and the Emperor and the Empress were dead before they hit the floor.

Diana Moon Glampers loaded the gun again. She aimed it at the musicians and told them they had ten seconds to get their handicaps back on.

It was then that the Bergerons' television tube burned out.

Hazel turned to comment about the blackout to George. But George had gone out into the kitchen for a can of beer.

George came back in with the beer, paused while a handicap signal shook him up. And then he sat down again. "You been crying?" he said to Hazel.

"Yup," she said.

"What about?" he said.

"I forget," she said. "Something real sad on television."

"What was it?" he said.

"It's all kind of mixed up in my mind," said Hazel.

"Forget sad things," said George.

"I always do," said Hazel.

"That's my girl," said George. He winced. There was the sound of a rivetting gun in his head.

"Gee—I could tell that one was a doozy," said Hazel.

"You can say that again," said George.

"Gee—" said Hazel, "I could tell that one was a doozy."

(1961)

WHO AM I
THIS TIME?

THE North Crawford Mask and Wig Club, an amateur theatrical society I belong to, voted to do Tennessee Williams' *A Streetcar Named Desire* for the spring play. Doris Sawyer, who always directs, said she couldn't direct this time because her mother was so sick. And she said the club ought to develop some other directors anyway, because she couldn't live forever, even though she'd made it safely to seventy-four.

So I got stuck with the directing job, even though the only thing I'd ever directed before was the installation of combination aluminum storm windows and screens I'd sold. That's what I am, a salesman of storm windows and doors, and here and there a bathtub enclosure. As far as acting goes, the highest rank I ever held on stage was either butler or policeman, whichever's higher.

I made a lot of conditions before I took the directing job, and the biggest one was that Harry Nash, the only real actor the club has, had to take the Marlon Brando part in the play. To give you an idea of how versatile Harry is, inside of one year he was Captain Queeg in *The Caine Mutiny Court Martial,* then Abe Lincoln in *Abe Lincoln in Illinois* and then the young architect in *The Moon is Blue.* The year after that, Harry Nash was Henry the Eighth in *Anne of the Thousand Days* and Doc in *Come Back Little Sheba,* and I was after him for Marlon Brando in *A Streetcar Named Desire.* Harry wasn't at the meeting to say whether he'd take the part or not. He never came to meetings. He was too shy. He didn't stay away from meetings because he had something else to do. He wasn't married, didn't go out with women—didn't have any close men friends either. He stayed away from all kinds of gatherings because he never could think of anything to say or do without a script.

So I had to go down to Miller's Hardware Store, where Harry was a clerk, the next day and ask him if he'd take the part. I stopped off at the telephone company to complain about a bill I'd gotten for a call to Honolulu, I'd never called Honolulu in my life.

And there was this beautiful girl I'd never seen before behind the counter at the phone company, and she explained that the company had put in an automatic billing machine and that the machine didn't have all the bugs out of it yet. It made mistakes. "Not only did I not call Honolulu," I told her, "I don't think anybody in North Crawford ever has or will."

So she took the charge off the bill, and I asked her if she was from around North Crawford. She said no. She said she just came with the new billing machine to teach local girls how to take care of it. After that, she said, she would go with some other machine to someplace else. "Well," I said, "as long as people have to come along with the machines, I guess we're all right."

"What?" she said.

"When machines start delivering themselves," I said, "I guess that's when the people better start really worrying."

"Oh," she said. She didn't seem very interested in that subject, and I wondered if she was interested in anything. She seemed kind of numb, almost a machine herself, an automatic phone-company politeness machine.

"How long will you be in town here?" I asked her.

"I stay in each town eight weeks, sir," she said. She had pretty blue eyes, but there sure wasn't much hope or curiosity in them. She told me she had been going from town to town like that for two years, always a stranger.

And I got it in my head that she might make a good Stella for the play. Stella was the wife of the Marlon Brando character, the wife of the character I wanted Harry Nash to play. So I told her where and when we were going to hold tryouts, and said the club would be very happy if she'd come.

She looked surprised, and she warmed up a little. "You know," she said, "that's the first time anybody ever asked me to participate in any community thing."

"Well," I said, "there isn't any other way to get to know a lot of nice people faster than to be in a play with 'em."

She said her name was Helene Shaw. She said she might just surprise me—and herself. She said she just might come.

You would think that North Crawford would be fed up with Harry Nash in plays after all the plays he'd been in. But the fact was that North Crawford probably could have gone on enjoying Harry forever, because he was never Harry on stage. When the maroon curtain went up on the stage in the gymnasium of the Consolidated Junior-Senior High School, Harry, body and soul, was exactly what the script and the director told him to be.

Somebody said one time that Harry ought to go to a psychiatrist so he could be something important and colorful in real life, too—so he could get married anyway, and maybe get a better job than just clerking in Miller's Hardware Store for fifty dollars a week. But I don't know what a psychiatrist could have turned up about him that the town didn't already know. The trouble with Harry was he'd been left on the doorstep of the Unitarian Church when he was a baby, and he never did find out who his parents were.

When I told him there in Miller's that I'd been appointed director, that I wanted him in my play, he said what he always said to anybody who asked him to be in a play—and it was kind of sad, if you think about it.

"Who am I this time?" he said.

So I held the tryouts where they're always held—in the meeting room on the second floor of the North Crawford Public Library. Doris Sawyer, the woman who usually directs, came to give me the benefit of all her experience. The two of us sat in state upstairs, while the people who wanted parts waited below. We called them upstairs one by one.

Harry Nash came to the tryouts, even though it was a

waste of time. I guess he wanted to get that little bit more acting in.

For Harry's pleasure, and our pleasure, too, we had him read from the scene where he beats up his wife. It was a play in itself, the way Harry did it, and Tennesse Williams hadn't written it all either. Tennessee Williams didn't write the part, for instance, where Harry, who weighs about one hundred forty-five, who's about five feet eight inches tall, added fifty pounds to his weight and four inches to his height by just picking up a playbook. He had a short little double-breasted bellows-back grade-school graduation suit coat on and a dinky little red tie with a horsehead on it. He took off the coat and tie, opened his collar, then turned his back to Doris and me, getting up steam for the part. There was a great big rip in the back of his shirt, and it looked like a fairly new shirt too. He'd ripped it on purpose, so he could be that much more like Marlon Brando, right from the first.

When he faced us again, he was huge and handsome and conceited and cruel. Doris read the part of Stella, the wife, and Harry bullied that old, old lady into believing that she was a sweet, pregnant girl married to a sexy gorilla who was going to beat her brains out. She had me believing it too. And I read the lines of Blanche, her sister in the play, and darned if Harry didn't scare me into feeling like a drunk and faded Southern belle.

And then, while Doris and I were getting over our emotional experiences, like people coming out from under ether, Harry put down the playbook, put on his coat and tie, and turned into the pale hardware-store clerk again.

"Was—was that all right?" he said, and he seemed pretty sure he wouldn't get the part.

"Well," I said, "for a first reading, that wasn't too bad."

"Is there a chance I'll get the part?" he said. I don't know why he always had to pretend there was some doubt about his getting a part, but he did.

"I think we can safely say we're leaning powerfully in your direction," I told him.

He was very pleased. "Thanks! Thanks a lot!" he said, and he shook my hand.

"Is there a pretty new girl downstairs?" I said, meaning Helene Shaw.

"I didn't notice," said Harry.

It turned out that Helene Shaw *had* come for the try-outs, and Doris and I had our hearts broken. We thought the North Crawford Mask and Wig Club was finally going to put a really good-looking, really young girl on stage, instead of one of the beat-up forty-year-old women we generally have to palm off as girls.

But Helene Shaw couldn't act for sour apples. No matter what we gave her to read, she was the same girl with the same smile for anybody who had a complaint about his phone bill.

Doris tried to coach her some, to make her understand that Stella in the play was a very passionate girl who loved a gorilla because she needed a gorilla. But Helene just read the lines the same way again. I don't think a volcano could have stirred her up enough to say, "Oo."

"Dear," said Doris, "I'm going to ask you a personal question."

"All right," said Helene.

"Have you ever been in love?" said Doris. "The reason I ask," she said, "remembering some old love might help you put more warmth in your acting."

Helene frowned and thought hard. "Well," she said, "I travel a lot, you know. And practically all the men in the different companies I visit are married and I never stay anyplace long enough to know many people who aren't."

"What about school?" said Doris. "What about puppy love and all the other kinds of love in school?"

So Helene thought hard about that, and then she said, "Even in school I was always moving around a lot. My father was a construction worker, following jobs around, so I was always saying hello or good-by to someplace, without anything in between."

"Um," said Doris.

"Would movie stars count?" said Helene. "I don't mean in real life. I never knew any. I just mean up on the screen."

Doris looked at me and rolled her eyes. "I guess that's love of a kind," she said.

And then Helene got a little enthusiastic. "I used to sit through movies over and over again," she said, "and pretend I was married to whoever the man movie star was. They were the only people who came with us. No matter where we moved, movie stars were there."

"Uh huh," said Doris.

"Well, thank you, Miss Shaw," I said. "You go downstairs and wait with the rest. We'll let you know."

So we tried to find another Stella. And there just wasn't one, not one woman in the club with the dew still on her. "All we've got are Blanches," I said, meaning all we had were faded women who could play the part of Blanche, Stella's faded sister. "That's life, I guess—twenty Blanches to one Stella."

"And when you find a Stella," said Doris, "it turns out she doesn't know what love is."

Doris and I decided there was one last thing we could try. We could get Harry Nash to play a scene along with Helene. "He just might make her bubble the least little bit," I said.

"That girl hasn't got a bubble in her," said Doris.

So we called down the stairs for Helene to come back on up, and we told somebody to go find Harry. Harry never sat with the rest of the people at tryouts—or at rehearsals either. The minute he didn't have a part to play, he'd disappear into some hiding place where he could hear people call him, but where he couldn't be seen. At tryouts in the library he generally hid in the reference room, passing the time looking at flags of different countries in the front of the dictionary.

Helene came back upstairs, and we were very sorry and surprised to see that she'd been crying.

"Oh, dear," said Doris. "Oh, my—now what on earth's the trouble, dear?"

"I was terrible, wasn't I?" said Helene, hanging her head.

Doris said the only thing anybody can say in an amateur

theatrical society when somebody cries. She said, "Why, no dear—you were marvelous."

"No, I wasn't," said Helene. "I'm a walking icebox, and I know it."

"Nobody could look at you and say that," said Doris.

"When they get to know me, they can say it," said Helene. "When people get to know me, that's what they *do* say." Her tears got worse. "I don't want to be the way I am," she said. "I just can't help it, living the way I've lived all my life. The only experiences I've had have been in crazy dreams of movie stars. When I meet somebody nice in real life, I feel as though I were in some kind of big bottle, as though I couldn't touch that person, no matter how hard I tried." And Helene pushed on air as though it were a big bottle all around her.

"You ask me if I've ever been in love," she said to Doris. "No—but I want to be. I know what this play's about. I know what Stella's supposed to feel and why she feels it. I—I—I—" she said, and her tears wouldn't let her go on.

"You what, dear?" said Doris gently.

"I——" said Helene, and she pushed on the imaginary bottle again. "I just don't know how to begin," she said.

There was heavy clumping on the library stairs. It sounded like a deep-sea diver coming upstairs in his lead shoes. It was Harry Nash, turning himself into Marlon Brando. In he came, practically dragging his knuckles on the floor. And he was so much in character that the sight of a weeping woman made him sneer.

"Harry," I said, "I'd like you to meet Helene Shaw. Helene—this is Harry Nash. If you get the part of Stella, he'll be your husband in the play." Harry didn't offer to shake hands. He put his hands in his pockets, and he hunched over, and he looked her up and down, gave her looks that left her naked. Her tears stopped right then and there.

"I wonder if you two would play the fight scene," I said, "and then the reunion scene right after it."

"Sure," said Harry, his eyes still on her. Those eyes

burned up clothes faster than she could put them on. "Sure," he said, "if Stell's game."

"What?" said Helene. She'd turned the color of cranberry juice.

"Stell—Stella," said Harry. "That's you. Stell's my wife."

I handed the two of them playbooks. Harry snatched his from me without a word of thanks. Helene's hands weren't working very well, and I had to kind of mold them around the book.

"I'll want something I can throw," said Harry.

"What?" I said.

"There's one place where I throw a radio out a window," said Harry. "What can I throw?"

So I said an iron paperweight was the radio, and I opened the window wide. Helene Shaw looked scared to death.

"Where you want us to start?" said Harry, and he rolled his shoulders like a prizefighter warming up.

"Start a few lines back from where you throw the radio out the window," I said.

"O.K., O.K.," said Harry, warming up, warming up. He scanned the stage directions. "Let's see," he said, "after I throw the radio, she runs off stage, and I chase her, and I sock her one."

"Right," I said.

"O.K., baby," Harry said to Helene, his eyelids drooping. What was about to happen was wilder than the chariot race in *Ben Hur*. "On your mark," said Harry. "Get ready, baby. Go!"

When the scene was over, Helene Shaw was as hot as a hod carrier, as limp as an eel. She sat down with her mouth open and her head hanging to one side. She wasn't in any bottle any more. There wasn't any bottle to hold her up and keep her safe and clean. The bottle was gone.

"Do I get the part or don't I?" Harry snarled at me.

"You'll do," I said.

"You said a mouthful!" he said. "I'll be going now. . . . See you around, Stella," he said to Helene, and he left. He slammed the door behind him.

"Helene?" I said. "Miss Shaw?"

"Mf?" she said.

"The part of Stella is yours," I said "You were great!"

"I was?" she said.

"I had no idea you had that much fire in you, dear," Doris said to her.

"Fire?" said Helene. She didn't know if she was afoot or on horseback.

"Skyrockets! Pinwheels! Roman candles!" said Doris.

"Mf," said Helene. And that was all she said. She looked as though she were going to sit in the chair with her mouth open forever.

"Stella," I said.

"Huh?" she said.

"You have my permission to go."

So we started having rehearsals four nights a week on the stage of the Consolidated School. And Harry and Helene set such a pace that everybody in the production was half crazy with excitement and exhaustion before we'd rehearsed four times. Usually a director has to beg people to learn their lines, but I had no such trouble. Harry and Helene were working so well together that everybody else in the cast regarded it as a duty and an honor and a pleasure to support them.

I was certainly lucky—or thought I was. Things were going so well, so hot and heavy, so early in the game that I had to say to Harry and Helene after one love scene, "Hold a little something back for the actual performance, would you please? You'll burn yourselves out."

I said that at the fourth or fifth rehearsal, and Lydia Miller, who was playing Blanche, the faded sister, was sitting next to me in the audience. In real life, she's the wife of Verne Miller. Verne owns Miller's Hardware Store. Verne was Harry's boss.

"Lydia," I said to her, "have we got a play or have we got a play?"

"Yes," she said, "you've got a play, all right." She made it sound as though I'd committed some kind of crime, done something just terrible. "You should be very proud of yourself."

"What do you mean by that?" I said.

Before Lydia could answer, Harry yelled at me from the stage, asked if I was through with him, asked if he could go home. I told him he could and, still Marlon Brando, he left, kicking furniture out of his way and slamming doors. Helene was left all alone on the stage, sitting on a couch with the same gaga look she'd had after the tryouts. That girl was drained.

I turned to Lydia again and I said, "Well—until now, I thought I had every reason to be happy and proud. Is there something going on I don't know about?"

"Do you know that girl's in love with Harry?" said Lydia.

"In the play?" I said.

"What play?" said Lydia. "There isn't any play going on now, and look at her up there." She gave a sad cackle. "You aren't directing this play."

"Who is?" I said.

"Mother Nature at her worst," said Lydia. "And think what it's going to do to that girl when she discovers what Harry really is." She corrected herself. "What Harry really isn't," she said.

I didn't do anything about it, because I didn't figure it was any of my business. I heard Lydia try to do something about it, but she didn't get very far.

"You know," Lydia said to Helene one night, "I once played Ann Rutledge, and Harry was Abraham Lincoln."

Helene clapped her hands. "That must have been heaven!" she said.

"It was, in a way," said Lydia. "Sometimes I'd get so worked up, I'd love Harry the way I'd love Abraham Lincoln. I'd have to come back to earth and remind myself that he wasn't ever going to free the slaves, that he was just a clerk in my husband's hardware store."

"He's the most marvelous man I ever met," said Helene.

"Of course, one thing you have to get set for, when you're in a play with Harry," said Lydia, "is what happens after the last performance."

"What are you talking about?" said Helene.

"Once the show's over," said Lydia, "whatever you

thought Harry was just evaporates into thin air."

"I don't believe it," said Helene.

"I admit it's hard to believe," said Lydia.

Then Helene got a little sore. "Anyway, why tell me about it?" she said. "Even if it is true, what do I care?"

"I—I don't know," said Lydia, backing away. "I—I just thought you might find it interesting."

"Well, I don't," said Helene.

And Lydia slunk away, feeling about as frowzy and unloved as she was supposed to feel in the play. After that nobody said anything more to Helene to warn her about Harry, not even when word got around that she'd told the telephone company that she didn't want to be moved around anymore, that she wanted to stay in North Crawford.

So the time finally came to put on the play. We ran it for three nights—Thursday, Friday, and Saturday—and we murdered those audiences. They believed every word that was said on stage, and when the maroon curtain came down they were ready to go to the nut house along with Blanche, the faded sister.

On Thursday night the other girls at the telephone company sent Helene a dozen red roses. When Helene and Harry were taking a curtain call together, I passed the roses over the footlights to her. She came forward for them, took one rose from the bouquet to give to Harry. But when she turned to give Harry the rose in front of everybody, Harry was gone. The curtain came down on that extra little scene—that girl offering a rose to nothing and nobody.

I went backstage, and I found her still holding that one rose. She'd put the rest of the bouquet aside. There were tears in her eyes. "What did I do wrong?" she said to me. "Did I insult him some way?"

"No," I said. "He always does that after a performance. The minute it's over, he clears out as fast as he can."

"And tomorrow he'll disappear again?"

"Without even taking off his makeup."

"And Saturday?" she said. "He'll stay for the cast party on Saturday, won't he?"

"Harry never goes to parties," I said. "When the curtain comes down on Saturday, that's the last anybody will see of him till he goes to work on Monday."

"How sad," she said.

Helene's performance on Friday night wasn't nearly so good as Thursday's. She seemed to be thinking about other things. She watched Harry take off after curtain call. She didn't say a word.

On Saturday she put on the best performance yet. Ordinarily it was Harry who set the pace. But on Saturday Harry had to work to keep up with Helene.

When the curtain came down on the final curtain call, Harry wanted to get away, but he couldn't. Helene wouldn't let go his hand. The rest of the cast and the stage crew and a lot of well-wishers from the audience were all standing around Harry and Helene, and Harry was trying to get his hand back.

"Well," he said, "I've got to go."

"Where?" she said.

"Oh," he said, "home."

"Won't you please take me to the cast party?" she said.

He got very red. "I'm afraid I'm not much on parties," he said. All the Marlon Brando in him was gone. He was tongue-tied, he was scared, he was shy—he was everything Harry was famous for being between plays.

"All right," she said. "I'll let you go—if you promise me one thing."

"What's that?" he said, and I thought he would jump out a window if she let go of him then.

"I want you to promise to stay here until I get you your present," she said.

"Present?" he said, getting even more panicky.

"Promise?" she said.

He promised. It was the only way he could get his hand back. And he stood there miserably while Helene went down to the ladies' dressing room for the present. While he waited, a lot of people congratulated him on being such a fine actor. But congratulations never made him happy. He just wanted to get away.

Helene came back with the present. It turned out to be a

little blue book with a big red ribbon for a place marker. It was a copy of *Romeo and Juliet*. Harry was very embarrassed. It was all he could do to say "Thank you."

"The marker marks my favorite scene," said Helene.

"Um," said Harry.

"Don't you want to see what my favorite scene is?" she said.

So Harry had to open the book to the red ribbon.

Helene got close to him, and read a line of Juliet's. " 'How cam'st thou hither, tell me, and wherefore?' " she read. " 'The orchard walls are high and hard to climb, and the place death, considering who thou art, if any of my kinsmen find thee here.' " She pointed to the next line. "Now, look what Romeo says," she said.

"Um," said Harry.

"Read what Romeo says," said Helene.

Harry cleared his throat. He didn't want to read the line, but he had to. " 'With love's light wings did I o'erperch these walls,' " he read out loud in his everyday voice. But then a change came over him. " 'For stony limits cannot hold love out,' " he read, and he straightened up, and eight years dropped away from him, and he was brave and gay. " 'And what love can do, that dares love attempt,' " he read, " 'therefore thy kinsmen are no let to me.' "

" 'If they do see thee they will murther thee,' " said Helene, and she started him walking toward the wings.

" 'Alack!' " said Harry, " 'there lies more peril in thine eye than twenty of their swords.' " Helene led him toward the backstage exit. " 'Look thou but sweet,' " said Harry, " 'and I am proof against their enmity.' "

" 'I would not for the world they saw thee here,' " said Helene, and that was the last we heard. The two of them were out the door and gone.

They never did show up at the cast party. One week later they were married.

They seem very happy, although they're kind of strange from time to time, depending on which play they're reading to each other at the time.

I dropped into the phone company office the other day,

on account of the billing machine was making dumb mistakes again. I asked her what plays she and Harry'd been reading lately.

"In the past week," she said, "I've been married to Othello, been loved by Faust and been kidnaped by Paris. Wouldn't you say I was the luckiest girl in town?"

I said I thought so, and I told her most of the women in town thought so too.

"They had their chance," she said.

"Most of 'em couldn't stand the excitement," I said. And I told her I'd been asked to direct another play. I asked if she and Harry would be available for the cast. She gave me a big smile and said, "Who are we this time?"

(1961)

WELCOME TO THE
MONKEY HOUSE

SO PETE CROCKER, the sheriff of Barnstable County, which
was the whole of Cape Cod, came into the Federal Ethical
Suicide Parlor in Hyannis one May afternoon—and she
told the two six-foot Hostesses there that they weren't to be
alarmed, but that a notorious nothinghead named Billy the
Poet was believed headed for the Cape.

A nothinghead was a person who refused to take his
ethical birth-control pills three times a day. The penalty
for that was $10,000 and ten years in jail.

This was at a time when the population on Earth was 17
billion human beings. That was far too many mammals
that big for a planet that small. The people were virtually
packed together like drupelets.

Drupelets are the pulpy little knobs that compose the
outside of a raspberry.

So the World Government was making a two-pronged
attack on overpopulation. One pronging was the encouragement of ethical suicide, which consisted of going to the
nearest Suicide Parlor and asking a Hostess to kill you
painlessly while you lay on a Barcalounger. The other
pronging was compulsory ethical birth control.

The sheriff told the Hostesses, who were pretty, tough-
minded, highly intelligent girls, that roadblocks were being
set up and house-to-house searches were being conducted
to catch Billy the Poet. The main difficulty was that the
police didn't know what he looked like. The few people
who had seen him and known him for what he was were
women—and they disagreed fantastically as to his height,
his hair color, his voice, his weight, the color of his skin.

"I don't need to remind you girls," the sheriff went on,

"that a nothinghead is very sensitive from the waist down. If Billy the Poet somehow slips in here and starts making trouble, one good kick in the right place will do wonders."

He was referring to the fact that ethical birth-control pills, the only legal form of birth control, made people numb from the waist down.

Most men said their bottom halves felt like cold iron or balsawood. Most women said their bottom halves felt like wet cotton or stale ginger ale. The pills were so effective that you could blindfold a man who had taken one, tell him to recite the Gettysburg Address, kick him in the balls while he was doing it, and he wouldn't miss a syllable.

The pills were ethical because they didn't interfere with a person's ability to reproduce, which would have been unnatural and immoral. All the pills did was take every bit of pleasure out of sex.

Thus did science and morals go hand in hand.

The two Hostesses there in Hyannis were Nancy McLuhan and Mary Kraft. Nancy was a strawberry blonde. Mary was a glossy brunette. Their uniforms were white lipstick, heavy eye makeup, purple body stockings with nothing underneath, and black-leather boots. They ran a small operation—with only six suicide booths. In a really good week, say the one before Christmas, they might put sixty people to sleep. It was done with a hypodermic syringe.

"My main message to you girls," said Sheriff Crocker, "is that everything's well under control. You can just go about your business here."

"Didn't you leave out part of your main message?" Nancy asked him.

"I don't get you."

"I didn't hear you say he was probably headed straight for us."

He shrugged in clumsy innocence. "We don't know that for sure."

"I thought that was all anybody *did* know about Billy the Poet: that he specializes in deflowering Hostesses in Ethical Suicide Parlors." Nancy was a virgin. All Hostesses were virgins. They also had to hold advanced degrees in psychology and nursing. They also had to be plump and rosy, and at least six feet tall.

America had changed in many ways, but it had yet to adopt the metric system.

Nancy McLuhan was burned up that the sheriff would try to protect her and Mary from the full truth about Bill the Poet—as though they might panic if they heard it. She told the sheriff so.

"How long do you think a girl would last in the E. S. S.," she said, meaning the Ethical Suicide Service, "if she scared that easy?"

The sheriff took a step backward, pulled in his chin. "Not very long, I guess."

"That's very true," said Nancy, closing the distance between them and offering him a sniff of the edge of her hand, which was poised for a karate chop. All Hostesses were experts at judo and karate. "If you'd like to find out how helpless we are, just come toward me, pretending you're Billy the Poet."

The sheriff shook his head, gave her a glassy smile. "I'd rather not."

"That's the smartest thing you've said today," said Nancy, turning her back on him while Mary laughed. "We're not scared—we're *angry*. Or we're not even *that*. He isn't *worth* that. We're *bored*. How boring that he should come a great distance, should cause all this fuss, in order to——" She let the sentence die there. "It's just too absurd."

"I'm not as mad at *him* as I am at the women who let him do it to them without a struggle"—said Mary—"who let him do it and then couldn't tell the police what he looked like. Suicide Hostesses at that!"

"Somebody hasn't been keeping up with her karate," said Nancy.

It wasn't just Billy the Poet who was attracted to Hostesses in Ethical Suicide Parlors. All nothingheads were. Bombed out of their skulls with the sex madness that came from taking nothing, they thought the white lips and big eyes and body stocking and boots of a Hostess spelled *sex, sex, sex.*

The truth was, of course, that sex was the last thing any Hostess ever had in mind.

"If Billy follows his usual M. O.," said the sheriff, "he'll study your habits and the neighborhood. And then he'll pick one or the other of you and he'll send her a dirty poem in the mail."

"Charming," said Nancy.

"He has also been known to use the telephone."

"How brave," said Nancy. Over the sheriff's shoulder, she could see the mailman coming.

A blue light went on over the door of a booth for which Nancy was responsible. The person in there wanted something. It was the only booth in use at the time.

The sheriff asked her if there was a possibility that the person in there was Billy the Poet, and Nancy said, "Well, if it is, I can break his neck with my thumb and forefinger."

"Foxy Grandpa," said Mary, who'd seen him, too. A Foxy Grandpa was any old man, cute and senile, who quibbled and joked and reminisced for hours before he let a Hostess put him to sleep.

Nancy groaned. "We've spent the past two hours trying to decide on a last meal."

And then the mailman came in with just one letter. It was addressed to Nancy in smeary pencil. She was splendid with anger and disgust as she opened it, knowing it would be a piece of filth from Billy.

She was right. Inside the envelope was a poem. It wasn't an original poem. It was a song from olden days that had taken on new meanings since the numbness of ethical birth control had become universal. It went like this, in smeary pencil again:

> *We were walking through the park,*
> A-goosing statues in the dark.
> If Sherman's horse can take it,
> So can you.

When Nancy came into the suicide booth to see what he wanted, the Foxy Grandpa was lying on the mint-green Barcalounger, where hundreds had died so peacefully over the years. He was studying the menu from the Howard Johnson's next door and beating time to the Muzak coming from the loudspeaker on the lemon-yellow wall. The room was painted cinder block. There was one barred window with a Venetian blind.

There was a Howard Johnson's next door to every Ethical Suicide Parlor, and vice versa. The Howard Johnson's had an orange roof and the Suicide Parlor had a purple roof, but they were both the Government. Practically everything was the Government.

Practically everything was automated, too. Nancy and Mary and the sheriff were lucky to have jobs. Most people didn't. The average citizen moped around home and watched television, which was the Government. Every fifteen minutes his television would urge him to vote intelligently or consume intelligently, or worship in the church of his choice, or love his fellowmen, or obey the laws—or pay a call to the nearest Ethical Suicide Parlor and find out how friendly and understanding a Hostess could be.

The Foxy Grandpa was something of a rarity, since he was marked by old age, was bald, was shaky, had spots on his hands. Most people looked twenty-two, thanks to anti-aging shots they took twice a year. That the old man looked old was proof that the shots had been discovered after his sweet bird of youth had flown.

"Have we decided on a last supper yet?" Nancy asked him. She heard peevishness in her own voice, heard herself betray her exasperation with Billy the Poet, her boredom with the old man. She was ashamed, for this was unprofessional of her. "The breaded veal cutlet is very good."

The old man cocked his head. With the greedy cunning of second childhood, he had caught her being unprofessional, unkind, and he was going to punish her for it. "You don't sound very friendly. I thought you were all supposed to be friendly. I thought this was supposed to be a pleasant place to come."

"I beg your pardon," she said. "If I seem unfriendly, it has nothing to do with you."

"I thought maybe I bored you."

"No, no," she said gamely, "not at all. You certainly know some very interesting history." Among other things, the Foxy Grandpa claimed to have known J. Edgar Nation, the Grand Rapids druggist who was the father of ethical birth control.

"Then *look* like you're interested," he told her. He could get away with that sort of impudence. The thing was, he could leave any time he wanted to, right up to the moment he asked for the needle—and he had to *ask* for the needle. That was the law.

Nancy's art, and the art of every Hostess, was to see that volunteers didn't leave, to coax and wheedle and flatter them patiently, every step of the way.

So Nancy had to sit down there in the booth, to pretend to marvel at the freshness of the yarn the old man told, a story everybody knew, about how J. Edgar Nation happened to experiment with ethical birth control.

"He didn't have the slightest idea his pills would be taken by human beings someday," said the Foxy Grandpa. "His dream was to introduce morality into the monkey house at the Grand Rapids Zoo. Did you realize that?" he inquired severely.

"No. No, I didn't. That's very interesting."

"He and his eleven kids went to church one Easter. And the day was so nice and the Easter service had been so beautiful and pure that they decided to take a walk through the zoo, and they were just walking on clouds."

"Um." The scene described was lifted from a play that was performed on television every Easter.

The Foxy Grandpa shoehorned himself into the scene, had himself chat with the Nations just before they got to the monkey house. " 'Good morning, Mr. Nation,' I said to him. 'It certainly is a nice morning.' 'And a good morning to *you*, Mr. Howard,' he said to me. 'There is nothing like an Easter morning to make a man feel clean and reborn and at one with God's intentions.' "

"Um." Nancy could hear the telephone ringing faintly, naggingly, through the nearly soundproof door.

"So we went on to the monkey house together, and what do you think we saw?"

"I can't imagine." Somebody had answered the phone.

"We saw a monkey playing with his private parts!"

"No!"

"Yes! And J. Edgar Nation was so upset he went straight home and he started developing a pill that would make monkeys in the springtime fit things for a Christian family to see."

There was a knock on the door.

"Yes——?" said Nancy.

"Nancy," said Mary, "telephone for you."

When Nancy came out of the booth, she found the sheriff choking on little squeals of law-enforcement delight. The telephone was tapped by agents hidden in the Howard Johnson's. Billy the Poet was believed to be on the line. His call had been traced. Police were already on their way to grab him.

"Keep him on, keep him on," the sheriff whispered to Nancy, and he gave her the telephone as though it were solid gold.

"Yes—?" said Nancy.

"Nancy McLuhan?" said a man. His voice was disguised. He might have been speaking through a kazoo. "I'm calling for a mutual friend."

"Oh?"

"He asked me to deliver a message."

"I see."

"It's a poem."

"All right."

"Ready?"

"Ready." Nancy could hear sirens screaming in the background of the call.

The caller must have heard the sirens, too, but he recited the poem without any emotion. It went like this:

> *"Soak yourself in Jergen's Lotion.*
> *Here comes the one-man population*
> *explosion."*

They got him. Nancy heard it all—the thumping and clumping, the argle-bargle and cries.

The depression she felt as she hung up was glandular. Her brave body had prepared for a fight that was not to be.

The sheriff bounded out of the Suicide Parlor, in such a hurry to see the famous criminal he'd helped catch that a sheaf of papers fell from the pocket of his trench coat.

Mary picked them up, called after the sheriff. He halted for a moment, said the papers didn't matter any more, asked her if maybe she wouldn't like to come along. There was a flurry between the two girls, with Nancy persuading Mary to go, declaring that she had no curiosity about Billy. So Mary left, irrelevantly handing the sheaf to Nancy.

The sheaf proved to be photocopies of poems Billy had sent to Hostesses in other places. Nancy read the top one. It made much of a peculiar side effect of ethical birth-control pills: They not only made people numb—they also made people piss blue. The poem was called *What the Somethinghead Said to the Suicide Hostess*, and it went like this:

> *I did not sow, I did not spin,*
> *And thanks to pills I did not sin.*
> *I loved the crowds, the stink, the noise.*
> *And when I peed, I peed turquoise.*
>
> *I ate beneath a roof of orange;*
> *Swung with progress like a door hinge.*
> *'Neath purple roof I've come today*
> *To piss my azure life away.*
>
> *Virgin hostess, death's recruiter,*
> *Life is cute, but you are cuter.*

Mourn my pecker, purple daughter—
All it passed was sky-blue water.

"You never heard that story before—about how J. Edgar Nation came to invent ethical birth control?" the Foxy Grandpa wanted to know. His voice cracked.

"Never did," lied Nancy.

"I thought everybody knew that."

"It was news to me."

"When he got through with the monkey house, you couldn't tell it from the Michigan Supreme Court. Meanwhile, there was this crisis going on in the United Nations. The people who understood science said people had to quit reproducing so much, and the people who understood morals said society would collapse if people used sex for nothing but pleasure."

The Foxy Grandpa got off his Barcalounger, went over to the window, pried two slats of the blind apart. There wasn't much to see out there. The view was blocked by the backside of a mocked-up thermometer twenty feet high, which faced the street. It was calibrated in billions of people on Earth, from zero to twenty. The make-believe column of liquid was a strip of translucent red plastic. It showed how many people there were on Earth. Very close to the bottom was a black arrow that showed what the scientists thought the population ought to be.

The Foxy Grandpa was looking at the setting sun through that red plastic, and through the blind, too, so that his face was banded with shadows and red.

"Tell me—" he said, "when I die, how much will that thermometer go down? A foot?"

"No."

"An inch?"

"Not quite."

"You know what the answer is, don't you?" he said, and he faced her. The senility had vanished from his voice and eyes. "One inch on that thing equals 83,333 people. You knew that, didn't you?"

"That—that might be true," said Nancy, "but that isn't the right way to look at it, in my opinion."

He didn't ask her what the right way was, in her opinion. He completed a thought of his own, instead. "I'll tell you something else that's true: I'm Billy the Poet, and you're a very good-looking woman."

With one hand, he drew a snub-nosed revolver from his belt. With the other, he peeled off his bald dome and wrinkled forehead, which proved to be rubber. Now he looked twenty-two.

"The police will want to know exactly what I look like when this is all over," he told Nancy with a malicious grin. "In case you're not good at describing people, and it's surprising how many women aren't:

> *I'm five foot two,*
> *With eyes of blue,*
> *With Brown hair to my shoulders—*
> *A manly elf*
> *So full of self*
> *The ladies say he smolders."*

Billy was ten inches shorter than Nancy was. She had about forty pounds on him. She told him he didn't have a chance, but Nancy was much mistaken. He had unbolted the bars on the window the night before and he made her go out the window and then down a manhole that was hidden from the street by the big thermometer.

He took her down into the sewers of Hyannis. He knew where he was going. He had a flashlight and a map. Nancy had to go before him along the narrow catwalk, her own shadow dancing mockingly in the lead. She tried to guess where they were, relative to the real world above. She guessed correctly when they passed under the Howard Johnson's, guessed from noises she heard. The machinery that processed and served the food there was silent. But, so people wouldn't feel too lonesome when eating there, the designers had provided sound effects for the kitchen. It was these Nancy heard—a tape recording of the clashing of silverware and the laughter of Negroes and Puerto Ricans.

After that she was lost. Billy had very little to say to her other than "Right," or, "Left," or "Don't try anything funny, Juno, or I'll blow your great big fucking head off."

Only once did they have anything resembling a conversation. Billy began it, and ended it, too. "What in hell is a girl with hips like yours doing selling death?" he asked her from behind.

She dared to stop. "I can answer that," she told him. She was confident that she could give him an answer that would shrivel him like napalm.

But he gave her a shove, offered to blow her fucking head off again.

"You don't even want to hear my answer," she taunted him. "You're afraid to hear it."

"I never listen to a woman till the pills wear off," sneered Billy. That was his plan, then—to keep her a prisoner for at least eight hours. That was how long it took for the pills to wear off.

"That's a silly rule."

"A woman's not a woman till the pills wear off."

"You certainly manage to make a woman feel like an object rather than a person."

"Thank the pills for that," said Billy.

There were 80 miles of sewers under Greater Hyannis, which had a population of 400,000 drupelets, 400,000 souls. Nancy lost track of the time down there. When Billy announced that they had at last reached their destination, it was possible for Nancy to imagine that a year had passed.

She tested this spooky impression by pinching her own thigh, by feeling what the chemical clock of her body said. Her thigh was still numb.

Billy ordered her to climb iron rungs that were set in wet masonry. There was a circle of sickly light above. It proved to be moonlight filtered through the plastic polygons of an enormous geodesic dome. Nancy didn't have to ask the traditional victim's question, "Where am I?" There was only one dome like that on Cape Cod. It was in Hyannis Port and it sheltered the ancient Kennedy Compound.

It was a museum of how life had been lived in more

expansive times. The museum was closed. It was open only in the summertime.

The manhole from which Nancy and then Billy emerged was set in an expanse of green cement, which showed where the Kennedy lawn had been. On the green cement, in front of the ancient frame houses, were statues representing the fourteen Kennedys who had been Presidents of the United States or the World. They were playing touch football.

The President of the World at the time of Nancy's abduction, incidentally, was an ex-Suicide Hostess named "Ma" Kennedy. Her statue would never join this particular touch-football game. Her name was Kennedy, all right, but she wasn't the real thing. People complained of her lack of style, found her vulgar. On the wall of her office was a sign that said, YOU DON'T HAVE TO BE CRAZY TO WORK HERE, BUT IT SURE HELPS, and another one that said THIMK!, and another one that said, SOME DAY WE'RE GOING TO HAVE TO GET ORGANIZED AROUND HERE.

Her office was in the Taj Mahal.

Until she arrived in the Kennedy Museum, Nancy McLuhan was confident that she would sooner or later get a chance to break every bone in Billy's little body, maybe even shoot him with his own gun. She wouldn't have minded doing those things. She thought he was more disgusting than a blood-filled tick.

It wasn't compassion that changed her mind. It was the discovery that Billy had a gang. There were at least eight people around the manhole, men and women in equal numbers, with stockings pulled over their heads. It was the women who laid firm hands on Nancy, told her to keep calm. They were all at least as tall as Nancy and they held her in places where they could hurt her like hell if they had to.

Nancy closed her eyes, but this didn't protect her from the obvious conclusion: These perverted women were sisters from the Ethical Suicide Service. This upset her so much that she asked loudly and bitterly, "How can you violate your oaths like this?"

She was promptly hurt so badly that she doubled up and burst into tears.

When she straightened up again, there was plenty more she wanted to say, but she kept her mouth shut. She speculated silently as to what on Earth could make Suicide Hostesses turn against every concept of human decency. Nothingheadedness alone couldn't begin to explain it. They had to be drugged besides.

Nancy went over in her mind all the terrible drugs she'd learned about in school, persuaded herself that the women had taken the worst one of all. That drug was so powerful, Nancy's teachers had told her, that even a person numb from the waist down would copulate repeatedly and enthusiastically after just one glass. That had to be the answer: The women, and probably the men, too, had been drinking gin.

They hastened Nancy into the middle frame house, which was dark like all the rest, and Nancy heard the men giving Billy the news. It was in this news that Nancy perceived a glint of hope. Help might be on its way.

The gang member who had phoned Nancy obscenely had fooled the police into believing that they had captured Billy the Poet, which was bad for Nancy. The police didn't know yet that Nancy was missing, two men told Billy, and a telegram had been sent to Mary Kraft in Nancy's name, declaring that Nancy had been called to New York City on urgent family business.

That was where Nancy saw the glint of hope: Mary wouldn't believe that telegram. Mary knew Nancy had no family in New York. Not one of the 63,000,000 people living there was a relative of Nancy's.

The gang had deactivated the burglar-alarm system of the museum. They had also cut through a lot of the chains and ropes that were meant to keep visitors from touching anything of value. There was no mystery as to who and what had done the cutting. One of the men was armed with brutal lopping shears.

They marched Nancy into a servant's bedroom upstairs. The man with the shears cut the ropes that fenced off the narrow bed. They put Nancy into the bed and two men held Nancy while a woman gave her a knockout shot.

Billy the Poet had disappeared.

As Nancy was going under, the woman who had given her the shot asked her how old she was.

Nancy was determined not to answer, but discovered that the drug had made her powerless not to answer. "Sixty-three," she murmured.

"How does it feel to be a virgin at sixty-three?"

Nancy heard her own answer through a velvet fog. She was amazed by the answer, wanted to protest that it couldn't possibly be hers. "Pointless," she'd said.

Moments later, she asked the woman thickly, "What was in that needle?"

"What was in the needle, honey bunch? Why, honey bunch, they call that 'truth serum.' "

The moon was down when Nancy woke up—but the night was still out there. The shades were drawn and there was candlelight. Nancy had never seen a lit candle before.

What awakened Nancy was a dream of mosquitoes and bees. Mosquitoes and bees were extinct. So were birds. But Nancy dreamed that millions of insects were swarming about her from the waist down. They didn't sting. They fanned her. Nancy was a nothinghead.

She went to sleep again. When she awoke next time, she was being led into a bathroom by three women, still with stockings over their heads. The bathroom was already filled with the steam from somebody else's bath. There were somebody else's wet footprints crisscrossing the floor and the air reeked of pine-needle perfume.

Her will and intelligence returned as she was bathed and perfumed and dressed in a white nightgown. When the women stepped back to admire her, she said to them quietly, "I may be a nothinghead now. But that doesn't mean I have to think like one or act like one."

Nobody argued with her.

Nancy was taken downstairs and out of the house. She fully expected to be sent down a manhole again. It would be the perfect setting for her violation by Billy, she was thinking—down in a sewer.

But they took her across the green cement, where the grass used to be, and then across the yellow cement, where the beach used to be, and then out onto the blue cement, where the harbor used to be. There were twenty-six yachts that had belonged to various Kennedys, sunk up to their water lines in blue cement. It was to the most ancient of these yachts, the Marlin, once the property of Joseph P. Kennedy, that they delivered Nancy.

It was dawn. Because of the high-rise apartments all around the Kennedy Museum, it would be an hour before any direct sunlight would reach the microcosm under the geodesic dome.

Nancy was escorted as far as the companionway to the forward cabin of the Marlin. The women pantomimed that she was expected to go down the five steps alone.

Nancy froze for the moment and so did the women. And there were two actual statues in the tableau on the bridge. Standing at the wheel was a statue of Frank Wirtanen, once skipper of the Marlin. And next to him was his son and first mate, Carly. They weren't paying any attention to poor Nancy. They were staring out through the windshield at the blue cement.

Nancy, barefoot and wearing a thin white nightgown, descended bravely into the forward cabin, which was a pool of candlelight and pine-needle perfume. The companionway hatch was closed and locked behind her.

Nancy's emotions and the antique furnishings of the cabin were so complex that Nancy could not at first separate Billy the Poet from his surroundings, from all the mahogany and leaded glass. And then she saw him at the far end of the cabin, with his back against the door to the forward cockpit. He was wearing purple silk pajamas with a Russian collar. They were piped in red, and writhing across Billy's silken breast was a golden dragon. It was belching fire.

Anticlimactically, Billy was wearing glasses. He was holding a book.

Nancy poised herself on the next-to-the-bottom step,

took a firm grip on the handholds in the companionway. She bared her teeth, calculated that it would take ten men Billy's size to dislodge her.

Between them was a great table. Nancy had expected the cabin to be dominated by a bed, possibly in the shape of a swan, but the Marlin was a day boat. The cabin was anything but a seraglio. It was about as voluptuous as a lower-middle-class dining room in Akron, Ohio, around 1910.

A candle was on the table. So were an ice bucket and two glasses and a quart of champagne. Champagne was as illegal as heroin.

Billy took off his glasses, gave her a shy, embarrassed smile, said, "Welcome."

"This is as far as I come."

He accepted that. "You're very beautiful there."

"And what am I supposed to say—that you're stunningly handsome? That I feel an overwhelming desire to throw myself into your manly arms?"

"If you wanted to make me happy, that would certainly be the way to do it." He said that humbly.

"And what about *my* happiness?"

The question seemed to puzzle him. "Nancy—that's what this is all about."

"What if my idea of happiness doesn't coincide with yours?"

"And what do you think my idea of happiness is?"

"I'm not going to throw myself into your arms, and I'm not going to drink that poison, and I'm not going to budge from here unless somebody makes me," said Nancy. "So I think your idea of happiness is going to turn out to be eight people holding me down on that table, while you bravely hold a cocked pistol to my head—and do what you want. That's the way it's going to have to be, so call your friends and get it over with!"

Which he did.

He didn't hurt her. He deflowered her with a clinical skill she found ghastly. When it was all over, he didn't seem cocky or proud. On the contrary, he was terribly depressed, and he said to Nancy, "Believe me, if there'd been any other way——"

Her reply to this was a face like stone—and silent tears of humiliation.

His helpers let down a folding bunk from the wall. It was scarcely wider than a bookshelf and hung on chains. Nancy allowed herself to be put to bed in it, and she was left alone with Billy the Poet again. Big as she was, like a double bass wedged on that narrow shelf, she felt like a pitiful little thing. A scratchy, war-surplus blanket had been tucked in around her. It was her own idea to pull up a corner of the blanket to hide her face.

Nancy sensed from sounds what Billy was doing, which wasn't much. He was sitting at the table, sighing occasionally, sniffing occasionally, turning the pages of a book. He lit a cigar and the stink of it seeped under the blanket. Billy inhaled the cigar, then coughed and coughed and coughed.

When the coughing died down, Nancy said loathingly through the blanket, "You're so strong, so masterful, so healthy. It must be wonderful to be so manly."

Billy only sighed at this.

"I'm not a very typical nothinghead," she said. "I hated it—hated everything about it."

Billy sniffed, turned a page.

"I suppose all the other women just loved it—couldn't get enough of it."

"Nope."

She uncovered her face. "What do you mean, 'Nope'?"

"They've all been like you."

This was enough to make Nancy sit up and stare at him. "The women who helped you tonight——"

"What about them?"

"You've done to them what you did to me?"

He didn't look up from his book. "That's right."

"Then why don't they kill you instead of helping you?"

"Because they understand." And then he added mildly, "They're *grateful*."

Nancy got out of bed, came to the table, gripped the

edge of the table, leaned close to him. And she said to him tautly, "I am not grateful."

"You will be."

"And what could possibly bring about that miracle?"

"Time," said Billy.

Billy closed his book, stood up. Nancy was confused by his magnetism. Somehow he was very much in charge again.

"What you've been through, Nancy," he said, "is a typical wedding night for a strait-laced girl of a hundred years ago, when everybody was a nothinghead. The groom did without helpers, because the bride wasn't customarily ready to kill him. Otherwise, the spirit of the occasion was much the same. These are the pajamas my great-great-grandfather wore on his wedding night in Niagara Falls.

"According to his diary, his bride cried all that night, and threw up twice. But, with the passage of time, she became a sexual enthusiast."

It was Nancy's turn to reply by not replying. She understood the tale. It frightened her to understand so easily that, from gruesome beginnings, sexual enthusiasm could grow and grow.

"You're a very typical nothinghead," said Billy. "If you dare to think about it now, you'll realize that you're angry because I'm such a bad lover, and a funny-looking shrimp besides. And what you can't help dreaming about from now on is a really suitable mate for a Juno like yourself.

"You'll find him, too—tall and strong and gentle. The nothinghead movement is growing by leaps and bounds."

"But——" said Nancy, and she stopped there. She looked out a porthole at the rising sun.

"But what?"

"The world is in the mess it is today because of the nothingheadedness of olden times. Don't you see?" She was pleading weakly. "The world can't afford sex anymore."

"Of course it can afford sex," said Billy. "All it can't afford anymore is reproduction."

"Then why the laws?"

"They're bad laws," said Billy. "If you go back through

history, you'll find that the people who have been most eager to rule, to make the laws, to enforce the laws and to tell everybody exactly how God Almighty wants things here on Earth—those people have forgiven themselves and their friends for anything and everything. But they have been absolutely disgusted and terrified by the natural sexuality of common men and women.

"Why this is, I do not know. That is one of the many questions I wish somebody would ask the machines. I do know this: The triumph of that sort of disgust and terror is now complete. Almost every man and woman looks and feels like something the cat dragged in. The only sexual beauty that an ordinary human being can see today is in the woman who will kill him. Sex is death. There's a short and nasty equation for you: 'Sex is death. Q. E. D.'

"So you see, Nancy," said Billy, "I have spent this night, and many others like it, attempting to restore a certain amount of innocent pleasure to the world, which is poorer in pleasure than it needs to be."

Nancy sat down quietly and bowed her head.

"I'll tell you what my grandfather did on the dawn of his wedding night," said Billy.

"I don't think I want to hear it."

"It isn't violent. It's—it's meant to be tender."

"Maybe that's why I don't want to hear it."

"He read his bride a poem." Billy took the book from the table, opened it. "His diary tells which poem it was. While we aren't bride and groom, and while we may not meet again for many years, I'd like to read this poem to you, to have you know I've loved you."

"Please—no. I couldn't stand it."

"All right, I'll leave the book here, with the place marked, in case you want to read it later. It's the poem beginning:

How do I love thee? Let me count the ways.
I love thee to the depth and breadth and height
My soul can reach, when feeling out of sight
For the ends of Being and ideal Grace."

Billy put a small bottle on top of the book. "I am also leaving you these pills. If you take one a month, you will never have children. And still you'll be a nothinghead."

And he left. And they all left but Nancy.

When Nancy raised her eyes at last to the book and bottle, she saw that there was a label on the bottle. What the label said was this: WELCOME TO THE MONKEY HOUSE.

(1968)

LONG WALK
TO FOREVER

THEY HAD GROWN UP next door to each other, on the fringe of a city, near fields and woods and orchards, within sight of a lovely bell tower that belonged to a school for the blind.

Now they were twenty, had not seen each other for nearly a year. There had always been playful, comfortable warmth between them, but never any talk of love.

His name was Newt. Her name was Catharine. In the early afternoon, Newt knocked on Catharine's front door.

Catharine came to the door. She was carrying a fat, glossy magazine she had been reading. The magazine was devoted entirely to brides. "Newt!" she said. She was surprised to see him.

"Could you come for a walk?" he said. He was a shy person, even with Catharine. He covered his shyness by speaking absently, as though what really concerned him were far away—as though he were a secret agent pausing briefly on a mission between beautiful, distant, and sinister points. This manner of speaking had always been Newt's style, even in matters that concerned him desperately.

"A walk?" said Catharine.

"One foot in front of the other," said Newt, "through leaves, over bridges——"

"I had no idea you were in town," she said.

"Just this minute got in," he said.

"Still in the Army, I see," she said.

"Seven more months to go," he said. He was a private first class in the Artillery. His uniform was rumpled. His shoes were dusty. He needed a shave. He held out his hand for the magazine. "Let's see the pretty book," he said.

She gave it to him. "I'm getting married, Newt," she said.

"I know," he said. "Let's go for a walk."

"I'm awfully busy, Newt," she said. "The wedding is only a week away."

"If we go for a walk," he said, "it will make you rosy. It will make you a rosy bride." He turned the pages of the magazine. "A rosy bride like her—like her—like her," he said, showing her rosy brides.

Catharine turned rosy, thinking about rosy brides.

"That will be my present to Henry Stewart Chasens," said Newt. "By taking you for a walk, I'll be giving him a rosy bride."

"You know his name?" said Catharine.

"Mother wrote," he said. "From Pittsburgh?"

"Yes," she said. "You'd like him."

"Maybe," he said.

"Can—can you come to the wedding, Newt?" she said.

"That I doubt," he said.

"Your furlough isn't for long enough?" she said.

"Furlough?" said Newt. He was studying a two-page ad for flat silver. "I'm not on furlough," he said.

"Oh?" she said.

"I'm what they call A.W.O.L.," said Newt.

"Oh, Newt! You're not!" she said.

"Sure I am," he said, still looking at the magazine.

"Why, Newt?" she said.

"I had to find out what your silver pattern is," he said. He read names of silver patterns from the magazine. "Albemarle? Heather?" he said. "Legend? Rambler Rose?" He looked up, smiled. "I plan to give you and your husband a spoon," he said.

"Newt, Newt—tell me really," she said.

"I want to go for a walk," he said.

She wrung her hands in sisterly anguish. "Oh, Newt—you're fooling me about being A.W.O.L.," she said.

Newt imitated a police siren softly, raised his eyebrows.

"Where—where from?" she said.

"Fort Bragg," he said.

"North Carolina?" she said.

"That's right," he said. "Near Fayetteville—where Scarlet O'Hara went to school."

"How did you get here, Newt?" she said.

He raised his thumb, jerked it in a hitchhike gesture. "Two days," he said.

"Does your mother know?" she said.

"I didn't come to see my mother," he told her.

"Who did you come to see?" she said.

"You," he said.

"Why me?" she said.

"Because I love you," he said. "Now can we take a walk?" he said. "One foot in front of the other—through leaves, over bridges——"

They were taking the walk now, were in a woods with a brown-leaf floor.

Catharine was angry and rattled, close to tears. "Newt," she said, "this is absolutely crazy."

"How so?" said Newt.

"What a crazy time to tell me you love me," she said. "You never talked that way before." She stopped walking.

"Let's keep walking," he said.

"No," she said. "So far, no farther. I shouldn't have come out with you at all," she said.

"You did," he said.

"To get you out of the house," she said. "If somebody walked in and heard you talking to me that way, a week before the wedding——"

"What would they think?" he said.

"They'd think you were crazy," she said.

"Why?" he said.

Catharine took a deep breath, made a speech. "Let me say that I'm deeply honored by this crazy thing you've done," she said. "I can't believe you're really A.W.O.L., but maybe you are. I can't believe you really love me, but maybe you do. But——"

"I do," said Newt.

"Well, I'm deeply honored," said Catharine, "and I'm very fond of you as a friend, Newt, extremely fond—but it's just too late." She took a step away from him. "You've never even kissed me," she said, and she protected herself with her hands. "I don't mean you should do it now. I just mean this is all so unexpected. I haven't got the remotest idea of how to respond."

"Just walk some more," he said. "Have a nice time."

They started walking again.

"How did you expect me to react?" she said.

"How would I know what to expect?" he said. "I've never done anything like this before."

"Did you think I would throw myself into your arms?" she said.

"Maybe," he said.

"I'm sorry to disappoint you," she said.

"I'm not disappointed," he said. "I wasn't counting on it. This is very nice, just walking."

Catharine stopped again. "You know what happens next?" she said.

"Nope," he said.

"We shake hands," she said. "We shake hands and part friends," she said. "That's what happens next."

Newt nodded. "All right," he said. "Remember me from time to time. Remember how much I loved you."

Involuntarily, Catharine burst into tears. She turned her back to Newt, looked into the infinite colonnade of the woods.

"What does that mean?" said Newt.

"Rage!" said Catharine. She clenched her hands. "You have no right——"

"I had to find out," he said.

"If I'd loved you," she said, "I would have let you know before now.

"You would?" he said.

"Yes," she said. She faced him, looked up at him, her face quite red. "You would have known," she said.

"How?" he said.

"You would have seen it," she said. "Women aren't very clever at hiding it."

Newt looked closely at Catharine's face now. To her consternation, she realized that what she had said was true, that a woman couldn't hide love.

Newt was seeing love now.

And he did what he had to do. He kissed her.

"You're hell to get along with!" she said when Newt let her go.

"I am?" said Newt.

"You shouldn't have done that," she said.

"You didn't like it?" he said.

"What did you expect," she said—"wild, abandoned passion?"

"I keep telling you," he said, "I never know what's going to happen next."

"We say good-by," she said.

He frowned slightly. "All right," he said.

She made another speech. "I'm not sorry we kissed," she said. "That was sweet. We should have kissed, we've been so close. I'll always remember you, Newt, and good luck."

"You too," he said.

"Thank you, Newt," she said.

"Thirty days," he said.

"What?" she said.

"Thirty days in the stockade," he said—"that's what one kiss will cost me."

"I—I'm sorry," she said, "but I didn't ask you to go A.W.O.L."

"I know," he said.

"You certainly don't deserve any hero's reward for doing something as foolish as that," she said.

"Must be nice to be a hero," said Newt. "Is Henry Stewart Chasens a hero?"

"He might be, if he got the chance," said Catharine. She noted uneasily that they had begun to walk again. The farewell had been forgotten.

"You really love him?" he said.

"Certainly I love him!" she said hotly. "I wouldn't marry him if I didn't love him!"

"What's good about him?" said Newt.

"Honestly!" she cried, stopping again. "Do you have any idea how offensive you're being? Many, many, many things are good about Henry! Yes," she said, "and many, many,

many things are probably bad too. But that isn't any of your business. I love Henry, and I don't have to argue his merits with you!"

"Sorry," said Newt.

"Honestly!" said Catharine.

Newt kissed her again. He kissed her again because she wanted him to.

They were now in a large orchard.

"How did we get so far from home, Newt?" said Catharine.

"One foot in front of the other—through leaves, over bridges," said Newt.

"They add up—the steps," she said.

Bells rang in the tower of the school for the blind nearby.

"School for the blind," said Newt.

"School for the blind," said Catharine. She shook her head in drowsy wonder. "I've got to go back now," she said.

"Say good-by," said Newt.

"Every time I do," said Catharine, "I seem to get kissed."

Newt sat down on the close-cropped grass under an apple tree. "Sit down," he said.

"No," she said.

"I won't touch you," he said.

"I don't believe you," she said.

She sat down under another tree, twenty feet away from him. She closed her eyes.

"Dream of Henry Stewart Chasens," he said.

"What?" she said.

"Dream of your wonderful husband-to-be," he said.

"All right, I will," she said. She closed her eyes tighter, caught glimpses of her husband-to-be.

Newt yawned.

The bees were humming in the trees, and Catharine almost fell asleep. When she opened her eyes she saw that Newt really was asleep.

He began to snore softly.

Catharine let Newt sleep for an hour, and while he slept she adored him with all her heart.

The shadows of the apple trees grew to the east. The bells in the tower of the school for the blind rang again.

"Chick-a-dee-dee-dee," went a chickadee.

Somewhere far away an automobile starter nagged and failed, nagged and failed, fell still.

Catharine came out from under her tree, knelt by Newt.

"Newt?" she said.

"H'm?" he said. He opened his eyes.

"Late," she said.

"Hello, Catharine," he said.

"Hello, Newt," she said.

"I love you," he said.

"I know," she said.

"Too late," he said.

"Too late," she said.

He stood, stretched groaningly. "A very nice walk," he said.

"I thought so," she said.

"Part company here?" he said.

"Where will you go?" she said.

"Hitch into town, turn myself in," he said.

"Good luck," she said.

"You, too," he said. "Marry me, Catharine?"

"No," she said.

He smiled, stared at her hard for a moment, then walked away quickly.

Catharine watched him grow smaller in the long perspective of shadows and trees, knew that if he stopped and turned now, if he called to her, she would run to him. She would have no choice.

Newt did stop. He did turn. He did call. "Catharine," he called.

She ran to him, put her arms around him, could not speak.

(1960)

THE FOSTER
PORTFOLIO

I'M A SALESMAN of good advice for rich people. I'm a contact man for an investment counseling firm. It's a living, but not a whale of a one—or at least not now, when I'm just starting out. To qualify for the job, I had to buy a Homburg, a navy-blue overcoat; a double-breasted banker's gray suit, black shoes, a regimental-stripe tie, half a dozen white shirts, half a dozen pairs of black socks and gray gloves.

When I call on a client, I come by cab, and I am sleek and clean and foursquare. I carry myself as though I've made a quiet killing on the stock market, and have come to call more as a public service than anything else. When I arrive in clean wool, with crackling certificates and confidential stock analyses in crisp Manila folders, the reaction —ideally and usually—is the same accorded a minister or physician. I am in charge, and everything is going to be just fine.

I deal mostly with old ladies—the meek, who by dint of castiron constitutions have inherited sizable portions of the earth. I thumb through the clients' lists of securities, and relay our experts' suggestions for ways of making their portfolios—or bonanzas or piles—thrive and increase. I can speak of tens of thousands of dollars without a catch in my throat, and look at a list of securities worth more than a hundred thousand with no more fuss than a judicious "Mmmmm, uh-huh."

Since *I* don't have a portfolio, my job is a little like being a hungry delivery boy for a candy store. But I never really felt that way about it until Herbert Foster asked me to have a look at his finances.

He called one evening to say a friend had recommended me, and could I come out to talk business. I washed, shaved, dusted my shoes, put on my uniform, and made my grave arrival by cab.

People in my business—and maybe people in general—have an unsavory habit of sizing up a man's house, car, and suit, and estimating his annual income. Herbert Foster was six thousand a year, or I'd never seen it. Understand, I have nothing against people in moderate circumstances, other than the crucial fact that I can't make any money off them. It made me a little sore that Foster would take my time, when the most he had to play around with, I guessed, was no more than a few hundred dollars. Say it was a thousand: my take would be a dollar or two at best.

Anyway, there I was in the Fosters' jerry-built postwar colonial with expansion attic. They had taken up a local furniture store on its offer of three rooms of furniture, including ashtrays, a humidor, and pictures for the wall, all for $199.99. Hell, I was there, and I figured I might as well go through with having a look at his pathetic problem.

"Nice place you have here, Mr. Foster," I said. "And this is your charming wife?"

A skinny, shrewish-looking woman smiled up at me vacuously. She wore a faded housecoat figured with a fox-hunting scene. The print was at war with the slipcover of the chair, and I had to squint to separate her features from the clash about her. "A pleasure, Mrs. Foster," I said. She was surrounded by underwear and socks to be mended, and Herbert said her name was Alma, which seemed entirely possible.

"And this is the young master," I said. "Bright little chap. Believe he favors his father." The two-year-old wiped his grubby hands on my trousers, snuffled, and padded off toward the piano. He stationed himself at the upper end of the keyboard, and hammered on the highest note for one minute, then two, then three.

"Musical—like his father," Alma said.

"You play, do you, Mr. Foster?"

"Classical," Herbert said. I took my first good look at

him. He was lightly built, with the round, freckled face and big teeth I usually associate with a show-off or wise guy. It was hard to believe that he had settled for so plain a wife, or that he could be as fond of family life as he seemed. It may have been that I only imagined a look of quiet desperation in his eyes.

"Shouldn't you be getting on to your meeting, dear?" Herbert said.

"It was called off at the last minute."

"Now, about your portfolio—" I began.

Herbert looked rattled. "How's that?"

"Your portfolio—your securities."

"Yes, well, I think we'd better talk in the bedroom. It's quieter in there."

Alma put down her sewing. "What securities?"

"The bonds, dear. The government bonds."

"Now, Herbert, you're not going to cash them in."

"No, Alma, just want to talk them over."

"I see," I said tentatively. "Uh—approximately how much in government bonds?"

"Three hundred and fifty dollars," Alma said proudly.

"Well," I said, "I don't see any need for going into the bedroom to talk. My advice, and I give it free, is to hang on to your nest egg until it matures. And now, if you'll let me phone a cab—"

"Please," Herbert said, standing in the bedroom door, "there are a couple of other things I'd like to discuss."

"What?" Alma said.

"Oh, long-range investment planning," Herbert said vaguely.

"We could use a little short-range planning for next month's grocery bill."

"Please," Herbert said to me again.

I shrugged and followed him into the bedroom. He closed the door behind me. I sat on the edge of the bed and watched him open a little door in the wall, which bared the pipes servicing the bathroom. He slid his arm up into the wall, grunted, and pulled down an envelope.

"Oho," I said apathetically, "so that's where we've got the bonds, eh? Very clever. You needn't have gone to that trouble, Mr. Foster. I have an idea what government bonds look like."

"Alma," he called.

"Yes, Herbert."

"Will you start some coffee for us?"

"I don't drink coffee at night," I said.

"We have some from dinner," Alma said.

"I can't sleep if I touch it after supper," I said.

"Fresh—we want some fresh," Herbert said.

The chair springs creaked, and her reluctant footsteps faded into the kitchen.

"Here," said Herbert, putting the envelope in my lap. "I don't know anything about this business, and I guess I ought to have professional help."

All right, so I'd give the poor guy a professional talk about his three hundred and fifty dollars in government bonds. "They're the most conservative investment you can make. They haven't the growth characteristics of many securities, and the return isn't great, but they're very safe. By all means hang onto them." I stood up. "And now, if you'll let me call a cab—"

"You haven't looked at them."

I sighed, and untwisted the red string holding the envelope shut. Nothing would do but that I admire the things. The bonds and a list of securities slid into my lap. I riffled through the bonds quickly, and then read the list of securities slowly.

"Well?"

I put the list down on the faded bedspread. I composed myself. "Mmmmm, uh-huh," I said. "Do you mind telling me where the securities listed here came from?"

"Grandfather left them to me two years ago. The lawyers who handled the estate have them. They sent me that list."

"Do you know what these stocks are worth?"

"They were appraised when I inherited them." He told me the figure, and, to my bewilderment, he looked sheepish, even a little unhappy about it.

"They've gone up a little since then."

"How much?"

"On today's market—maybe they're worth seven hundred and fifty thousand dollars, Mr. Foster. Sir."

His expression didn't change. My news moved him about as much as if I'd told him it'd been a chilly winter. He raised his eyebrows as Alma's footsteps came back into the living room. "Shhhh!"

"She doesn't know?"

"Lord, no!" He seemed to have surprised himself with his vehemence. "I mean the time isn't ripe."

"If you'll let me have this list of securities, I'll have our New York office give you a complete analysis and recommendations," I whispered. "May I call you Herbert, sir?"

My client, Herbert Foster, hadn't had a new suit in three years; he had never owned more than one pair of shoes at a time. He worried about payments on his second-hand car, and ate tuna and cheese instead of meat, because meat was too expensive. His wife made her own clothes, and those of Herbert, Jr., and the curtains and slipcovers —all cut from the same bargain bolt. The Fosters were going through hell, trying to choose between new tires or retreads for the car; and television was something they had to go two doors down the street to watch. Determinedly, they kept within the small salary Herbert made as a bookkeeper for a wholesale grocery house.

God knows it's no disgrace to live that way, which is better than the way I live, but it was pretty disturbing to watch, knowing Herbert had an income, after taxes, of perhaps twenty thousand a year.

I had our securities analysts look over Foster's holdings, and report on the stocks' growth possibilities, prospective earnings, the effect of war and peace, inflation and deflation, and so on. The report ran to twenty pages, a record for any of my clients. Usually, the reports are bound in cardboard covers. Herbert's was done up in red leatherette.

It arrived at my place on a Saturday afternoon, and I called up Herbert to ask if I could bring it out. I had exciting news for him. My by-eye estimate of the values had been off, and his portfolio, as of that day, was worth close to eight hundred and fifty thousand.

"I've got the analysis and recommendations," I said, "and things look good, Mr. Foster—*very* good. You need a little diversification here and there, and maybe more emphasis on growth, but—"

"Just go ahead and do whatever needs to be done," he said.

"When could we talk about this? It's something we ought to go over together, certainly. Tonight would be fine with me."

"I work tonight."

"Overtime at the wholesale house?"

"Another job—in a restaurant. Work Friday, Saturday, and Sunday nights."

I winced. The man had maybe seventy-five dollars a day coming in from his securities, and he worked three nights a week to make ends meet! "Monday?"

"Play organ for choir practice at the church."

"Tuesday?"

"Volunteer Fire Department drill."

"Wednesday?"

"Play piano for folk dancing at the church."

"Thursday?"

"Movie night for Alma and me."

"When, then?"

"You go ahead and do whatever needs to be done."

"Don't you want to be in on what I'm doing?"

"Do I have to be?"

"I'd feel better if you were."

"All right, Tuesday noon, lunch."

"Fine with me. Maybe you'd better have a good look at this report before then, so you can have questions ready."

He sounded annoyed. "Okay, okay, okay. I'll be here tonight until nine. Drop it off before then."

"One more thing, Herbert." I'd saved the kicker for last. "I was way off about what the stocks are worth. They're now up to about eight hundred and fifty thousand dollars."

"Um."

"I said, you're about a hundred thousand dollars richer than you thought!"

"Uh-huh. Well, you just go ahead and do whatever needs to be done."

"Yes, sir." The phone was dead.

I was delayed by other business, and I didn't get out to the Fosters' until quarter of ten. Herbert was gone. Alma answered the door, and, to my surprise, she asked for the report, which I was hiding under my coat.

"Herbert said I wasn't supposed to look at it," she said, "so you don't need to worry about me peeking."

"Herbert told you about this?" I said carefully.

"Yes. He said it's confidential reports on stocks you want to sell him."

"Yes, uh-huh—well, if he said to leave it with you, here it is."

"He told me he had to promise you not to let *anybody* look at it."

"Mmm? Oh, yes, yes. Sorry, company rules."

She was a shade hostile. "I'll tell you one thing without looking at any reports, and that is he's not going to cash those bonds to buy any stocks with."

"I'd be the last one to recommend that, Mrs. Foster."

"Then why do you keep after him?"

"He may be a good customer at a later date." I looked at my hands, which I realized had become inkstained on the earlier call. "I wonder if I might wash up?"

Reluctantly, she let me in, keeping as far away from me as the modest floor pl..n would permit.

As I washed up, I thought of the list of securities Herbert had taken from between the plasterboard walls. Those securities meant winters in Florida, *filet mignon* and twelve-year-old bourbon, Jaguars, silk underwear and handmade shoes, a trip around the world. . . . Name it; Herbert Foster could have it. I sighed heavily. The soap in the Foster soap dish was mottled and dingy—a dozen little chips moistened and pressed together to make a new bar.

I thanked Alma, and started to leave. On my way out, I

paused by the mantel to look at a small tinted photograph. "Good picture of you," I said. A feeble effort at public relations. "I like that."

"Everybody says that. It isn't me; it's Herbert's mother."

"Amazing likeness." And it was. Herbert had married a girl just like the girl that married dear old dad. "And this picture is his father?"

"*My* father. We don't want a picture of *his* father."

This looked like a sore point that might prove informative. "Herbert is such a wonderful person, his father must have been wonderful, too, eh?"

"He deserted his wife and child. That's how wonderful he was. You'll be smart not to mention him to Herbert."

"Sorry. Everything good about Herbert comes from his mother?"

"She was a saint. She taught Herbert to be decent and respectable and God-fearing." Alma was grim about it.

"Was she musical, too?"

"He gets that from his father. But what he does with it is something quite different. His taste in music is his mother's —the classics."

"His father was a jazz man, I take it?" I hinted.

"He preferred playing piano in dives, and breathing smoke and drinking gin, to his wife and child and home and job. Herbert's mother finally said he had to choose one life or the other."

I nodded sympathetically. Maybe Herbert looked on his fortune as filthy, untouchable, since it came from his father's side of the family. "This grandfather of Herbert's, who died two years ago—?"

"He supported Herbert and his mother after his son deserted them. Herbert worshipped him." She shook her head sadly. "He was penniless when he died."

"What a shame."

"I'd so hoped he would leave us a little something, so Herbert wouldn't have to work weekends."

We were trying to talk above the clatter, tinkle, and crash of the cafeteria where Herbert ate every day.

Lunch was on me—or on my expense account—and I'd picked up his check for eighty-seven cents. I said, "Now, Herbert, before we go any further, we'd better decide what you want from your investments: growth or income." It was a cliché of the counseling business. God knows what *he* wanted from the securities. It didn't seem to be what everybody else wanted—money.

"Whatever you say," Herbert said absently. He was upset about something, and not paying much attention to me.

"Herbert—look, you've got to face this thing. You're a rich man. You've got to concentrate on making the most of your holdings."

"That's why I called you. I want *you* to concentrate. I want you to run things for me, so I won't have to bother with the deposits and proxies and taxes. Don't trouble me with it at all."

"Your lawyers have been banking the dividends, eh?"

"Most of them. Took out thirty-two dollars for Christmas, and gave a hundred to the church."

"So what's your balance?"

He handed me the deposit book.

"Not bad," I said. Despite his Christmas splurge and largess toward the church, he'd managed to salt away $50,227.33. "May I ask what a man with a balance like that can be blue about?"

"Got bawled out at work again."

"Buy the place and burn it down," I suggested.

"I could, couldn't I?" A wild look came into his eyes, then disappeared.

"Herbert, you can do anything your heart desires."

"Oh, I suppose so. It's all in the way you look at it."

I leaned forward. "How *do* you look at it, Herbert?"

"I think every man, for his own self-respect, should earn what he lives on."

"But, Herbert—"

"I have a wonderful wife and child, a nice house for them, and a car. And I've earned every penny of the way. I'm living up to the full measure of my responsibilities. I'm proud to say I'm everything my mother wanted me to be, and nothing my father was."

"Do you mind my asking what your father was?"

"I don't enjoy talking about him. Home and family meant nothing to him. His real love was for low-down music and honky-tonks, and for the trash in them."

"Was he a good musician, do you think?"

"Good?" For an instant, there was excitement in his voice, and he tensed, as though he were going to make an important point. But he relaxed again. "Good?" he repeated, flatly this time. "Yes, in a crude way, I suppose he was passable—technically, that is."

"And that much you inherited from him."

"His wrists and hands, maybe. God help me if there's any more of him in me."

"You've got his love of music, too."

"I love music, but I'd never let it get like dope to me!" he said, with more force than seemed necessary.

"Uh-huh. Well—"

"Never!"

"Beg your pardon?"

His eyes were wide. "I said I'll never let music get like dope to me. It's important to me, but I'm master of it, and not the other way around."

Apparently it was a treacherous subject, so I switched back to the matter of his finances. "Yes, well, now about your portfolio again: just what use do you expect to make of it?"

"Use some of it for Alma's and my old age; leave most of it to the boy."

"The least you can do is take enough out of the kitty to let you out of working weekends."

He stood up suddenly. "Look. I want you to handle my securities, not my life. If you can't do one without the other, I'll find someone who can."

"Please, Herbert, Mr. Foster. I'm sorry, sir. I was only trying to get the whole picture for planning."

He sat down, red-faced. "All right then, respect my

convictions. I want to make my own way. If I have to hold a second job to make ends meet, then that's my cross to bear."

"Sure, sure, certainly. And you're dead right, Herbert. I respect you for it." I thought he belonged in the bughouse for it. "You leave everything to me from now on. I'll invest those dividends and run the whole show." As I puzzled over Herbert, I glanced at a passing blonde. Herbert said something I missed. "What was that, Herbert?"

"I said, 'If thy right eye offend thee, pluck it out and cast it from thee.'"

I laughed appreciatively, then cut it short. Herbert was deadly serious. "Well, pretty soon you'll have the car paid for, and then you can take a well-earned rest on the weekends. And you'll really have something to be proud of, eh? Earned the whole car by the sweat of your brow, right down to the tip of the exhaust pipe."

"One more payment."

"*Then* by-by, restaurant."

"There'll still be Alma's birthday present to pay for. I'm getting her television."

"Going to earn that, too, are you?"

"Think how much more meaningful it will be as a gift, if I do."

"Yes, sir, and it'll give her something to do on weekends, too."

"If I have to work weekends for twenty-eight more months, God knows it's little enough to do for her."

If the stock market kept doing what it had been doing for the past three years, Herbert would be a millionaire just about the time he made the last payment on Alma's birthday present. "Fine."

"I love my family," Herbert said earnestly.

"I'm sure you do."

"And I wouldn't trade the life I've got for anything."

"I can certainly see why," I said. I had the impression that he was arguing with me, that it was important to him that I be convinced.

"When I consider what my father was, and then see the

life I've made for myself, it's the biggest thrill in all my experience."

A very small thrill could qualify for the biggest in Herbert's experience, I thought. "I envy you. It must be gratifying."

"Gratifying," he repeated determinedly. "It is, it is, it is."

My firm began managing Herbert's portfolio, converting some of the slower-moving securities into more lucrative ones, investing the accumulated dividends, diversifying his holdings so he'd be in better shape to weather economic shifts—and in general making his fortune altogether ship-shape. A sound portfolio is a thing of beauty in its way, aside from its cash value. Putting one together is a creative act, if done right, with solid major themes of industrials, rails, and utilities, and with the lighter, more exciting themes of electronics, frozen foods, magic drugs, oil and gas, aviation, and other more speculative items. Herbert's portfolio was our masterpiece. I was thrilled and proud of what the firm had done, and not being able to show it off, even to him, was depressing.

It was too much for me, and I decided to engineer a coincidence. I would find out in which restaurant Herbert worked, and then drop in, like any other citizen, for something to eat. I would happen to have a report on his overhauled portfolio with me.

I telephoned Alma, who told me the name of the place, one I'd never heard of. Herbert hadn't wanted to talk about the place, so I gathered that it was pretty grim—as he said, his cross to bear.

It was worse than I'd expected: tough, brassy, dark, and noisy. Herbert had picked one hell of a place, indeed, to do penance for a wayward father, or to demonstrate his gratitude to his wife, or to maintain his self-respect by earning his own way—or to do whatever it was he was doing there.

I elbowed my way between bored-looking women and racetrack types to the bar. I had to shout at the bartender to be heard. When I did get through to him, he yelled back that he'd never heard of no Herbert Foster. Herbert, then, was about as minor an employee as there was in the establishment. He was probably doing something greasy in the kitchen or basement. Typical.

In the kitchen, a crone was making questionable-looking hamburgers, and nipping at a quart of beer.

"I'm looking for Herbert Foster."

"Ain' no damn' Herbert Foster in here."

"In the basement?"

"Ain' no damn' basement."

"Ever hear of Herbert Foster?"

"Ain't never heard of no damn' Herbert Foster."

"Thanks."

I sat in a booth to think it over. Herbert had apparently picked the joint out of a telephone book, and told Alma it was where he spent his weekend evenings. In a way, it made me feel better, because it began to look as though Herbert maybe had better reasons than he'd given me for letting eight hundred and fifty thousand dollars get musty. I remembered that every time I'd mentioned his giving up the weekend job, he'd reacted like a man hearing a dentist tune up his drill. I saw it now: the minute he let Alma know he was rich, he'd lose his excuse for getting away from her on weekends.

But what was it that was worth more to Herbert than eight hundred and fifty thousand? Binges? Dope? Women? I sighed, and admitted I was kidding myself, that I was no closer to the answer than I'd ever been. Moral turpitude on Herbert's part was inconceivable. Whatever he was up to, it had to be for a good cause. His mother had done such a thorough job on him, and he was so awfully ashamed of his father's failings, that I was sure he couldn't operate any other way but righteously. I gave up on the puzzle, and ordered a nightcap.

And then Herbert Foster, looking drab and hunted, picked his way through the crowd. His expression was one of disapproval, of a holy man in Babylon. He was oddly stiff-necked and held his arms at his sides as he pointedly kept from brushing against anyone or from meeting any of the gazes that fell upon him. There was no question that being in the place was absolute, humiliating hell for him.

I called to him, but he paid no attention. There was no communicating with him. Herbert was in a near coma of seen-no-evil, speak-no-evil, hear-no-evil.

The crowd in the rear parted for him, and I expected to see Herbert go into a dark corner for a broom or a mop. But a light flashed on at the far end of the aisle the crowd made for him, and a tiny white piano sparkled there like jewelry. The bartender set a drink on the piano, and went back to his post.

Herbert dusted off the piano bench with his handkerchief, and sat down gingerly. He took a cigarette from his breast pocket and lighted it. And then the cigarette started to droop slowly from his lips; and, as it drooped, Herbert hunched over the keyboard and his eyes narrowed as though he were focusing on something beautiful on a faraway horizon.

Startlingly, Herbert Foster disappeared. In his place sat an excited stranger, his hands poised like claws. Suddenly he struck, and a spasm of dirty, low-down, gorgeous jazz shook the air, a hot, clanging wraith of the twenties.

Late that night I went over my masterpiece, the portfolio of Herbert Foster, alias "Firehouse" Harris. I hadn't bothered Firehouse with it or with myself.

In a week or so, there would be a juicy melon from one of his steel companies. Three of his oil stocks were paying extra dividends. The farm machinery company in which he owned five thousand shares was about to offer him rights worth three dollars apiece.

Thanks to me and my company and an economy in full bloom, Herbert was about to be several thousand dollars richer than he'd been a month before. I had a right to be proud, but my triumph—except for the commission—was gall and wormwood.

Nobody could do anything for Herbert. Herbert already had what he wanted. He had had it long before the inheritance or I intruded. He had the respectability his mother had hammered into him. But just as priceless as that was an income not quite big enough to go around. It left him no alternative but—in the holy names of wife, child, and home—to play piano in a dive, and breathe smoke, and drink gin, to be Firehouse Harris, his father's son, three nights out of seven.

(1951)

MISS
TEMPTATION

Puritanism had fallen into such disrepair that not even the oldest spinster thought of putting Susanna in a ducking stool; not even the oldest farmer suspected that Susanna's diabolical beauty had made his cow run dry.

Susanna was a bit-part actress in the summer theater near the village, and she rented a room over the firehouse. She was a part of village life all summer, but the villagers never got used to her. She was forever as startling and desirable as a piece of big-city fire apparatus.

Susanna's feathery hair and saucer eyes were as black as midnight. Her skin was the color of cream. Her hips were like a lyre, and her bosom made men dream of peace and plenty for ever and ever. She wore barbaric golden hoops on her shell-pink ears, and around her ankles were chains with little bells on them.

She went barefoot and slept until noon every day. And, as noon drew near, the villagers on the main street would grow as restless as beagles with a thunderstorm on the way.

At noon, Susanna would appear on the porch outside her room. She would stretch languidly, pour a bowl of milk for her black cat, kiss the cat, fluff her hair, put on her earrings, lock her door, and hide the key in her bosom.

And then, barefoot, she would begin her stately, undulating, titillating, tinkling walk—down the outside stairway, past the liquor store, the insurance agency, the real-estate office, the diner, the American Legion post, and the church, to the crowded drugstore. There she would get the New York papers.

She seemed to nod to all the world in a dim, queenly way. But the only person she spoke to during her daily walk was Bearse Hinkley, the seventy-two-year-old pharmacist.

The old man always had her papers ready for her.

"Thank you, Mr. Hinkley. You're an angel," she would say, opening a paper at random. "Now, let's see what's going on back in civilization." While the old man would watch, fuddled by her perfume, Susanna would laugh or gasp or frown at items in the paper—items she never explained.

Then she would take the papers, and return to her nest over the firehouse. She would pause on the porch outside her room, dip her hand into her bosom, bring out the key, unlock the door, pick up the black cat, kiss it again, and disappear inside.

The one-girl pageant had a ritual sameness until one day toward the end of summer, when the air of the drugstore was cut by a cruel, sustained screech from a dry bearing in a revolving soda-fountain stool.

The screech cut right through Susanna's speech about Mr. Hinkley's being an angel. The screech made scalps tingle and teeth ache. Susanna looked indulgently in the direction of the screech, forgiving the screecher. She found that the screecher wasn't a person to be indulged.

The screech had been made by the stool of Cpl. Norman Fuller, who had come home the night before from eighteen bleak months in Korea. They had been eighteen months without war—but eighteen months without cheer, all the same. Fuller had turned on the stool slowly, to look at Susanna with indignation. When the screech died, the drugstore was deathly still.

Fuller had broken the enchantment of summer by the seaside—had reminded all in the drugstore of the black, mysterious passions that were so often the mainsprings of life.

He might have been a brother, come to rescue his idiot sister from the tenderloin; or an irate husband, come to a saloon to horsewhip his wife back to where she belonged, with the baby. The truth was that Corporal Fuller had never seen Susanna before.

He hadn't consciously meant to make a scene. He hadn't known, consciously, that his stool would screech. He had meant to underplay his indignation, to make it a small detail in the background of Susanna's pageant—a detail noticed by only one or two connoisseurs of the human comedy.

But the screech had made his indignation the center of the solar system for all in the drugstore—particularly for Susanna. Time had stopped, and it could not proceed until Fuller had explained the expression on his granite Yankee face.

Fuller felt his skin glowing like hot brass. He was comprehending destiny. Destiny had suddenly given him an audience, and a situation about which he had a bitter lot to say.

Fuller felt his lips move, heard the words come out. "Who do you think you are?" he said to Susanna.

"I beg your pardon?" said Susanna. She drew her newspapers about herself protectively.

"I saw you come down the street like you were a circus parade, and I just wondered who you thought you were," said Fuller.

Susanna blushed gloriously. "I—I'm an actress," she said.

"You can say that again," said Fuller. "Greatest actresses in the world. American women."

"You're very nice to say so," said Susanna uneasily.

Fuller's skin glowed brighter and hotter. His mind had become a fountain of apt, intricate phrases. "I'm not talking about theaters with seats in 'em. I'm talking about the stage of life. American women act and dress like they're gonna give you the world. Then, when you stick out your hand, they put an ice cube in it."

"They do?" said Susanna emptily.

"They do," said Fuller, "and it's about time somebody said so." He looked challengingly from spectator to spectator, and found what he took to be dazed encouragement. "It isn't fair," he said.

"What isn't?" said Susanna, lost.

"You come in here with bells on your ankles, so's I'll have to look at your ankles and your pretty pink feet," said Fuller. "You kiss the cat, so's I'll have to think about how it'd be to be that cat," said Fuller. "You call an old man an angel, so's I'll have to think about what it'd be like to be called an angel by you,'" said Fuller. "You hide your key in front of everybody, so's I'll have to think about where that key is," said Fuller.

He stood. "Miss," he said, his voice full of pain, "you do everything you can to give lonely, ordinary people like me indigestion and the heeby-jeebies, and you wouldn't even hold hands with me to keep me from falling off a cliff."

He strode to the door. All eyes were on him. Hardly anyone noticed that his indictment had reduced Susanna to ashes of what she'd been moments before. Susanna now looked like what she really was—a muddle-headed nineteen-year-old clinging to a tiny corner of sophistication.

"It isn't fair," said Fuller. "There ought to be a law against girls acting and dressing like you do. It makes more people unhappy than it does happy. You know what I say to you, for going around making everybody want to kiss you?"

"No," piped Susanna, every fuse in her nervous system blown.

"I say to you what you'd say to me, if I was to try and kiss you," said Fuller grandly. He swung his arms in an umpire's gesture for "out." "The hell with you," he said. He left, slamming the screen door.

He didn't look back when the door slammed again a moment later, when the patter of running bare feet and the wild tinkling of little bells faded away in the direction of the firehouse.

That evening, Corporal Fuller's widowed mother put a candle on the table, and fed him sirloin steak and strawberry shortcake in honor of his homecoming. Fuller ate the meal as though it were wet blotting paper, and he answered his mother's cheery questions in a voice that was dead.

"Aren't you glad to be home?" said his mother, when they'd finished their coffee,

"Sure," said Fuller.

"What did you do today?" she said.

"Walked," he said.

"Seeing all your old friends?" she said.

"Haven't got any friends," said Fuller.

His mother threw up her hands. "No friends?" she said. "You?"

"Times change, ma," said Fuller heavily. "Eighteen months is a long time. People leave town, people get married——"

"Marriage doesn't kill people, does it?" she said.

Fuller didn't smile. "Maybe not," he said. "But it makes it awful hard for 'em to find any place to fit old friends in."

"Dougie isn't married, is he?"

"He's out west, ma—with the Strategic Air Command," said Fuller. The little dining room became as lonely as a bomber in the thin, cold stratosphere.

"Oh," said his mother. "There must be somebody left."

"Nope," said Fuller. "I spent the whole morning on the phone, ma. I might as well have been back in Korea. Nobody home."

"I can't believe it," she said. "Why, you couldn't walk down Main Street without being almost trampled by friends."

"Ma," said Fuller hollowly, "after I ran out of numbers to call, you know what I did? I went down to the drugstore, ma, and just sat there by the soda fountain, waiting for somebody to walk in—somebody I knew maybe just even a little. Ma," he said in anguish, "all I knew was poor old Bearse Hinkley. I'm not kidding you one bit." He stood, crumpling his napkin into a ball. "Ma, will you please excuse me?"

"Yes. Of course," she said. "Where are you going now?" She beamed. "Out to call on some nice girl, I hope?"

Fuller threw the napkin down. "I'm going to get a cigar!" he said. "I don't know any girls. They're all married too."

His mother paled. "I—I see," she said. "I—I didn't even know you smoked."

"Ma," said Fuller tautly, "can't you get it through your head? I been away for eighteen months, ma—eighteen months!"

"It is a long time, isn't it?" said his mother, humbled by his passion. "Well, you go get your cigar." She touched his arm. "And please don't feel so lonesome. You just wait. Your life will be so full of people again, you won't know which one to turn to. And, before you know it, you'll meet some pretty young girl, and you'll be married too."

"I don't intend to get married for some time, mother," said Fuller stuffily. "Not until I get through divinity school."

"Divinity school!" said his mother. "When did you decide that?"

"This noon," said Fuller.

"What happened this noon?"

"I had kind of a religious experience, ma," he said. "Something just made me speak out."

"About what?" she said, bewildered.

In Fuller's buzzing head there whirled a rhapsody of Susannas. He saw again all the professional temptresses who had tormented him in Korea, who had beckoned from makeshift bed-sheet movie screens, from curling pin-ups on damp tent walls, from ragged magazines in sand-bagged pits. The Susannas had made fortunes, beckoning to lonely Corporal Fullers everywhere—beckoning with stunning beauty, beckoning the Fullers to come nowhere for nothing.

The wraith of a Puritan ancestor, stiff-necked, dressed in black, took possession of Fuller's tongue. Fuller spoke with a voice that came across the centuries, the voice of a witch hanger, a voice redolent with frustration, self-righteousness, and doom.

"What did I speak out against?" he said. "Temp-ta-tion."

Fuller's cigar in the night was a beacon warning care-free, frivolous people away. It was plainly a cigar smoked in anger. Even the moths had sense enough to stay away.

Like a restless, searching red eye, it went up and down every street in the village, coming to rest at last, a wet, dead butt, before the firehouse.

Bearse Hinkley, the old pharmacist, sat at the wheel of the pumper, his eyes glazed with nostalgia—nostalgia for the days when he had been young enough to drive. And on his face, for all to see, was a dream of one more catastrophe, with all the young men away, when an old man or nobody would drive the pumper to glory one more time. He spent warm evenings there, behind the wheel—and had for years.

"Want a light for that thing?" he said to Corporal Fuller, seeing the dead cigar between Fuller's lips.

"No, thanks, Mr. Hinkley," he said. "All the pleasure's out of it."

"Beats me how anybody finds any pleasure in cigars in the first place," said the old man.

"Matter of taste," said Fuller. "No accounting for tastes."

"One man's meat's another man's poison," said Hinkley. "Live and let live, I always say." He glanced at the ceiling. Above it was the fragrant nest of Susanna and her black cat. "Me? All my pleasures are looking at what used to be pleasures."

Fuller looked at the ceiling, too, meeting the unmentioned issue squarely. "If you were young," he said, "you'd know why I said what I said to her. Beautiful, stuck-up girls give me a big pain."

"Oh, I remember that," said Hinkley. "I'm not so old I don't remember the big pain."

"If I have a daughter, I hope she isn't beautiful," said Fuller. "The beautiful girls at high school—by God, if they didn't think they were something extra-special."

"By God, if I don't think so, too," said Hinkley.

"They wouldn't even look at you if you didn't have a car and an allowance of twenty bucks a week to spend on 'em," said Fuller.

"Why should they?" said the old man cheerfully. "If I was a beautiful girl, I wouldn't." He nodded to himself.

"Well—anyway, I guess you came home from the wars and settled that score. I guess you told her."

"Ah-h-h," said Fuller. "You can't make any impression on them."

"I dunno," said Hinkley. "There's a fine old tradition in the theater: The show must go on. You know, even if you got pneumonia or your baby's dying, you still put on the show."

"I'm all right," said Fuller. "Who's complaining? I feel fine."

The old man's white eyebrows went up. "Who's talking about you?" he said. "I'm talking about her."

Fuller reddened, mousetrapped by egoism. "She'll be all right," he said.

"She will?" said Hinkley. "Maybe she will. All I know is, the show's started at the theater. She's supposed to be in it and she's still upstairs."

"She is?" said Fuller, amazed.

"Has been," said Hinkley, "ever since you paddled her and sent her home."

Fuller tried to grin ironically. "Now, isn't that too bad?" he said. His grin felt queasy and weak. "Well, good-night, Mr. Hinkley."

"Good-night, soldier boy," said Hinkley. "Good-night."

As noon drew near on the next day, the villagers along the main street seemed to grow stupid. Yankee shopkeepers made change lackadaisically, as though money didn't matter any more. All thoughts were of the great cuckoo clock the firehouse had become. The question was: Had Corporal Fuller broken it or, at noon, would the little door on top fly open, would Susanna appear?

In the drugstore, old Bearse Hinkley fussed with Susanna's New York papers, rumpling them in his anxiety to make them attractive. They were bait for Susanna.

Moments before noon, Corporal Fuller—the vandal himself—came into the drugstore. On his face was a strange mixture of guilt and soreheadedness. He had spent the better part of the night awake, reviewing his grievances against beautiful women. *All they think about is how beautiful they are,* he'd said to himself at dawn. *They wouldn't even give you the time of day.*

He walked along the row of soda-fountain stools and gave each empty stool a seemingly idle twist. He found the stool that had screeched so loudly the day before. He sat down on it, a monument of righteousness. No one spoke to him.

The fire siren gave its perfunctory wheeze for noon. And then, hearselike, a truck from the express company drove up to the firehouse. Two men got out and climbed the stairs. Susanna's hungry black cat jumped to the porch railing and arched its back as the expressmen disappeared into Susanna's room. The cat spat when they staggered out with Susanna's trunk.

Fuller was shocked. He glanced at Bearse Hinkley, and he saw that the old man's look of anxiety had become the look of double pneumonia—dizzy, blind, drowning.

"Satisfied, corporal?" said the old man.

"I didn't tell her to leave," said Fuller.

"You didn't leave her much choice," said Hinkley.

"What does she care what I think?" said Fuller. "I didn't know she was such a tender blossom."

The old man touched Fuller's arm lightly. "We all are, corporal—we all are," he said. "I thought that was one of the few good things about sending a boy off to the Army. I thought that was where he could find out for sure he wasn't the only tender blossom on earth. Didn't you find that out?"

"I never thought I was a tender blossom," said Fuller. "I'm sorry it turned out this way, but she asked for it." His head was down. His ears were hot crimson.

"She really scared you stiff, didn't she?" said Hinkley.

Smiles bloomed on the faces of the small audience that had drawn near on one pretext or another. Fuller appraised the smiles, and found that the old man had left him only one weapon—utterly humorless good citizenship.

"Who's afraid?" he said stuffily. "I'm not afraid. I just think it's a problem somebody ought to bring up and discuss."

"It's sure the one subject nobody gets tired of," said Hinkley.

Fuller's gaze, which had become a very shifty thing, passed over the magazine rack. There was tier upon tier of Susannas, a thousand square feet of wet-lipped smiles and sooty eyes and skin like cream. He ransacked his mind for a ringing phrase that would give dignity to his cause.

"I'm thinking about juvenile delinquency!" he said. He pointed to the magazines. "No wonder kids go crazy."

"I know I did," said the old man quietly. "I was as scared as you are."

"I told you, I'm not afraid of her," said Fuller.

"Good!" said Hinkley. "Then you're just the man to take her papers to her. They're paid for." He dumped the papers in Fuller's lap.

Fuller opened his mouth to reply. But he closed it again. His throat had tightened, and he knew that, if he tried to speak, he would quack like a duck.

"If you're really not afraid, corporal," said the old man, "that would be a very nice thing to do—a Christian thing to do."

As he mounted the stairway to Susanna's nest, Fuller was almost spastic in his efforts to seem casual.

Susanna's door was unlatched. When Fuller knocked on it, it swung open. In Fuller's imagination, her nest had been dark and still, reeking of incense, a labyrinth of heavy hangings and mirrors, with somewhere a Turkish corner, with somewhere a billowy bed in the form of a swan.

He saw Susanna and her room in truth now. The truth was the cheerless truth of a dirt-cheap Yankee summer rental—bare wood walls, three coat hooks, a linoleum rug. Two gas burners, an iron cot, an icebox. A tiny sink with naked pipes, a plastic drinking glass, two plates, a murky mirror. A frying pan, a saucepan, a can of soap powder.

The only harem touch was a white circle of talcum powder before the murky mirror. In the center of the circle were the prints of two bare feet. The marks of the toes were no bigger than pearls.

Fuller looked from the pearls to the truth of Susanna. Her back was to him. She was packing the last of her things into a suitcase.

She was now dressed for travel—dressed as properly as a missionary's wife.

"Papers," croaked Fuller. "Mr. Hinkley sent 'em."

"How very nice of Mr. Hinkley," said Susanna. She turned. "Tell him——" No more words came. She recognized him. She pursed her lips and her small nose reddened.

"Papers," said Fuller emptily. "From Mr. Hinkley."

"I heard you," she said. "You just said that. Is that all you've got to say?"

Fuller flapped his hands limply at his sides. "I'm—I—I didn't mean to make you leave," he said. "I didn't mean that."

"You suggest I stay?" said Susanna wretchedly. "After I've been denounced in public as a scarlet woman? A tart? A wench?"

"Holy smokes, I never called you those things!" said Fuller.

"Did you ever stop to think what it's like to be me?" she said. She patted her bosom. "There's somebody living inside here, too, you know."

"I know," said Fuller. He hadn't known, up to then.

"I have a soul," she said.

"Sure you do," said Fuller, trembling. He trembled because the room was filled with a profound intimacy. Susanna, the golden girl of a thousand tortured daydreams, was now discussing her soul, passionately, with Fuller the lonely, Fuller the homely, Fuller the bleak.

"I didn't sleep a wink last night because of you," said Susanna.

"Me?" He wished she'd get out of his life again. He wished she were in black and white, a thousandth of an inch thick on a magazine page. He wished he could turn the page and read about baseball or foreign affairs.

"What did you expect?" said Susanna. "I talked to you all night. You know what I said to you?"

"No," said Fuller, backing away. She followed, and seemed to throw off heat like a big iron radiator. She was appallingly human.

"I'm not Yellowstone Park!" she said. "I'm not supported by taxes! I don't belong to everybody! You don't have any right to say anything about the way I look!"

"Good gravy!" said Fuller.

"I'm so tired of dumb toots like you!" said Susanna. She stamped her foot and suddenly looked haggard. "I can't help it if you want to kiss me! Whose fault is that?"

Fuller could now glimpse his side of the question only dimly, like a diver glimpsing the sun from the ocean floor. "All I was trying to say was, you could be a little more conservative," he said.

Susanna opened her arms. "Am I conservative enough now?" she said. "Is this all right with you?"

The appeal of the lovely girl made the marrow of Fuller's bones ache. In his chest was a sigh like the lost chord. "Yes," he said. And then he murmured, "Forget about me."

Susanna tossed her head. "Forget about being run over by a truck," she said. "What makes you so mean?"

"I just say what I think," said Fuller.

"You think such mean things," said Susanna, bewildered. Her eyes widened. "All through high school, people like you would look at me as if they wished I'd drop dead. They'd never dance with me, they'd never talk to me, they'd never even smile back." She shuddered. "They'd just go slinking around like small-town cops. They'd look at me the way you did—like I'd just done something terrible."

The truth of the indictment made Fuller itch all over. "Probably thinking about something else," he said.

"I don't think so," said Susanna. "You sure weren't. All of a sudden, you started yelling at me in the drugstore, and I'd never even seen you before." She burst into tears. "What is the matter with you?"

Fuller looked down at the floor. "Never had a chance with a girl like you—that's all," he said. "That hurts."

Susanna looked at him wonderingly. "You don't know what a chance is," she said.

"A chance is a late-model convertible, a new suit, and twenty bucks," said Fuller.

Susanna turned her back to him and closed her suitcase. "A chance is a girl," she said. "You smile at her, you be friendly, you be glad she's a girl." She turned and opened her arms again. "I'm a girl. Girls are shaped this way," she said. "If men are nice to me and make me happy, I kiss them sometimes. Is that all right with you?"

"Yes," said Fuller humbly. She had rubbed his nose in the sweet reason that governed the universe. He shrugged. "I better be going. Good-by."

"Wait!" she said. "You can't do that—just walk out, leaving me feeling so wicked." She shook her head. "I don't deserve to feel wicked."

"What can I do?" said Fuller helplessly.

"You can take me for a walk down the main street, as though you were proud of me," said Susanna. "You can welcome me back to the human race." She nodded to herself. "You owe that to me."

Cpl. Norman Fuller, who had come home two nights before from eighteen bleak months in Korea, waited on the porch outside Susanna's nest, with all the village watching.

Susanna had ordered him out while she changed, while she changed for her return to the human race. She had also called the express company and told them to bring her trunk back.

Fuller passed the time by stroking Susanna's cat. "Hello, kitty, kitty, kitty, kitty," he said, over and over again. Saying, "Kitty, kitty, kitty, kitty," numbed him like a merciful drug.

He was saying it when Susanna came out of her nest. He couldn't stop saying it, and she had to take the cat away from him, firmly, before she could get him to look at her, to offer his arm.

"So long, kitty, kitty, kitty, kitty, kitty, kitty," said Fuller.

Susanna was barefoot, and she wore barbaric hoop earrings, and ankle bells. Holding Fuller's arm lightly, she led him down the stairs, and began her stately, undulating, titillating, tinkling walk past the liquor store, the insurance agency, the real-estate office, the diner, the American Legion post, and the church, to the crowded drugstore.

"Now, smile and be nice," said Susanna. "Show you're not ashamed of me."

"Mind if I smoke?" said Fuller.

"That's very considerate of you to ask," said Susanna. "No, I don't mind at all."

By steadying his right hand with his left, Corporal Fuller managed to light a cigar.

(1956)

ALL THE
KING'S HORSES

COLONEL BRYAN KELLY, his huge figure blocking off the light that filtered down the narrow corridor behind him, leaned for a moment against the locked door in an agony of anxiety and helpless rage. The small Oriental guard sorted through a ring of keys, searching for the one that would open the door. Colonel Kelly listened to the voices inside the room.

"Sarge, they wouldn't dare do anything to Americans, would they?" The voice was youthful, unsure. "I mean, there'd be hell to pay if they hurt—"

"Shut up. Want to wake up Kelly's kids and have them hear you running off at the mouth that way?" The voice was gruff, tired.

"They'll turn us loose pretty quick, whaddya bet, Sarge?" insisted the young voice.

"Oh, sure, kid, they love Americans around here. That's probably what they wanted to talk to Kelly about, and they're packing the beer and ham sandwiches into box lunches for us right now. All that's holding things up is they don't know how many with mustard, how many without. How d'ya want yours?"

"I'd just like to—"

"Shut up."

"Okay, I'd just—"

"Shut up."

"I'd just like to know what's going on, is all." The young corporal coughed.

"Pipe down and pass the butt along," said a third voice irritably. "There's ten good puffs left in it. Don't hog the

84

whole thing, kid." A few other voices muttered in agreement.

Colonel Kelly opened and closed his hands nervously, wondering how he could tell the fifteen human beings behind the door about the interview with Pi Ying and the lunatic ordeal they were going to have to endure. Pi Ying said that their fight against death would be no different, philosophically, from what all of them, except Kelly's wife and children, had known in battle. In a cold way, it was true—no different, philosophically. But Colonel Kelly was more shaken than he had ever been in battle.

Colonel Kelly and the fifteen on the other side of the door had crash-landed two days before on the Asiatic mainland, after they had been blown off course by a sudden storm and their radio had gone dead. Colonel Kelly had been on his way, with his family, to a post as military attaché in India. On board the Army transport plane with them had been a group of enlisted men, technical specialists needed in the Middle East. The plane had come to earth in territory held by a Communist guerrilla chief, Pi Ying.

All had survived the crash—Kelly, his wife Margaret, his ten-year-old twin sons, the pilot and copilot, and the ten enlisted men. A dozen of Pi Ying's ragged riflemen had been waiting for them when they climbed from the plane. Unable to communicate with their captors, the Americans had been marched for a day through rice fields and near-jungle to come at sunset to a decaying palace. There they had been locked in a subterranean room, with no idea of what their fates might be.

Now, Colonel Kelly was returning from an interview with Pi Ying, who had told him what was to become of the sixteen American prisoners. *Sixteen*—Kelly shook his head as the number repeated itself in his thoughts.

The guard prodded him to one side with his pistol and thrust the key into the lock, and the door swung open. Kelly stood silently in the doorway.

A cigarette was being passed from hand to hand. It cast its glow for an instant on each expectant face in turn. Now it lighted the ruddy face of the talkative young corporal from Minneapolis, now cast rugged shadows over the eye sockets and heavy brows of the pilot from Salt Lake, now bloomed red at the thin lips of the sergeant.

Kelly looked from the men to what seemed in the twilight to be a small hillock by the door. There his wife Margaret sat, with the blond heads of her sleeping sons cradled in her lap. She smiled up at him, her face misty white. "Darling—you're all right?" Margaret asked quietly.

"Yes, I'm all right."

"Sarge," said the corporal, "ask him what Pi Ying said."

"Shut up." The sergeant paused. "What about it, sir—good news or bad?"

Kelly stroked his wife's shoulder, trying to make the right words come—words to carry courage he wasn't sure he had. "Bad news," he said at last. "Rotten news."

"Well, let's have it," said the transport pilot loudly. Kelly supposed he was trying to reassure himself with the boom of his own voice, with brusqueness. "The worst he can do is kill us. Is that it?" He stood and dug his hands into his pockets.

"He wouldn't dare!" said the young corporal in a threatening voice—as though he could bring the wraths of the United States Army to bear on Pi Ying with a snap of his fingers.

Colonel Kelly looked at the youngster with curiosity and dejection. "Let's face it. The little man upstairs has all the trumps." An expression borrowed from another game, he thought irrelevantly. "He's an outlaw. He hasn't got a thing to lose by getting the United States sore at him."

"If he's going to kill us, say so!" the pilot said explosively. "So he's got us cold! What's he going to do?"

"He considers us prisoners of war," said Kelly, trying to keep his voice even. "He'd like to shoot us all." He shrugged. "I haven't been trying to keep you in suspense, I've been looking for the right words—and there aren't any. Pi Ying wants more entertainment out of us than shooting us would provide. He'd like to prove that he's smarter than we are in the bargain."

"How?" asked Margaret. Her eyes were wide. The two children were waking up.

"In a little while, Pi Ying and I are going to play chess for your lives." He closed his fist over his wife's limp hand. "And for my four lives. It's the only chance Pi Ying will give us." He shrugged, and smiled wryly. "I play a better-than-average game—a little better than average."

"Is he nuts?" said the sergeant.

"You'll all see for yourselves," said Colonel Kelly simply. "You'll see him when the game begins—Pi Ying and his friend, Major Barzov." He raised his eyebrows. "The major claims to be sorry that, in his capacity as a military observer for the Russian army, he is powerless to intervene in our behalf. He also says we have his sympathy. I suspect he's a damn liar on both counts. Pi Ying is scared stiff of him."

"We get to watch the game?" whispered the corporal tensely.

"The sixteen of us, soldier, are the chessmen I'll be playing with."

The door swung open. . . .

"Can you see the whole board from down there, White King?" called Pi Ying cheerfully from a balcony overlooking the azure-domed chamber. He was smiling down at Colonel Bryan Kelly, his family, and his men. "You must be the White King, you know. Otherwise, we couldn't be sure that you'd be with us for the whole game." The guerrilla chief's face was flushed. His smile was one of mock solicitousness. "Delighted to see all of you!"

To Pi Ying's right, indistinct in the shadows, stood Major Barzov, the taciturn Russian military observer. He acknowledged Kelly's stare with a slow nod. Kelly continued to stare fixedly. The arrogant, bristle-haired major became restless, folding and unfolding his arms, repeatedly rocking back and forth in his black boots. "I wish I could help you," he said at last. It wasn't an amenity but a contemptuous jest. "I am only an observer here." Barzov said it heavily. "I wish you luck, Colonel," he added, and turned his back.

Seated on Pi Ying's left was a delicate young Oriental woman. She gazed expressionlessly at the wall over the Americans' heads. She and Barzov had been present when Pi Ying had first told Colonel Kelly of the game he wanted to play. When Kelly had begged Pi Ying to leave his wife and children out of it, he had thought he saw a spark of pity in her eyes. As he looked up at the motionless, ornamental girl now, he knew he must have been mistaken.

"This room was a whim of my predecessors, who for generations held the people in slavery," said Pi Ying sententiously. "It served nicely as a throne room. But the floor is inlaid with squares, sixty-four of them—a chessboard, you see? The former tenants had those handsome, man-sized chessmen before you built so that they and their friends could sit up here and order servants to move them about." He twisted a ring on his finger. "Imaginative as that was, it remained for us to hit upon this new twist. Today, of couse, we will use only the black chessmen, my pieces." He turned to the restive Major Barzov. "The Americans have furnished their own chessmen. Fascinating idea." His smile faded when he saw that Barzov wasn't smiling with him. Pi Ying seemed eager to please the Russian. Barzov, in turn, appeared to regard Pi Ying as hardly worth listening to.

The twelve American soldiers stood against a wall under heavy guard. Instinctively, they bunched together and glared sullenly at their patronizing host. "Take it easy," said Colonel Kelly, "or we'll lose the one chance we've got." He looked quickly at his twin sons, Jerry and Paul, who gazed about the room, unruffled, interested, blinking sleepily at the side of their stunned mother. Kelly wondered why he felt so little as he watched his family in the face of death. The fear he had felt while they were waiting in their dark prison was gone. Now he recognized the eerie calm—an old wartime friend—that left only the cold machinery of his wits and senses alive. It was the narcotic of generalship. It was the essence of war.

"Now, my friends, your attention," said Pi Ying importantly. He stood. "The rules of the game are easy to remember. You are all to behave as Colonel Kelly tells you. Those of you who are so unfortunate as to be taken by one of my chessmen will be killed quickly, painlessly, promptly." Major Barzov looked at the ceiling as though he were inwardly criticizing everything Pi Ying said.

The corporal suddenly released a blistering stream of obscenities—half abuse, half self-pity. The sergeant clapped his hand over the youngster's mouth.

Pi Ying leaned over the balustrade and pointed a finger at the struggling soldier. "For those who run from the board or make an outcry, a special form of death can be arranged," he said sharply. "Colonel Kelly and I must have complete silence in which to concentrate. If the colonel is clever enough to win, then all of you who are still with us when I am checkmated will get safe transport out of my territory. If he loses—" Pi Ying shrugged. He settled back on a mound of cushions. "Now, you must all be good sports," he said briskly. "Americans are noted for that, I believe. As Colonel Kelly can tell you, a chess game can very rarely be won—any more than a battle can be won—without sacrifices. Isn't that so, Colonel?"

Colonel Kelly nodded mechanically. He was recalling what Pi Ying had said earlier—that the game he was about to play was no different, philosophically, from what he had known in war.

"How can you do this to children!" cried Margaret suddenly, twisting free of a guard and striding across the squares to stand directly below Pi Ying's balcony. "For the love of God—" she began.

Pi Ying interrupted angrily: "Is it for the love of God that Americans make bombs and jet planes and tanks?" He waved her away impatiently. "Drag her back." He covered his eyes. "Where was I? We were talking about sacrifices, weren't we? I was going to ask you who you had chosen to be your king's pawn," said Pi Ying. "If you haven't chosen one, Colonel, I'd like to recommend the noisy young man down there—the one the sergeant is holding. A delicate position, king's pawn."

The corporal began to kick and twist with new fury. The sergeant tightened his arms about him. "The kid'll calm down in a minute," he said under his breath. He turned his head toward Colonel Kelly. "Whatever the hell the king's pawn is, that's me. Where do I stand, sir?" The youngster relaxed and the sergeant freed him.

Kelly pointed to the fourth square in the second row of the huge chessboard. The sergeant strode to the square and hunched his broad shoulders. The corporal mumbled something incoherent, and took his place in the square next to the sergeant—a second dependable pawn. The rest still hung back.

"Colonel, you tell us where to go," said a lanky T-4 uncertainly. "What do we know about chess? You put us where you want us." His Adam's apple bobbed. "Save the soft spots for your wife and kids. They're the ones that count. You tell us what to do."

"There are no soft spots," said the pilot sardonically, "no soft spots for anybody. Pick a square, any square." He stepped onto the board. "What does this square make me?"

"You're a bishop, Lieutenant, the king's bishop," said Kelly.

He found himself thinking of the lieutenant in those terms—no longer human, but a piece capable of moving diagonally across the board; capable, when attacking with the queen, of terrible damage to the black men across the board.

"And me in church only twice in my life. Hey, Pi Ying," called the pilot insolently, "what's a bishop worth?"

Pi Ying was amused. "A knight and a pawn, my boy; a knight and a pawn."

Thank God for the lieutenant, thought Kelly. One of the American soldiers grinned. They had been sticking close together, backed against the wall. Now they began to talk among themselves—like a baseball team warming up. At Kelly's direction, seeming almost unconscious of the mean-

ing of their actions, they moved out onto the board to fill
out the ranks.

Pi Ying was speaking again. "All of your pieces are in
place now, except your knights and your queen, Colonel.
And you, of course, are the king. Come, come. The game
must be over before suppertime."

Gently, shepherding them with his long arms, Kelly led
his wife and Jerry and Paul to their proper squares. He
detested himself for the calm, the detachment with which
he did it. He saw the fear and reproach in Margaret's
eyes. She couldn't understand that he had to be this way—
that in his coldness was their only hope for survival. He
looked away from Margaret.

Pi Ying clapped his hands for silence. "There, good;
now we can begin." He tugged at his ear reflectively. "I
think this is an excellent way of bringing together the
Eastern and Western minds, don't you, Colonel? Here we
indulge the American's love for gambling with our appre-
ciation of profound drama and philosophy." Major Barzov whispered impatiently to him. "Oh, yes," said Pi Ying,
"two more rules: We are allowed ten minutes a move,
and—this goes without saying—no moves may be taken
back. Very well," he said, pressing the button on a stop
watch and setting it on the balustrade, "the honor of the
first move belongs to the white men." He grinned. "An
ancient tradition."

"Sergeant," said Colonel Kelly, his throat tight, "move
two squares forward." He looked down at his hands. They
were starting to tremble.

"I believe I'll be slightly unconventional," said Pi Ying,
half turning his head toward the young girl, as though to
make sure that she was sharing his enjoyment. "Move my
queen's pawn forward two squares," he instructed a servant.

Colonel Kelly watched the servant slide the massive
carving forward—to a point threatening the sergeant. The
sergeant looked quizzically at Kelly. "Everything okay,
sir?" He smiled faintly.

"I hope so," said Kelly. "Here's your protection . . ."

Soldier," he ordered the young corporal, "step forward one square." There—it was all he could do. Now there was no advantage in Pi Ying's taking the pawn he threatened—the sergeant. Tactically it would be a pointless trade, pawn for pawn. No advantage so far as good chess went.

"This is very bad form, I know," said Pi Ying blandly. He paused. "Well, then again, I'm not so sure I'd be wise to trade. With so brilliant an opponent, perhaps I'd better play flawless chess, and forget the many temptations." Major Barzov murmured something to him. "But it would get us into the spirit of the game right off, wouldn't it?"

"What's he talking about, sir?" asked the sergeant apprehensively.

Before Kelly could order his thoughts, Pi Ying gave the order. "Take his king's pawn."

"Colonel! What'd you do?" cried the sergeant. Two guards pulled him from the board and out of the room. A studded door banged shut behind them.

"Kill me!" shouted Kelly, starting off his square after them. A half-dozen bayonets hemmed him in.

Impassively, the servant slid Pi Ying's wooden pawn onto the square where the sergeant had stood. A shot reverberated on the other side of the thick door, and the guards reappeared. Pi Ying was no longer smiling. "Your move, Colonel. Come, come—four minutes have gone already."

Kelly's calm was shattered, and with it the illusion of the game. The pieces in his power were human beings again. The precious, brutal stuff of command was gone from Colonel Kelly. He was no more fit to make decisions of life and death than the rawest recruit. Giddily, he realized that Pi Ying's object was not to win the game quickly, but to thin out the Americans in harrowing, pointless forays. Another two minutes crept by as he struggled to force himself to be rational. "I can't do it," he whispered at last. He slouched now.

"You wish me to have all of you shot right now?" asked Pi Ying. "I must say that I find you a rather pathetic colonel. Do all American officers give in so easily?"

"Pin his ears back, Colonel," said the pilot. "Let's go. Sharpen up. Let's go!"

"You're in no danger now," said Kelly to the corporal. "Take his pawn."

"How do I know you're not lying?" said the youngster bitterly. "Now I'm going to get it!"

"Get over there!" said the transport pilot sharply.

"No!"

The sergeant's two executioners pinned the corporal's arms to his sides. They looked up expectantly at Pi Ying.

"Young man," said Pi Ying solicitously, "would you enjoy being tortured to death, or would you rather do as Colonel Kelly tells you?"

The corporal spun suddenly and set both guards sprawling. He stepped onto the square occupied by the pawn that had taken the sergeant, kicked the piece over, and stood there with his feet apart.

Major Barzov guffawed. "He'll learn to be a pawn yet," he roared. "It's an Oriental skill Americans could do well to learn for the days ahead, eh?"

Pi Ying laughed with Barzov, and stroked the knee of the young girl, who had been sitting, expressionless, at his side. "Well, it's been perfectly even so far—a pawn for a pawn. Let's begin our offensives in earnest." He snapped his fingers for the attention of the servant. "King's pawn to king three," he commanded. "There! Now my queen and bishop are ready for an expedition into white man's territory." He pressed the button on the stop watch. "Your move, Colonel." . . .

It was an old reflex that made Colonel Bryan Kelly look to his wife for compassion, courage. He looked away again —Margaret was a frightening, heartbreaking sight, and there was nothing he could do for her but win. Nothing. Her stare was vacant, almost idiotic. She had taken refuge in deaf, blind, unfeeling shock.

Kelly counted the figures still surviving on the board. An hour had passed since the game's beginning. Five pawns were still alive, among them the young corporal;

one bishop, the nervy pilot; two rooks; two knights—ten-year-old frightened knights; Margaret, a rigid, staring queen; and himself, the king. The missing four? Butchered —butchered in senseless exchanges that had cost Pi Ying only blocks of wood. The other soldiers had fallen silent, sullen in their own separate worlds.

"I think it's time for you to concede," said Pi Ying. "It's just about over, I'm afraid. Do you concede, Colonel?" Major Barzov frowned wisely at the chessmen, shook his head slowly, and yawned.

Colonel Kelly tried to bring his mind and eyes back into focus. He had the sensation of burrowing, burrowing, burrowing his way through a mountain of hot sand, of having to keep going on and on, digging, squirming, suffocated, blinded. "Go to hell," he muttered. He concentrated on the pattern of the chessmen. As chess, the ghastly game had been absurd. Pi Ying had moved with no strategy other than to destroy white men. Kelly had moved to defend each of his chessmen at any cost, had risked none in offense. His powerful queen, knights, and rooks stood unused in the relative safety of the two rear rows of squares. He clenched and unclenched his fists in frustration. His opponent's haphazard ranks were wide open. A checkmate of Pi Ying's king would be possible, if only the black knight weren't dominating the center of the board.

"Your move, Colonel. Two minutes." coaxed Pi Ying.

And then Kelly saw it—the price he would pay, that they all would pay, for the curse of conscience. Pi Ying had only to move his queen diagonally, three squares to the left, to put him in check. After that he needed to make one more move—inevitable, irresistible—and then checkmate, the end. And Pi Ying would move his queen. The game seemed to have lost its piquancy for him; he had the air of a man eager to busy himself elsewhere.

The guerrilla chief was standing now, leaning over the balustrade. Major Barzov stood behind him, fitting a cigarette into an ornate ivory holder. "It's a very distressing thing about chess," said Barzov, admiring the holder, turning it this way and that. "There isn't a grain of luck in the game, you know. There's no excuse for the loser." His tone was pedantic, with the superciliousness of a teacher imparting profound truths to students too immature to understand.

Pi Ying shrugged. "Winning this game gives me very little satisfaction. Colonel Kelly has been a disappointment. By risking nothing, he has deprived the game of its subtlety and wit. I could expect more brilliance from my cook."

The hot red of anger blazed over Kelly's cheeks, inflamed his ears. The muscles of his belly knotted; his legs moved apart. Pi Ying must not move his queen. If Pi Ying moved his queen, Kelly would lose; if Pi Ying moved his knight from Kelly's line of attack, Kelly would win. Only one thing might induce Pi Ying to move his knight—a fresh, poignant opportunity for sadism.

"Concede, Colonel. My time is valuable," said Pi Ying.

"Is it all over?" asked the young corporal querulously.

"Keep your mouth shut and stay where you are," said Kelly. He stared through shrewd, narrowed eyes at Pi Ying's knight, standing in the midst of the living chessmen. The horse's carved neck arched. Its nostrils flared.

The pure geometry of the white chessmen's fate burst upon Kelly's consciousness. Its simplicity had the effect of a refreshing, chilling wind. A sacrifice had to be offered to Pi Ying's knight. If Pi Ying accepted the sacrifice, the game would be Kelly's. The trap was perfect and deadly save for one detail—bait.

"One minute, Colonel," said Pi Ying.

Kelly looked quickly from face to face, unmoved by the hostility or distrust or fear that he saw in each pair of eyes. One by one he eliminated the candidates for death. These four were vital to the sudden, crushing offense, and these must guard the king. Necessity, like a child counting eeny, meeny, miney, moe around a circle, pointed its finger at the one chessman who could be sacrificed. There was only one.

Kelly didn't permit himself to think of the chessman as anything but a cipher in a rigid mathematical proposition:

if x is dead, the rest shall live. He perceived the tragedy of his decision only as man who knew the definition of tragedy, not as one who felt it.

"Twenty seconds!" said Barzov. He had taken the stop watch from Pi Ying.

The cold resolve deserted Kelly for an instant, and he saw the utter pathos of his position—a dilemma as old as mankind, as new as the struggle between East and West. When human beings are attacked, x, multiplied by hundreds and thousands, must die—x to death by those who love them most. Kelly's profession was the choosing of x.

"Ten seconds," said Barzov.

"Jerry," said Kelly, his voice loud and sure, "move forward one square and two to your left." Trustingly, his son stepped out of the back rank and into the shadow of the black knight. Awareness seemed to be filtering back into Margaret's eyes. She turned her head when her husband spoke.

Pi Ying stared down at the board in bafflement. "Are you in your right mind, Colonel?" he asked at last. "Do you realize what you've just done?"

A faint smile crossed Barzov's face. He bent forward as though to whisper to Pi Ying, but apparently thought better of it. He leaned back against a pillar to watch Kelly's every move through a gauze of cigarette smoke.

Kelly pretended to be mystified by Pi Ying's words. And then he buried his face in his hands and gave an agonized cry. "Oh, God, no!"

"An exquisite mistake, to be sure," said Pi Ying. He excitedly explained the blunder to the young girl beside him. She turned away. He seemed infuriated by the gesture.

"You've got to let me take him back," begged Kelly brokenly.

Pi Ying rapped on the balustrade with his knuckles. "Without rules, my friend, games become nonsense. We agreed that all moves would be final, and so they are." He motioned to a servant. "King's knight to king's bishop six!" The servant moved the piece onto the square where Jerry stood. The bait was taken, the game was Colonel Kelly's from here on in.

"What is he talking about?" murmured Margaret.

"Why keep your wife in suspense, Colonel?" said Pi Ying. "Be a good husband and answer her question, or should I?"

"Your husband sacrificed a knight," said Barzov, his voice overriding Pi Ying's. "You've just lost your son." His expression was that of an experimenter, keen, expectant, entranced.

Kelly heard the choking sound in Margaret's throat, caught her as she fell. He rubbed her wrists. "Darling, please—listen to me!" He shook her more roughly than he had intended. Her reaction was explosive. Words cascaded from her—hysterical babble condemning him. Kelly locked her wrists together in his hands and listened dumbly to her broken abuse.

Pi Ying's eyes bulged, transfixed by the fantastic drama below, oblivious of the tearful frenzy of the young girl behind him. She tugged at his blouse, pleading. He pushed her back without looking away from the board.

The tall T-4 suddenly dived at the nearest guard, driving his shoulder into the man's chest, his fist into his belly. Pi Ying's soldiers converged, hammered him to the floor and dragged him back to his square.

In the midst of the bedlam, Jerry burst into tears and raced terrified to his father and mother. Kelly freed Margaret, who dropped to her knees to hug the quaking child. Paul, Jerry's twin, held his ground, trembled, stared stolidly at the floor.

"Shall we get on with the game, Colonel?" asked Pi Ying, his voice high. Barzov turned his back to the board, unwilling to prevent the next step, apparently reluctant to watch it.

Kelly closed his eyes, and waited for Pi Ying to give the order to the executioners. He couldn't bring himself to look at Margaret and Jerry. Pi Ying waved his hand for silence. "It is with deep regret—" he began. His lips closed.

The menace suddenly went out of his face, leaving only surprise and stupidity. The small man slumped on the balustrade, slithered over it to crash among his soldiers.

Major Barzov struggled with the Chinese girl. In her small hand, still free of his grasp, was a slender knife. She drove it into her breast and fell against the major. Barzov let her fall. He strode to the balustrade. "Keep the prisoners where they are!" he shouted at the guards. "Is he alive?" There was no anger in his voice, no sorrow—only irritation, resentment of inconvenience. A servant looked up and shook his head.

Barzov ordered servants and soldiers to carry out the bodies of Pi Ying and the girl. It was more the act of a scrupulous housekeeper than a pious mourner. No one questioned his brisk authority.

"So this is your party after all," said Kelly.

"The peoples of Asia have lost a very great leader," Barzov said severely. He smiled at Kelly oddly. "Though he wasn't without weaknesses, was he, Colonel?" He shrugged. "However, you've won only the initiative, not the game; and now you have me to reckon with instead of Pi Ying. Stay where you are, Colonel. I'll be back shortly."

He ground out his cigarette on the ornamented balustrade, returned the holder to his pocket with a flourish, and disappeared through the curtains.

"Is Jerry going to be all right?" whispered Margaret. It was a plea, not a question, as though mercy were Kelly's to dole out or to withhold.

"Only Barzov knows," he said. He was bursting to explain the moves to her, to make her understand why he had had no choice; but he knew that an explanation would only make the tragedy infinitely more cruel for her. Death through a blunder she might be able to understand; but death as a product of cool reason, a step in logic, she could never accept. Rather than accept it, she would have had them all die.

"Only Barzov knows," he repeated wearily. The bargain was still in force, the price of victory agreed to. Barzov apparently had yet to realize what it was that Kelly was buying with a life.

"How do we know Barzov will let us go if we do win?" said T-4.

"We don't, soldier. We don't." And then another doubt began to worm into his consciousness. Perhaps he had won no more than a brief reprieve. . . .

Colonel Kelly had lost track of how long they'd waited there on the chessboard for Barzov's return. His nerves were deadened by surge after surge of remorse and by the steady pressure of terrible responsibility. His consciousness had lapsed into twilight. Margaret slept in utter exhaustion, with Jerry, his life yet to be claimed, in her arms. Paul had curled up on his square, covered by the young corporal's field jacket. On what had been Jerry's square, the horse's carved head snarling as though fire would burst from its nostrils, stood Pi Ying's black knight.

Kelly barely heard the voice from the balcony—mistook it for another jagged fragment in a nightmare. His mind attached no sense to the words, heard only their sound. And then he opened his eyes and saw Major Barzov's lips moving. He saw the arrogant challenge in his eyes, understood the words. "Since so much blood has been shed in this game, it would be a pitiful waste to leave it unresolved."

Barzov settled regally on Pi Ying's cushions, his black boots crossed. "I propose to beat you, Colonel, and I will be surprised if you give me trouble. It would be very upsetting to have you win by the transparent ruse that fooled Pi Ying. It isn't that easy any more. You're playing me now, Colonel. You won the initiative for a moment. I'll take it and the game now, without any more delay."

Kelly rose to his feet, his great frame monumental above the white chessmen sitting on the squares about him. Major Barzov wasn't above the kind of entertainment Pi Ying had found so diverting. But Kelly sensed the difference between the major's demeanor and that of the guerrilla chief. The major was resuming the game, not because he liked it, but because he wanted to prove that he was one hell of a bright fellow, and that the Americans were dirt. Apparently, he didn't realize that Pi Ying had already lost the game. Either that, or Kelly had miscalculated.

In his mind, Kelly moved every piece on the board, driving his imagination to show him the flaw in his plan, if a flaw existed—if the hellish, heartbreaking sacrifice was for nothing. In an ordinary game, with nothing at stake but bits of wood, he would have called upon his opponent to concede, and the game would have ended there. But now, playing for flesh and blood, an aching, ineradicable doubt overshadowed the cleancut logic of the outcome. Kelly dared not reveal that he planned to attack and win in three moves—not until he had made the moves, not until Barzov had lost every chance to exploit the flaw, if there was one.

"What about Jerry?" cried Margaret.

"Jerry? Oh, of course, the little boy. Well, what about Jerry, Colonel?" asked Barzov. "I'll make a special concession, if you like. Would you want to take the move back?" The major was urbane, a caricature of cheerful hospitality.

"Without rules, Major, games become nonsense," said Kelly flatly. "I'd be the last to ask you to break them."

Barzov's expression became one of profound sympathy. "Your husband, madame, has made the decision, not I." He pressed the button on the stop watch. "You may keep the boy with you until the Colonel has fumbled all of your lives away. Your move, Colonel. Ten minutes."

"Take his pawn," Kelly ordered Margaret. She didn't move. "Margaret! Do you hear me?"

"Help her, Colonel, help her," chided Barzov.

Kelly took Margaret by the elbow, led her unresisting to the square where a black pawn stood. Jerry tagged along, keeping his mother between himself and Kelly. Kelly returned to his square, dug his hands into his pockets, and watched a servant take the black pawn from the board. "Check, Major. Your king is in check."

Barzov raised an eyebrow. "Check, did you say? What shall I do about this annoyance? How shall I get you back to some of the more interesting problems on the board?" He gestured to a servant. "Move my king over one square to the left."

"Move diagonally one square toward me, Lieutenant," Kelly ordered the pilot. The pilot hesitated. "Move! Do you hear?"

"Yessir." The tone was mocking. "Retreating, eh, sir?" The lieutenant slouched into the square, slowly, insolently.

"Check again, Major," Kelly said evenly. He motioned at the lieutenant. "Now my bishop has your king in check." He closed his eyes and told himself again and again that he had made no miscalculation, that the sacrifice *had* won the game, that there *could* be no out for Barzov. This was it—the last of the three moves.

"Well," said Barzov, "is that the best you can do? I'll simply move my queen in front of my king." The servant moved the piece. "Now it will be a different story."

"Take his queen," said Kelly to his farthest-advanced pawn, the battered T-4.

Barzov jumped to his feet. "Wait!"

"You didn't see it? You'd like to take it back?" taunted Kelly.

Barzov paced back and forth on his balcony, breathing hard. "Of course I saw it!"

"It was the only thing you could do to save your king," said Kelly. "You may take it back if you like, but you'll find it's the only move you can make."

"Take the queen and get on with the game," shouted Barzov. "Take her!"

"Take her," echoed Kelly, and the servant trundled the huge piece to the side lines. The T-4 now stood blinking at Barzov's king, inches away. Colonel Kelly said it very softly this time: "Check."

Barzov exhaled in exasperation. "Check indeed." His voice grew louder. "No credit to you, Colonel Kelly, but to the monumental stupidity of Pi Ying."

"And that's the game, Major."

T-4 laughed idiotically, the corporal sat down, the lieutenant threw his arms around Colonel Kelly. The two children gave a cheer. Only Margaret stood fast, still rigid, frightened.

"The price of your victory, of course, has yet to be paid," said Barzov acidly. "I presume you're ready to pay now?"

Kelly whitened. "That was the understanding, if it would give you satisfaction to hold me to it."

Barzov placed another cigarette in his ivory holder, taking a scowling minute to do it. When he spoke, it was in the tone of the pedant once more, the wielder of profundities. "No, I won't take the boy. I feel as Pi Ying felt about you—that you, as Americans, are the enemy, whether an official state of war exists or not. I look upon you as prisoners of war.

"However, as long as there is no official state of war, I have no choice, as a representative of my government, but to see that all of you are conducted safely through the lines. This was my plan when I resumed the game where Pi Ying left off. Your being freed has nothing to do with my personal feelings, nor with the outcome of the game. My winning would have delighted me and taught you a valuable lesson. But it would have made no difference in your fates." He lighted his cigarette and continued to look at them with severity.

"That's very chivalrous of you, Major," said Kelly.

"A matter of practical politics, I assure you. It wouldn't do to precipitate an incident between our countries just now. For a Russian to be chivalrous with an American is a spiritual impossibility, a contradiction in terms. In a long and bitter history, we've learned and learned well to reserve our chivalry for Russians." His expression became one of complete contempt. "Perhaps you'd like to play another game, Colonel—plain chess with wooden chessmen, without Pi Ying's refinement. I don't like to have you leave here thinking you play a better game than I."

"That's nice of you, but not this evening."

"Well, then, some other time." Major Barzov motioned for the guards to open the door of the throne room. "Some other time," he said again. "There will be others like Pi Ying eager to play you with live men, and I hope I will again be privileged to be an observer." He smiled brightly. "When and where would you like it to be?"

"Unfortunately, the time and the place are up to you," said Colonel Kelly wearily. "If you insist on arranging another game, issue an invitation, Major, and I'll be there."

(1953)

TOM EDISON'S
SHAGGY DOG

TWO OLD MEN sat on a park bench one morning in the sunshine of Tampa, Florida—one trying doggedly to read a book he was plainly enjoying while the other, Harold K. Bullard, told him the story of his life in the full, round, head tones of a public address system. At their feet lay Bullard's Labrador retriever, who further tormented the aged listener by probing his ankles with a large, wet nose.

Bullard, who had been, before he retired, successful in many fields, enjoyed reviewing his important past. But he faced the problem that complicates the lives of cannibals —namely: that a single victim cannot be used over and over. Anyone who had passed the time of day with him and his dog refused to share a bench with them again.

So Bullard and his dog set out through the park each day in quest of new faces. They had had good luck this morning, for they had found this stranger right away, clearly a new arrival in Florida, still buttoned up tight in heavy serge, stiff collar and necktie, and with nothing better to do than read.

"Yes," said Bullard, rounding out the first hour of his lecture, "made and lost five fortunes in my time."

"So you said," said the stranger, whose name Bullard had neglected to ask. "Easy, boy. No, no, no, boy," he said to the dog, who was growing more aggressive toward his ankles.

"Oh? Already told you that, did I?" said Bullard.

"Twice."

"Two in real estate, one in scrap iron, and one in oil and one in trucking."

"So you said."

"I did? Yes, guess I did. Two in real estate, one in scrap iron, one in oil, and one in trucking. Wouldn't take back a day of it."

"No, I suppose not," said the stranger. "Pardon me, but do you suppose you could move your dog somewhere else? He keeps—"

"Him?" said Bullard, heartily. "Friendliest dog in the world. Don't need to be afraid of him."

"I'm not afraid of him. It's just that he drives me crazy, sniffing at my ankles."

"Plastic," said Bullard, chuckling.

"What?"

"Plastic. Must be something plastic on your garters. By golly, I'll bet it's those little buttons. Sure as we're sitting here, those buttons must be plastic. That dog is nuts about plastic. Don't know why that is, but he'll sniff it out and find it if there's a speck around. Must be a deficiency in his diet, though, by gosh, he eats better than I do. Once he chewed up a whole plastic humidor. Can you beat it? *That's* the business I'd go into now, by glory, if the pill rollers hadn't told me to let up, to give the old ticker a rest."

"You could tie the dog to that tree over there," said the stranger.

"I get so darn' sore at all the youngsters these days!" said Bullard. "All of 'em mooning around about no frontiers any more. There never have been so many frontiers as there are today. You know what Horace Greeley would say today?"

"His nose is wet," said the stranger, and he pulled his ankles away, but the dog humped forward in patient pursuit. "Stop it, boy!"

"His wet nose shows he's healthy," said Bullard. " 'Go plastic, young man!' That's what Greeley'd say. 'Go atom, young man!' "

The dog had definitely located the plastic buttons on the stranger's garters and was cocking his head one way and another, thinking out ways of bringing his teeth to bear on those delicacies.

"Scat!" said the stranger.

" 'Go electronic, young man!' " said Bullard. "Don't talk to me about no opportunity any more. Opportunity's knocking down every door in the country, trying to get in. When I was young, a man had to go out and find opportunity and drag it home by the ears. Nowadays—"

"Sorry," said the stranger, evenly. He slammed his book shut, stood and jerked his ankle away from the dog. "I've got to be on my way. So good day, sir."

He stalked across the park, found another bench, sat down with a sigh and began to read. His respiration had just returned to normal, when he felt the wet sponge of the dog's nose on his ankles again.

"Oh—it's you!" said Bullard, sitting down beside him. "He was tracking you. He was on the scent of something, and I just let him have his head. What'd I tell you about plastic?" He looked about contentedly. "Don't blame you for moving on. It was stuffy back there. No shade to speak of and not a sign of a breeze."

"Would the dog go away if I bought him a humidor?" said the stranger.

"Pretty good joke, pretty good joke," said Bullard, amiably. Suddenly he clapped the stranger on his knee. "Sa-ay, you aren't in plastics, are you? Here I've been blowing off about plastics, and for all I know that's your line."

"My line?" said the stranger crisply, laying down his book. "Sorry—I've never had a line. I've been a drifter since the age of nine, since Edison set up his laboratory next to my home, and showed me the intelligence analyzer."

"Edison?" said Bullard. "Thomas Edison, the inventor?"

"If you want to call him that, go ahead," said the stranger.

"If I *want* to call him that?"—Bullard guffawed—"I guess I just will! Father of the light bulb and I don't know what all."

"If you want to think he invented the light bulb, go ahead. No harm in it." The stranger resumed his reading.

"Say, what is this?" said Bullard, suspiciously. "You

pulling my leg? What's this about an intelligence analyzer?
I never heard of that."

"Of course you haven't," said the stranger. "Mr. Edison
and I promised to keep it a secret. I've never told anyone.
Mr. Edison broke his promise and told Henry Ford, but
Ford made him promise not to tell anybody else—for the
good of humanity."

Bullard was entranced. "Uh, this intelligence analyzer,"
he said, "it analyzed intelligence, did it?"

"It was an electric butter churn," said the stranger.

"Seriously now," Bullard coaxed.

"Maybe it *would* be better to talk it over with someone,"
said the stranger. "It's a terrible thing to keep bottled up
inside me, year in and year out. But how can I be sure that
it won't go any further?"

"My word as a gentleman," Bullard assured him.

"I don't suppose I could find a stronger guarantee than
that, could I?" said the stranger, judiciously.

"There is no stronger guarantee," said Bullard,
proudly. "Cross my heart and hope to die!"

"Very well." The stranger leaned back and closed his
eyes, seeming to travel backward through time. He was
silent for a full minute, during which Bullard watched with
respect.

"It was back in the fall of eighteen seventy-nine," said
the stranger at last, softly. "Back in the village of Menlo
Park, New Jersey. I was a boy of nine. A young man we
all thought was a wizard had set up a laboratory next door
to my home, and there were flashes and crashes inside, and
all sorts of scary goings on. The neighborhood children
were warned to keep away, not to make any noise that
would bother the wizard.

"I didn't get to know Edison right off, but his dog
Sparky and I got to be steady pals. A dog a whole lot like
yours, Sparky was, and we used to wrestle all over the
neighborhood. Yes, sir, your dog is the image of Sparky."

"Is that so?" said Bullard, flattered.

"Gospel," replied the stranger. "Well, one day Sparky
and I were wrestling around, and we wrestled right up to
the door of Edison's laboratory. The next thing I knew,

Sparky had pushed me in through the door, and bam! I was sitting on the laboratory floor, looking up at Mr. Edison himself."

"Bet he was sore," said Bullard, delighted.

"You can bet I was scared," said the stranger. "*I* thought I was face to face with Satan himself. Edison had wires hooked to his ears and running down to a little black box in his lap! I started to scoot, but he caught me by my collar and made me sit down.

" 'Boy,' said Edison, "it's always darkest before the dawn. I want you to remember that.'

" 'Yes, sir,' I said.

" 'For over a year, my boy,' Edison said to me, 'I've been trying to find a filament that will last in an incandescent lamp. Hair, string, splinters—nothing works. So while I was trying to think of something else to try, I started tinkering with another idea of mine, just letting off steam. I put this together,' he said, showing me the little black box. 'I thought maybe intelligence was just a certain kind of electricity, so I made this intelligence analyzer here. It works! You're the first one to know about it, my boy. But I don't know why you shouldn't be. It will be your generation that will grow up in the glorious new era when people will be as easily graded as oranges.' "

"I don't believe it!" said Bullard.

"May I be struck by lightning this very instant!" said the stranger. "And it did work, too. Edison had tried out the analyzer on the men in his shop, without telling them what he was up to. The smarter a man was, by gosh, the farther the needle on the indicator in the little black box swung to the right. I let him try it on me, and the needle just lay where it was and trembled. But dumb as I was, then is when I made my one and only contribution to the world. As I say, I haven't lifted a finger since."

"Whadja do?" said Bullard, eagerly.

"I said, 'Mr. Edison, sir, let's try it on the dog.' And I wish you could have seen the show that dog put on when I said it! Old Sparky barked and howled and scratched to get out. When he saw we meant business, that he wasn't going to get out, he made a beeline right for the intelligence analyzer and knocked it out of Edison's hands. But we cornered him, and Edison held him down while I touched the wires to his ears. And would you believe it, that needle sailed clear across the dial, way past a little red pencil marker on the dial face!"

"The dog busted it," said Bullard.

" 'Mr. Edison, sir,' I said, 'what's the red mark mean?'

" 'My boy,' said Edison, 'it means that the instrument is broken, because that red mark is me.' "

"I'll say it was broken," said Bullard.

The stranger said gravely, "But it wasn't broken. No, sir. Edison checked the whole thing, and it was in apple-pie order. When Edison told me that, it was then that Sparky, crazy to get out, gave himself away."

"How?" said Bullard, suspiciously.

"We really had him locked in, see? There were three locks on the door—a hook and eye, a bolt, and a regular knob and latch. That dog stood up, unhooked the hook, pushed the bolt back and had the knob in his teeth when Edison stopped him."

"No!" said Bullard.

"Yes!" said the stranger, his eyes shining. "And then is when Edison showed me what a great scientist he was. He was willing to face the truth, no matter how unpleasant it might be.

" 'So!' said Edison to Sparky. 'Man's best friend, huh? Dumb animal, huh?'

"That Sparky was a caution. He pretended not to hear. He scratched himself and bit fleas and went around growling at ratholes—anything to get out of looking Edison in the eye.

" 'Pretty soft, isn't it, Sparky?' said Edison. 'Let somebody else worry about getting food, building shelters and keeping warm, while you sleep in front of a fire or go chasing after the girls or raise hell with the boys. No mortgages, no politics, no war, no work, no worry. Just wag the old tail or lick a hand, and you're all taken care of.'

" 'Mr. Edison,' I said, 'do you mean to tell me that dogs are smarter than people?'

" 'Smarter?' said Edison. 'I'll tell the world! And what have I been doing for the past year? Slaving to work out a light bulb so dogs can play at night!'

" 'Look, Mr. Edison,' said Sparky, 'why not—' "

"Hold on!" roared Bullard.

"Silence!" shouted the stranger, triumphantly. " 'Look, Mr. Edison,' said Sparky, 'why not keep quiet about this? It's been working out to everybody's satisfaction for hundreds of thousands of years. Let sleeping dogs lie. You forget all about it, destroy the intelligence analyzer, and I'll tell you what to use for a lamp filament.' "

"Hogwash!" said Bullard, his face purple.

The stranger stood. "You have my solemn word as a gentleman. That dog rewarded *me* for my silence with a stock-market tip that made me independently wealthy for the rest of my days. And the last words that Sparky ever spoke were to Thomas Edison. 'Try a piece of carbonized cotton thread,' he said. Later, he was torn to bits by a pack of dogs that had gathered outside the door, listening."

The stranger removed his garters and handed them to Bullard's dog. "A small token of esteem, sir, for an ancestor of yours who talked himself to death. Good day." He tucked his book under his arm and walked away.

(1953)

NEW DICTIONARY

I WONDER NOW what Ernest Hemingway's dictionary looked like, since he got along so well with dinky words that everybody can spell and truly understand. Mr. Hotchner, was it a frazzled wreck? My own is a tossed salad of instant coffee and tobacco crumbs and India paper, and anybody seeing it might fairly conclude that I ransack it hourly for a vocabulary like Arnold J. Toynbee's. The truth is that I have broken its spine looking up the difference between *principle* and *principal,* and how to spell *cashmere.* It is a dear leviathan left to me by my father, "Webster's New International Dictionary of the English Language," based on the "International Dictionary" of 1890 and 1900. It doesn't have *radar* in it, or *Wernher von Braun* or *sulfathiazole,* but I *know* what *they* are. One time I actually *took* sulfathiazole.

And now I have this enormous and beautiful new bomb from Random House. I don't mean "bomb" in a pejorative sense, or in any dictionary sense, for that matter. I mean that the book is heavy and pregnant, and makes you think. One of the things it makes you think is that any gang of bright people with scads of money behind them can become appalling competitors in the American-unabridged-dictionary industry. They can make certain that they have all the words the other dictionaries have, then add words which have joined the language since the others were published, and then avoid mistakes that the others have caught particular hell for.

Random House has thrown in a color atlas of the world, as well, and concise dictionaries of French, Spanish, German, and Italian. And would you look at the price? And, lawsy me, Christmas is coming.

When Mario Pei reviewed the savagely-bopped third revised edition of the "Merriam-Webster" for The Times in 1961, he complained of the "residual prudishness" which still excluded certain four-letter words, "despite their copious appearance in numerous works of contemporary 'literature' as well as on rest-room walls." Random House has satisfied this complaint somewhat. They haven't included enough of the words to allow a Pakistani to decode "Last Exit to Brooklyn," or "Ulysses," either—but they have made brave beginnings, dealing, wisely I think, with the alimentary canal. I found only one abrupt verb for sexually congressing a woman, and we surely have Edward Albee to thank for its currency, though he gets no credit for it. The verb is *hump*, as in "hump the hostess."

If my emphasis on dirty words so early in this review seems childish, I can only reply that I, as a child, would never have started going through unabridged dictionaries if I hadn't suspected that there were dirty words hidden in there, where only grownups were supposed to find them. I always ended the searches feeling hot and stuffy inside, and looking at the queer illustrations—at the *trammel wheel,* the *arbalest,* and the *dugong.*

Of course, one dictionary is as good as another to most people, who use them for spellers and bet-settlers and accessories to crossword puzzles and Scrabble games. But some people use them for more than that, or *mean* to. This was brought home to me only the other evening, whilst I was supping with the novelist and short-story writer, Richard Yates, and Prof. Robert Scholes, the famous praiser of John Barth's "Giles Goat-Boy." Yates asked Scholes anxiously it seemed to me, which unabridged dictionary he should buy. He had just received a gorgeous grant for creative writing from the Federal Gumment, and the first thing he was going to buy was his entire language between hard covers. He was afraid that he might get a clunker—a word, by the way, not in this Random House job.

Scholes replied judiciously that Yates should get the second edition of the "Merriam-Webster," which was *pre-*

scriptive rather than *descriptive*. Prescriptive, as nearly as I could tell, was like an honest cop, and descriptive was like a boozed-up war buddy from Mobile, Ala. Yates said he would get the tough one; but, my goodness, *he* doesn't need official instructions in English any more than he needs training wheels on his bicycle. As Scholes said later, Yates is the sort of man lexicographers read in order to discover what pretty new things the language is up to.

To find out in a rush whether a dictionary is prescriptive or descriptive, you look up *ain't* and *like*. I learned this trick of horseback logomachy from reviews of the "Merriam-Webster" third edition. And here is the rundown on *ain't:* the "Merriam-Webster" first edition says that it is colloquial or illiterate, the second says it is dialect or illiterate, and the third says that *ain't* is, "though disapproved by many and more common in less educated speech, used orally . . . by many cultivated speakers esp. in the phrase *ain't I.*" I submit that this nation is so uniformly populated by parvenus with the heebie-jeebies that the phrase *ain't I* is heard about as frequently as the mating cry of the heath hen.

Random House says this about *ain't:* "*Ain't* is so traditionally and widely regarded as a nonstandard form that it should be shunned by all who prefer to avoid being considered illiterate. *Ain't* occurs occasionally in the informal speech of some educated users, especially in self-consciously [sic] or folksy or humorous contexts *(Ain't it the truth! She ain't what she used to be!)*, but it is completely unacceptable in formal writing and speech. Although the expression *ain't I* is perhaps defensible—and it is considered more logical than *aren't I?* and more euphonious than *amn't I?*—the well-advised person will avoid any use of *ain't.*" How's that for advice to parvenus?

My mother isn't mentioned, but what she taught me to say in place of *ain't I?* or *aren't I?* or *amn't I?* was *am I not?* Speed isn't everything. So I lost a micro-second here and there. The main thing is to be a *graceful* parvenu.

As for the use of *like* as though it were interchangeable with *as:* "M-W-1" says, "The use of *like* as a conjunction meaning *as* (as, *Do like I do*), though occasionally found in good writers, is a provincialism and contrary to good usage." "M-W-2" says that the same thing "is freely used only in illiterate speech and is now regarded as incorrect." "M-W-3" issues no warnings whatsoever, and flaunts models of current, O.K. usage from the St. Petersburg (Fla.) Independent, "wore his clothes like he was . . . afraid of getting dirt on them," and Art Linkletter, "impromptu programs where they ask questions much like I do on the air." "M-W-3," incidentally, came out during the dying days of the Eisenhower Administration, when simply *everybody* was talking like Art Linkletter.

Random House, in the catbird seat, since it gets to recite last, declares in 1966, "The use of *like* in place of *as* is universally condemned by teachers and editors, notwithstanding its wide currency, especially in advertising slogans. *Do as I say, not as I do* does not admit of *like* instead of *as*. In an occasional idiomatic phrase, it is somewhat less offensive when substituted for *as if* (*He raced down the street like crazy*), but this example is clearly colloquial and not likely to be found in any but the most informal written contexts." I find this excellent. It even tells who will hurt you if you make a mistake, and it witholds aid and comfort from those friends of cancer and money, those greedy enemies of the language who teach our children to say after school, "Winston tastes good like a cigarette should."

Random House is damned if it will set that slogan in type.

As you rumple through this new dictionary, looking for dirty words and schoolmarmisms tempered by worldliness, you will discover that biographies and major place names and even the names of famous works of art are integrated with the vocabulary: *A Streetcar Named Desire, Ralph Ellison, Mona Lisa, Kiselevsk*. I worry about the biographies and the works of art, since they seem a mixed bag, possibly locked for all eternity in a matrix of type. *Norman Mailer* is there, for instance, but not *William Styron* or *James Jones* or *Vance Bourjaily* or *Ed-*

ward Lewis Wallant. And are we to be told throughout eternity this and no more about *Alger Hiss:* "born 1904, U.S. public official"? And why is there no entry for *Whittaker Chambers?* And who promoted Peress?

It is the biographical inclusions and exclusions, in fact, which make this dictionary an ideal gift for the paranoiac on everybody's Christmas list. He will find dark entertainments without end between pages i and 2,059. Why are we informed about Joe Kennedy, Sr., and Jack and Bobby, but not about Teddy or Jacqueline? What is somebody trying to tell us when T. S. Eliot is called a *British* poet and W. H. Auden is called an *English* poet? (Maybe the distinction aims at accounting for Auden's American citizenship.) And when Robert Welch Jr., is tagged as a "retired U.S. candy manufacturer," is this meant to make him look silly? And why is the memory of John Dillinger perpetuated, while of Adolf Eichmann there is neither gibber nor squeak?

Whoever decides to crash the unabridged dictionary game next—and it will probably be General Motors or Ford—they will winnow this work heartlessly for bloopers. There can't be many, since Random House has winnowed its noble predecessors. The big blooper, it seems to me, is not putting the biographies and works of art in an appendix, where they can be cheaply revised or junked or added to.

Have I made it clear that this book is a beauty? You can't beat the contents, and you can't beat the price. Somebody will beat both sooner or later, of course, because that is good old Free Enterprise, where the consumer benefits from battles between jolly green giants.

And, as I've said, one dictionary is as good as another for most people. *Homo Americanus* is going to go on speaking and writing the way he always has, no matter what dictionary he owns. Consider the citizen who was asked recently what he thought of President Johnson's use of the slang expression "cool it" in a major speech:

"It's fine with me," he replied. "Now's not the time for the President of the United States to worry about the King's English. After all, we're living in an informal age.

Politicians don't go around in top hats any more. There's no reason why the English language shouldn't wear sports clothes, too. I don't say the President should speak like an illiterate. But 'cool it' is folksy, and the Chief Executive should be allowed to sound human. You can't be too corny for the American people—all the decent sentiments in life are corny. But linguistically speaking, Disraeli is dullsville."

These words, by the way, came from the larynx of Bennett Cerf, publisher of "The Random House Dictionary of the English Language." Moral: Everybody associated with a new dictionary ain't necessarily a new Samuel Johnson.

(1967)

NEXT DOOR

THE OLD HOUSE was divided into two dwellings by a thin wall that passed on, with high fidelity, sounds on either side. On the north side were the Leonards. On the south side were the Hargers.

The Leonards—husband, wife, and eight-year-old son—had just moved in. And, aware of the wall, they kept their voices down as they argued in a friendly way as to whether or not the boy, Paul, was old enough to be left alone for the evening.

"Shhhhh!" said Paul's father.

"Was I shouting?" said his mother. "I was talking in a perfectly normal tone."

"If I could hear Harger pulling a cork, he can certainly hear you," said his father.

"I didn't say anything I'd be ashamed to have anybody hear," said Mrs. Leonard.

"You called Paul a baby," said Mr. Leonard. "That certainly embarrasses Paul—and it embarrasses me."

"It's just a way of talking," she said.

"It's a way we've got to stop," he said. "And we can stop treating him like a baby, too—*tonight*. We simply shake his hand, walk out, and go to the movie." He turned to Paul. "You're not afraid—are you boy?"

"I'll be all right," said Paul. He was very tall for his age, and thin, and had a soft, sleepy, radiant sweetness engendered by his mother. "I'm fine."

"Damn right!" said his father, clouting him on the back. "It'll be an adventure."

"I'd feel better about this adventure, if we could get a sitter," said his mother.

"If it's going to spoil the picture for you," said the father, "let's take him with us."

Mrs. Leonard was shocked. "Oh—it isn't for children."

"I don't care," said Paul amiably. The why of their not wanting him to see certain movies, certain magazines, certain books, certain television shows was a mystery he respected—even relished a little.

"It wouldn't kill him to see it," said his father.

"You *know* what it's about," she said.

"What *is* it about?" said Paul innocently.

Mrs. Leonard looked to her husband for help, and got none. "It's about a girl who chooses her friends unwisely," she said.

"Oh," said Paul. "That doesn't sound very interesting."

"Are we going, or aren't we?" said Mr. Leonard impatiently. "The show starts in ten minutes."

Mrs. Leonard bit her lip. "All right!" she said bravely. "You lock the windows and the back door, and I'll write down the telephone numbers for the police and the fire department and the theater and Dr. Failey." She turned to Paul. "You *can* dial, can't you, dear?"

"He's been dialing for years!" cried Mr. Leonard.

"Sssssssh!" said Mrs. Leonard.

"Sorry," Mr. Leonard bowed to the wall. "My apologies."

"Paul, dear," said Mrs. Leonard, "what are you going to do while we're gone?"

"Oh—look through my microscope, I guess," said Paul.

"You're not going to be looking at germs, are you?" she said.

"Nope—just hair, sugar, pepper, stuff like that," said Paul.

His mother frowned judiciously. "I think that would be all right, don't you?" she said to Mr. Leonard.

"Fine!" said Mr. Leonard. "Just as long as the pepper doesn't make him sneeze!"

"I'll be careful," said Paul.

Mr. Leonard winced. "Shhhhh!" he said.

Soon after Paul's parents left, the radio in the Harger

apartment went on. It was on softly at first—so softly that Paul, looking through his microscope on the living room coffee table, couldn't make out the announcer's words. The music was frail and dissonant—unidentifiable.

Gamely, Paul tried to listen to the music rather than to the man and woman who were fighting.

Paul squinted through the eyepiece of his microscope at a bit of his hair far below, and he turned a knob to bring the hair into focus. It looked like a glistening brown eel, flecked here and there with tiny spectra where the light struck the hair just so.

There—the voices of the man and woman were getting louder again, drowning out the radio. Paul twisted the microscope knob nervously, and the objective lens ground into the glass slide on which the hair rested.

The woman was shouting now.

Paul unscrewed the lens, and examined it for damage.

Now the man shouted back—shouted something awful, unbelievable.

Paul got a sheet of lens tissue from his bedroom, and dusted at the frosted dot on the lens, where the lens had bitten into the slide. He screwed the lens back in place.

All was quiet again next door—except for the radio.

Paul looked down into the microscope, down into the milky mist of the damaged lens.

Now the fight was beginning again—louder and louder, cruel and crazy.

Trembling, Paul sprinkled grains of salt on a fresh slide, and put it under the microscope.

The woman shouted again, a high, ragged, poisonous shout.

Paul turned the knob too hard, and the fresh slide cracked and fell in triangles to the floor. Paul stood, shaking, wanting to shout, too—to shout in terror and bewilderment. It had to stop. Whatever it was, it *had* to stop!

"If you're going to yell, turn up the radio!" the man cried.

Paul heard the clicking of the woman's heels across the floor. The radio volume swelled until the boom of the bass made Paul feel like he was trapped in a drum.

"And now!" bellowed the radio, "for Katy from Fred! For Nancy from Bob, who thinks she's swell! For Arthur, from one who's worshipped him from afar for six weeks! Here's the old Glenn Miller Band and that all-time favorite, *Stardust!* Remember! If you have a dedication, call Milton nine-three-thousand! Ask for All-Night Sam, the record man!"

The music picked up the house and shook it.

A door slammed next door. Now someone hammered on a door.

Paul looked down into his microscope once more, looked at nothing—while a prickling sensation spread over his skin. He faced the truth: The man and woman would kill each other, if he didn't stop them.

He beat on the wall with his fist. "Mr. Harger! Stop it!" he cried. "Mrs. Harger! Stop it!"

"For Ollie from Lavinia!" All-Night Sam cried back at him. "For Ruth from Carl, who'll never forget last Tuesday! For Wilber from Mary, who's lonesome tonight! Here's the Sauter-Finnegan Band asking, *Love, What Are You Doing to My Heart?*"

Next door, crockery smashed, filling a split second of radio silence. And then the tidal wave of music drowned everything again.

Paul stood by the wall, trembling in his helplessness. "Mr. Harger! Mrs. Harger! Please!"

"Remember the number!" said All-Night Sam. "Milton nine-three-thousand!

Dazed, Paul went to the phone and dialed the number.

"WJCD," said the switchboard operator.

"Would you kindly connect me with All-Night Sam?" said Paul.

"Hello!" said All-Night Sam. He was eating, talking with a full mouth. In the background, Paul could hear sweet, bleating music, the original of what was rending the radio next door.

"I wonder if I might make a dedication," said Paul.

"Dunno why not," said Sam. "Ever belong to any organization listed as subversive by the Attorney General's office?"

Paul thought a moment. "Nossir—I don't think so, sir," he said.

"Shoot," said Sam.

"From Mr. Lemuel K. Harger to Mrs. Harger," said Paul.

"What's the message?" said Sam.

"I love you," said Paul. "Let's make up and start all over again."

The woman's voice was so shrill with passion that it cut through the din of the radio, and even Sam heard it.

"Kid—are you in trouble?" said Sam. "Your folks fighting?"

Paul was afraid that Sam would hang up on him if he found out that Paul wasn't a blood relative of the Hargers. "Yessir," he said.

"And you're trying to pull 'em back together again with this dedication?" said Sam.

"Yessir," said Paul.

Sam became very emotional. "O.K., kid," he said hoarsely, "I'll give it everything I've got. Maybe it'll work. I once saved a guy from shooting himself the same way."

"How did you do that?" said Paul, fascinated.

"He called up and said he was gonna blow his brains out," said Sam, "and I played *The Bluebird of Happiness*." He hung up.

Paul dropped the telephone into its cradle. The music stopped, and Paul's hair stood on end. For the first time, the fantastic speed of modern communications was real to him, and he was appalled.

"Folks!" said Sam, "I guess everybody stops and wonders sometimes what the heck he thinks he's doin' with the life the good Lord gave him! It may seem funny to you folks, because I always keep a cheerful front, no matter how I feel inside, that I wonder sometimes, too! And then, just like some angel was trying to tell me, 'Keep going, Sam, keep going,' something like this comes along."

"Folks!" said Sam, "I've been asked to bring a man and his wife back together again through the miracle of radio!

I guess there's no sense in kidding ourselves about marriage! It isn't any bowl of cherries! There's ups and downs, and sometimes folks don't see how they can go on!"

Paul was impressed with the wisdom and authority of Sam. Having the radio turned up high made sense now, for Sam was speaking like the right-hand man of God.

When Sam paused for effect, all was still next door. Already the miracle was working.

"Now," said Sam, "a guy in my business has to be half musician, half philosopher, half psychiatrist, and half electrical engineer! And! If I've learned one thing from working with all you wonderful people out there, it's this: if folks would swallow their self-respect and pride, there wouldn't be any more divorces!"

There were affectionate cooings from next door. A lump grew in Paul's throat as he thought about the beautiful thing he and Sam were bringing to pass.

"Folks!" said Sam, "that's all I'm gonna say about love and marriage! That's all anybody needs to know! And now, for Mrs. Lemuel K. Harger, from Mr. Harger—I love you! Let's make up and start all over again!" Sam choked up. "Here's Eartha Kitt, and *Somebody Bad Stole De Wedding Bell!*"

The radio next door went off.

The world lay still.

A purple emotion flooded Paul's being. Childhood dropped away, and he hung, dizzy, on the brink of life, rich, violent, rewarding.

There was movement next door—slow, foot-dragging movement.

"So," said the woman.

"Charlotte—" said the man uneasily. "Honey—I swear."

" 'I love you,' " she said bitterly. " 'let's make up and start all over again.' "

"B by," said the man desperately, "it's another Lemuel K. Harger. It's got to be!"

"You want your wife back?" she said. "All right—I won't get in her way. She can have you, Lemuel—you jewel beyond price, you."

"*She* must have called the station," said the man.

"She can have you, you philandering, two-timing, two-bit Lochinvar," she said. "But you won't be in very good condition."

"Charlotte—put down that gun," said the man. "Don't do anything you'll be sorry for."

"That's all behind me, you worm," she said.

There were three shots.

Paul ran out into the hall, and bumped into the woman as she burst from the Harger apartment. She was a big, blonde woman, all soft and awry, like an unmade bed.

She and Paul screamed at the same time, and then she grabbed him as he started to run.

"You want candy?" she said wildly. "Bicycle?"

"No, thank you," said Paul shrilly. "Not at this time."

"You haven't seen or heard a thing!" she said. "You know what happens to squealers?"

"Yes!" cried Paul.

She dug into her purse, and brought out a perfumed mulch of face tissues, bobbypins and cash. "Here!" she panted. "It's yours! And there's more where that came from, if you keep your mouth shut." She stuffed it into his trousers pocket.

She looked at him fiercely, then fled into the street.

Paul ran back into his apartment, jumped into bed, and pulled the covers up over his head. In the hot, dark cave of the bed, he cried because he and All-Night Sam had helped to kill a man.

A policeman came clumping into the house very soon, and he knocked on both apartment doors with his billy-club.

Numb, Paul crept out of the hot, dark cave, and answered the door. Just as he did, the door across the hall opened, and there stood Mr. Harger, haggard but whole.

"Yes, sir?" said Harger. He was a small, balding man, with a hairline mustache. "Can I help you?"

"The neighbors heard some shots," said the policeman.

"Really?" said Harger urbanely. He dampened his mustache with the tip of his little finger. "How bizarre. I heard nothing." He looked at Paul sharply. "Have you been playing with your father's guns again, young man?"

"Oh, nossir!" said Paul, horrified.

"Where are your folks?" said the policeman to Paul.

"At the movies," said Paul.

"You're all alone?" said the policeman.

"Yessir," said Paul. "It's an adventure."

"I'm sorry I said that about the guns," said Harger. "I certainly would have heard any shots in this house. The walls are thin as paper, and I heard nothing."

Paul looked at him gratefully.

"And you didn't hear any shots, either, kid?" said the policeman.

Before Paul could find an answer, there was a disturbance out on the street. A big, motherly woman was getting out of a taxicab and wailing at the top of her lungs. "Lem! Lem, baby."

She barged into the foyer, a suitcase bumping against her leg and tearing her stocking to shreds. She dropped the suitcase, and ran to Harger, throwing her arms around him.

"I got your message, darling," she said, "and I did just what All-Night Sam told me to do. I swallowed my self-respect, and here I am!"

"Rose, Rose, Rose—my little Rose," said Harger. "Don't ever leave me again." They grappled with each other affectionately, and staggered into their apartment.

"Just look at this apartment!" said Mrs. Harger. "Men are just lost without women!" As she closed the door, Paul could see that she was awfully pleased with the mess.

"You *sure* you didn't hear any shots?" said the policeman to Paul.

The ball of money in Paul's pocket seemed to swell to the size of a watermelon. "Yessir," he croaked.

The policeman left.

Paul shut his apartment door, shuffled into his bedroom, and collapsed on the bed.

The next voices Paul heard came from his own side of

the wall. The voices were sunny—the voices of his mother and father. His mother was singing a nursery rhyme and his father was undressing him.

"Diddle-diddle-dumpling, my son John," piped his mother, "Went to bed with his stockings on. One shoe off, and one shoe on—diddle-diddle-dumpling, my son John."

Paul opened his eyes.

"Hi, big boy," said his father, "you went to sleep with all your clothes on."

"How's my little adventurer?" said his mother.

"O.K.," said Paul sleepily. "How was the show?"

"It wasn't for children, honey," said his mother. "You would have liked the short subject, though. It was all about bears—cunning little cubs."

Paul's father handed her Paul's trousers, and she shook them out, and hung them neatly on the back of a chair by the bed. She patted them smooth, and felt the ball of money in the pocket. "Little boys' pockets!" she said, delighted. "Full of childhood's mysteries. An enchanted frog? A magic pocketknife from a fairy princess?" She caressed the lump.

"He's not a little boy—he's a big boy," said Paul's father. "And he's too old to be thinking about fairy princesses."

Paul's mother held up her hands. "Don't rush it, don't rush it. When I saw him asleep there, I realized all over again how dreadfully short childhood is." She reached into the pocket and sighed wistfully. "Little boys are so hard on clothes—especially pockets."

She brought out the ball and held it under Paul's nose. "Now, would you mind telling Mommy what we have here?" she said gaily.

The ball bloomed like a frowzy chrysanthemum, with ones, fives, tens, twenties, and lipstick-stained Kleenex for petals. And rising from it, befuddling Paul's young mind, was the pungent musk of perfume.

Paul's father sniffed the air. "What's that smell?" he said.

Paul's mother rolled her eyes. *"Tabu,"* she said.

(1955)

MORE STATELY
MANSIONS

WE'VE KNOWN the McClellans, Grace and George, for about two years now. They were the first neighbors to call on us and welcome us to the village.

I expected that initial conversation to lag uncomfortably after the first pleasantries, but not at all. Grace, her eyes quick and bright as a sparrow's, found subject matter enough to keep her talking for hours.

"You know," she said excitedly, "your living room could be a perfect dream! Couldn't it, George? Can't you see it?"

"Yup," said her husband. "Nice, all right."

"Just tear out all this white-painted woodwork," Grace said, her eyes narrowing. "Panel it all in knotty pine wiped with linseed oil with a little umber added. Cover the couch in lipstick red—*red* red. Know what I mean?"

"Red?" said Anne, my wife.

"Red! Don't be afraid of color."

"I'll try not to be," Anne said.

"And just cover the whole wall there, those two ugly little windows and all, with bottle-green curtains. Can't you see it? It'd be almost exactly like that problem living room in the February *Better House and Garden.* You remember that, of course."

"I must have missed that," said Anne. The month was August.

"Or was it *Good Homelife,* George?" Grace said.

"Don't remember offhand," said George.

"Well, I can look it up in my files and put my hand right on it." Grace stood up suddenly, and, uninvited, started a tour through the rest of the house.

She went from room to room, consigning a piece of furniture to the Salvation Army, detecting a fraudulent antique, shrugging partitions out of existence, and pacing off a chartreuse, wall-to-wall carpet we would have to order before we did another thing. "Start with the carpet," she said firmly, "and build from there. It'll pull your whole downstairs together if you build from the carpet."

"Um," said Anne.

"I hope you saw Nineteen Basic Carpet Errors in the June *Home Beautiful.*"

"Oh yes, yes indeed," Anne said.

"Good. Then I don't have to tell you how wrong you can go, *not* building from the carpet. George—Oh, he's still in the living room."

I caught a glimpse of George on the living-room couch, lost in his own thoughts. He straightened up and smiled.

I followed Grace, trying to change the subject. "Let's see, you are on our north side. Who's to our south?"

Grace held up her hands. "Oh! You haven't met them —the Jenkinses. George," she called, "they want to know about the Jenkinses." From her voice, I gathered that our southerly neighbors were sort of lovable beachcombers.

"Now, Grace, they're nice enough people," George said.

"Oooh, George," Grace said, "you know how the Jenkinses are. Yes, they're nice, but . . ." She laughed and shook her head.

"But what?" I said. The possibilities raced through my mind. Nudists? Heroin addicts? Anarchists? Hamster raisers?

"In 1945 they moved in," Grace said, "and right off the bat they bought two beautful Hitchcock chairs, and . . ." This time she sighed and shrugged.

"And what?" I demanded. And spilled India ink on them? And found a bundle of thousand-dollar bills rolled up in a hollow leg?

"And that's all," Grace said. "They just stopped right there."

"How's that?" said Anne.

"Don't you see? They started out beautifully with those two chairs; then they just petered out."

"Oh," said Anne slowly. "I see—a flash in the pan. So *that's* what's wrong with the Jenkinses. Aha!"

"Fie on the Jenkinses," I said.

Grace didn't hear me. She was patrolling between the living room and dining room, and I noticed that every time she entered or left the living room, she made a jog in her course, always at exactly the same place. Curious, I went over to the spot she avoided, and bounced up and down a couple of times to see if the floor was unsound at that point, or what.

In she came again, and she looked at me with surprise. "Oh!"

"Did I do something wrong?" I asked.

"I just didn't expect to find *you* there."

"Sorry."

"That's where the cobbler's bench goes, you know."

I stepped aside, and watched uncomfortably as she bent over the phantom cobbler's bench. I think it was then that she first alarmed me, made me feel a little less like laughing.

"With one or two little nail drawers open, and ivy growing out of them," she explained. "Cute?" She stepped around it, being careful not to bark her shins, and went up the stairs to the second floor. "Do you mind if I have a look around up here?" she asked gaily.

"Go right ahead," said Anne.

George had gotten up off the sofa. He stood looking up the stairs for a minute; then he held up his empty highball glass. "Mind if I have another?"

"Say, I'm sorry, George. We haven't been taking very good care of you. You bet. Help yourself. The bottle's there in the dining room."

He went straight to it, and poured himself a good inch and a half of whisky in the bottom of the tumbler.

"The tile in this bathroom is all wrong for your towels, of course," Grace said from upstairs.

Anne, who had padded after her like a housemaid, agreed bleakly. "Of course."

George lifted his glass, winked, and drained it. "Don't

let her throw you," he said. "Just her way of talking. Got a damn' nice house here. *I* like it, and so does she."

"Thanks, George. That's nice of you."

Anne and Grace came downstairs again, Anne looking quite bushed. "Oh, you men!" Grace said. "You just think we're silly, don't you?" She smiled companionably at Anne. "They just don't understand what interests women. What were you two talking about while we were having such a good time?"

"I was telling him he ought to wallpaper his trees and make chintz curtains for his keyholes," George said.

"Mmmmm," said Grace. "Well, time to go home, dear."

She paused outside the front door. "Nice basic lines to this door," she said. "That gingerbread will come right off, if you get a chisel under it. And you can lighten it by rubbing on white paint, then rubbing it off again right away. It'll look more like *you*."

"You've been awfully helpful," said Anne.

"Well, it's a dandy house the way it is," George said.

"I swear," Grace said, "I'll never understand how so many artists are men. No man I ever met had a grain of artistic temperament in him."

"Bushwa," said George quietly. And then he surprised me. The glance he gave Grace was affectionate and possessive.

"It *is* a dull little dump, I guess," said Anne gloomily, after the McClellans had left.

"Oh, listen—it's a swell house."

"I guess. But it needs so much done to it. I didn't realize. Golly, their place must be something. They've been in it for five years, she said. You can imagine what she could do to a place in five years—everything right, right down to the last nailhead."

"It isn't much from the outside. Anyway, Anne, this isn't like you."

She shook her head, as though to wake herself up. "It isn't, is it? Never in my life have I had the slightest interest in keeping up with the neighbors. But there's something about that woman."

"To hell with her! Let's throw in our lot with the Jenkinses."

Anne laughed. Grace's spell was wearing off. "Are you mad? Be friends with those two-chair people, those quitters?"

"Well, we'd make our friendship contingent on their getting a new couch to go with the chairs."

"And not any couch, but the *right* couch."

"If they want to be friends of ours, they mustn't be afraid of color, and they'd better build from the carpet."

"That goes without saying," said Anne crisply.

But it was a long time before we found leisure for more than a nod at the Jenkinses. Grace McClellan spent most of her waking hours at our house. Almost every morning, as I was leaving for work, she would stagger into our house under a load of home magazines and insist that Anne pore over them with her in search of just the right solutions for our particular problem house.

"They must be awfully rich," Anne said at dinner one night.

"I don't think so," I said. "George has a little leather-goods store that you hardly ever see anybody in."

"Well, then every cent must go into the house."

"That I can believe. But what makes you think they're rich?"

"To hear that woman talk, you'd think money was nothing! Without batting an eyelash, she talks about ten-dollar-a-yard floor-to-ceiling draperies, says fixing up the kitchen shouldn't cost more than a lousy fifteen hundred dollars—without the fieldstone fireplace, of course."

"What's a kitchen without a fieldstone fireplace?"

"And a circular couch."

"Isn't there some way you can keep her away, Anne? She's wearing you out. Can't you just tell her you're too busy to see her?"

"I haven't the heart, she's so kind and friendly and lonely," said Anne helplessly. "Besides, there's no getting through to her. She doesn't hear what I say. Her head is just crammed full of blueprints, cloth, furniture, wall-paper, and paint."

"Change the subject."

"Change the course of the Mississippi! Talk about poli-tics, and she talks about remodeling the White House; talk about dogs, and she talks about doghouses."

The telephone rang, and I answered it. It was Grace McClellan. "Yes, Grace?"

"You're in the office-furniture business, aren't you?"

"That's right."

"Do you ever get old filing cabinets in trade?"

"Yes. I don't like to, but sometimes I have to take them."

"Could you let me have one?"

I thought a minute. I had an old wooden wreck I was about to haul to the dump. I told her about it.

"Oh, that'll be divine! There's an article in last month's *Better House* about what to do with old filing cabinets. You can make them just darling by wallpapering them, then putting a coat of clear shellac over the paper. Can't you just see it?"

"Yep. Darling, all right. I'll bring it out tomorrow night."

"That's awfully nice of you. I wonder if you and Anne couldn't drop in for a drink then."

I accepted and hung up. "Well, the time has come," I said. "Marie Antoinette has finally invited us to have a look at Versailles."

"I'm afraid," Anne said. "It's going to make our home look so sad."

"There's more to life than decorating."

"I know, I know. I just wish you'd stay home in the daytime and keep telling me that while she's here."

The next evening, I drove the pickup truck home instead of my car, so I could deliver the old filing cabinet to Grace. Anne was already inside the McClellan house, and George came out to give me a hand.

The cabinet was an old-fashioned oak monster, and, with all the sweating and grunting, I didn't really pay much attention to the house until we'd put down our burden in the front hall.

The first thing I noticed was that there were already two dilapidated filing cabinets in the hall, ungraced by wall-paper or clear shellac. I looked into the living room. Anne was sitting on the couch with a queer smile on her face. The couch springs had burst through the bottom and were resting nakedly on the floor. The chief illumination came from a single light bulb in a cobwebbed chandelier with sockets for six. An electric extension cord, patched with friction tape, hung from another of the sockets and led to an iron on an ironing board in the middle of the living room.

A small throw rug, the type generally seen in bath-rooms, was the only floor covering, and the planks of the floor were scarred and dull from long neglect. Dust and cobwebs were everywhere, and the windows were dirty. The only sign of order or opulence was on the coffee table, where dozens of fat, slick decoration magazines were spread out like a fan.

George was nervous and more taciturn than usual, and I gathered that he was uneasy about having us in. After mixing us drinks, he sat down and maintained a fidgeting silence.

Not so with Grace. She was at a high pitch of excite-ment, and, seemingly, full of irrepressible pride. Sitting, rising, and sitting again a dozen times a minute, she did a sort of ballet about the room, describing exactly the way she was going to do the room over. She rubbed imaginary fabrics between her fingers, stretched out luxuriously in a wicker chair that would one day be a plum-colored chaise longue, held her hands as far apart as she could reach to indicate the span of a limed-oak television-radio-phono-graph console that was to stand against one wall.

She clapped her hands and closed her eyes. "Can you see it? Can you *see* it?"

"Simply lovely," said Anne.

"And every night, just as George is coming up the walk. I'll have Martinis ready in a frosty pewter pitcher, and I'll have a record playing on the phonograph." Grace knelt before the thin air where the console would be, selected a record from nothingness, put it on the imaginary turntable, pressed a nonexistent button, and retired to the wicker chair. To my dismay, she began to rock her head back and forth in time to the phantom music.

After a minute of this, George seemed disturbed, too. "Grace! You're going to sleep." He tried to make his tone light, but real concern showed through.

Grace shook her head and opened her eyes lazily. "I wasn't sleeping; I was listening."

"It will certainly be a charming room," Anne said, looking worriedly at me.

Grace was suddenly on her feet again, charged with new energy. "And the dining room!" Impatiently, she picked up a magazine and thumbed through it. "Now, wait, where is it, where is it? No, not that one." She let the magazine drop. "Oh, of course, I clipped it last night and put it in the files. Remember, George? The dining-room table with the glass top and the place for potted flowers underneath?"

"Uh-huh."

"That's what goes in the dining room," Grace said happily. "See? You look right through the table, and there, underneath, are geraniums, African violets, or anything you want to put there. Fun?" She hurried to the filing cabinets. "You've got to see it in color, really."

Anne and I followed her politely, and waited while she ran her finger along the dividers in the drawers. The drawers, I saw, were jammed with cloth and wallpaper samples, paint color cards, and pages taken from magazines. She had already filled two cabinets, and was ready to overflow into the third, the one I'd brought. The drawers were labeled, simply, "Living room," "Kitchen," "Dining room," and so on.

"Quite a filing system," I said to George, who was just brushing by with a fresh drink in his hand.

He looked at me closely, as though he was trying to make up his mind whether I was kidding him or not. "It is," he said at last. "There's even a section about the workshop she wants me to have in the basement." He sighed. "Someday."

Grace held up a little square of transparent blue plastic. "And this is the material for the kitchen curtains, over the sink and automatic dishwasher. Waterproof, and it wipes clean."

"It's darling," Anne said. "You have an automatic dishwasher?"

"Mmmmm?" Grace said, smiling at some distant horizon. "Oh—dishwasher? No, but I know exactly the one we want. We've made up our minds on that, haven't we, George?"

"Yes, dear."

"And someday . . ." said Grace happily, running her fingers over the contents of a file drawer.

"Someday . . ." said George.

As I say, two years have passed since then, since we first met the McClellans. Anne, with compassion and tenderness, invented harmless ways of keeping Grace from spending all her time at our house with her magazines. But we formed a neighborly habit of having a drink with the McClellans once or twice a month.

I liked George, and he grew friendly and talkative when he'd made sure we weren't going to bait his wife about interior decorating, something almost everyone else in the neighborhood was fond of doing. He adored Grace, and made light of her preoccupation, as he had done at our first meeting, only when he didn't know the people before whom she was performing. Among friends, he did nothing to discourage or disparage her dreaming.

Anne bore the brunt of Grace's one-track conversations as sort of a Christian service, listening with tact and patience. George and I ignored them, and had a pleasant enough time talking about everything but interior decoration.

In these talks it came out bit by bit that George had been in a bad financial jam for years, and that things refused to get better. The "someday" that Grace had been planning for for five years, George said, seemed to recede another month as each new home magazine appeared on the newsstands. It was this, I decided, not Grace, that kept him drinking more than his share.

And the filing cabinets got fuller and fuller, and the McClellan house got dowdier and dowdier. But not once did Grace's excitement about what their house was going to be like flag. If anything, it increased, and time and again we would have to follow her about the house to hear just how it was all going to be.

And then a fairly sad thing and an awfully nice thing happened to the McClellans. The sad thing was that Grace came down with a virus infection that kept her in the hospital two months. The nice thing was that George inherited a little money from a relative he'd never met.

While Grace was in the hospital, George often had supper with us; and the day he received his legacy, his taciturnity dropped away completely. To our surprise, *he* now talked interior decoration with fervor and to the exclusion of everything else.

"You've got the bug too, now," Anne said, laughing.

"Bug, hell! I've got the money! I'm going to surprise Grace by having that house just the way she wants it, when she comes home."

"Exactly, George?"

"Eggs-zactly!"

And Anne and I were willingly drafted to help him. We went through Grace's files and found detailed specifications for every room, right down to bookends and soap dishes. It was a tough job tracking down every item, but George was indefatigable, and so was Anne, and money was no object.

Time was everything, money was nothing. Electricians, plasterers, masons, and carpenters worked around the clock for bonus wages; and Anne, for no pay at all, harassed department stores into hurrying with the houseful of furniture she'd ordered.

Two days before Grace was to come home, the inheritance was gone, and the house was magnificent. George was unquestionably the happiest, proudest man on earth. The job was flawless, save for one tiny detail not worth mentioning. Anne had failed to match exactly the yellow square of cloth Grace had wanted for her living-room curtains and the cover for the couch. The shade Anne had had to settle for was just a little bit lighter. George and I couldn't see the difference at all.

And then Grace came home, cheerful but weak, leaning on George's arm. It was late in the afternoon, and Anne and I were waiting in the living room, literally trembling with excitement. As George helped Grace up the walk, Anne fussed nervously with a bouquet of red roses she had brought and placed in a massive glass vase in the center of the coffee table.

We heard George's hand on the latch, the door swung open, and the McClellans stood on the threshold of their dream house.

"Oh, George," Grace murmured. She let go of his arm, and, as though miraculously drawing strength from her surroundings, she walked from room to room, looking all about her as we had seen her do a thousand times. But this time of times she was speechless.

She returned at last to the living room, and sank onto the plum-colored chaise longue.

George turned down the volume of the phonograph to a sweet whisper. "Well?"

Grace sighed. "Don't rush me," she said. "I'm trying to find the words, the exact words."

"You like it?" George asked.

Grace looked at him and laughed incredulously. "Oh, George, George, of course I like it! You darling, it's wonderful! I'm home, home at last." Her lip trembled, and we all began to cloud up.

"Nothing wrong?" George asked huskily.

"You've taken wonderful care of it. Everything's so clean and beautiful."

"Well, it'd sure be a surprise if things *weren't* clean," George said. He clapped his hands together. "Now then, you well enough for a drink?"

"I'm not dead."

"Leave us out, George," I said. "We're leaving. We just had to see her expression when she walked in, but now we'll clear out."

"Oh, say now—" George said.

"No. I mean it. We're going. You two ought to be alone —you *three*, including the house."

"Stay right where you are," George said. He hurried into the dazzling white kitchen to mix the drinks.

"All right, so we'll sneak out," Anne said. We started for the front door. "Don't get up, Grace."

"Well, if you really won't stay, good-by," Grace said from the chaise longue. "I hardly know how to thank you."

"It was the most fun I've had in years," said Anne. She looked proudly around the room, and went over to the coffee table to rearrange the roses slightly. "The only thing that worried me was the color of the slipcover and curtains. Are they all right?"

"Why, Anne, did you notice them too? I wasn't even going to mention them. It would certainly be silly to let a little thing like that spoil my homecoming." She frowned a little.

Anne was crestfallen. "Oh dear, I hope they didn't spoil it."

"No, no, of course they didn't," Grace said. "I don't quite understand it, but it doesn't matter a bit."

"Well, I can explain," Anne said.

"Something in the air, I suppose."

"In the air?" Anne said.

"Well, how else can you explain it? That material held its color just perfectly for years, and then, poof, it fades like this in a few weeks."

George walked in with a frosty pewter pitcher. "Now, you'll stay for a quick one, won't you?"

Anne and I took glasses hungrily, gratefully, wordlessly.

"There's a new *Home Beautiful* that came today, sweetheart," George said.

Grace shrugged. "Read one and you've read them all." She lifted her glass. "Happy days, and thanks, darlings, so much for the roses."

(1951)

THE HYANNIS PORT
STORY

THE FARTHEST WAY from home I ever sold a storm
window was in Hyannis Port, Massachusetts, practically in
the front yard of President Kennedy's summer home. My
field of operation is usually within about twenty-five miles of
my home, which is in North Crawford, New Hampshire.

The Hyannis Port thing happened because somebody
misunderstood something I said, and thought I was an
ardent Goldwater Republican. Actually, I hadn't made up
my mind one way or the other about Goldwater.

What happened was this: The program chairman of the
North Crawford Lions Club was a Goldwater man, and
he had this college boy named Robert Taft Rumfoord
come talk to a meeting one day about the Democratic mess
in Washington and Hyannis Port. The boy was national
president of some kind of student organization that was
trying to get the country back to what he called First
Principles. One of the First Principles, I remember, was
getting rid of the income tax. You should have heard the
applause.

I got a funny feeling that the boy didn't care much more
about politics than I did. He had circles under his eyes,
and he looked as though he'd just as soon be somewhere
else. He would say strong things, but they came out sound-
ing like music on a kazoo. The only time he got really
interesting was when he told about being in sailboat races
and golf and tennis matches with different Kennedys and
their friends. He said that there was a lot of propaganda
around about what a fine golfer Bobby Kennedy was,
whereas Bobby actually couldn't golf for sour apples. He

said Pierre Salinger was one of the worst golfers in the world, and didn't care for sailing or tennis at all.

Robert Taft Rumfoord's parents were there to hear him. They had come all the way from Hyannis Port. They were both very proud of him—or at least the father was. The father had on white flannel trousers and white shoes, even though there was snow on the ground, and a double-breasted blue coat with brass buttons. The boy introduced him as *Commodore* William Rumfoord. The Commodore was a short man with very shaggy eyebrows and pale blue eyes. He looked like a gruff, friendly teddybear, and so did his son. I found out later, from a Secret Service man, that the Kennedys sometimes called the Rumfoords *"the Pooh people,"* on account of they were so much like the bear in the children's book *Winnie the Pooh.*

The Commodore's wife wasn't a Pooh person, though. She was thin and quick, and maybe two inches taller than the Commodore. Bears have a way of looking as though they're pretty much satisfied with everything. The Commodore's lady didn't have that look. I could tell she was jumpy about a lot of things.

After the boy was through pouring fire and brimstone on the Kennedys, with his father applauding everything he said, Hay Boyden, the building mover stood up. He was a Kennedy Democrat, and he said some terrible things to the boy. The only one I remember is the first thing he said: "Son, if you keep blowing off steam like this during your Boy Scout days, you aren't going to have an ounce of pressure left when you're old enough to vote." It got worse from there on.

The boy didn't get mad. He just got embarrassed, and answered back with some more kazoo music. It was the Commodore who really cared. He turned the color of tomato juice. He stood up and he argued back, did it pretty well, even though his wife was pulling at the bottom of his brass-buttoned coat the whole time. She was trying to get him to stop raising such an uproar, but the Commodore loved the uproar.

The meeting broke up with practically everybody embarrassed, and I went over to Hay Boyden to talk to him about something that didn't have anything to do with Kennedy *or* Goldwater. It was about a bathtub enclosure I had sold him. He had insisted on installing it himself, saving himself about seven dollars and a half. Only it leaked, and his dining-room ceiling fell down, and Hay claimed that was the fault of the merchandise and not the installation. Hay had some poison left in his system from his argument with the boy, so he used it up on me. I answered him back with the truth, and walked away from him, and Commodore Rumfoord grabbed my hand and shook it. He thought I'd been defending his boy and Barry Goldwater.

"What business you in?" he asked me.

I told him, and, the next thing I knew, I had an order for storm windows all around on a four-story house in Hyannis Port.

The Commodore called that big old house a cottage.

"You're a Commodore in the Navy?" I asked him.

"No," he said. "My father, however, was Secretary of the Navy under William Howard Taft. That's my full name: Commodore William Howard Taft Rumfoord."

"You're in the Coast Guard?" I said.

"You mean the *Kennedy Private Fleet?*" he said.

"Pardon me?" I said.

"That's what they ought to call the Coast Guard these days," he said. "Its sole mission seems to be to protect Kennedys while they water-ski behind high-powered stink-pots."

"You're *not* in the Coast Guard?" I said. I couldn't imagine what was left.

"I was Commodore of the Hyannis Port Yacht Club in 1946," he said.

He didn't smile, and neither did I, and neither did his wife, whose name was Clarice. But Clarice *did* give a little sigh that sounded like the whistle on a freight train far, far away on a wet morning.

I didn't know what the trouble was at the time, but Clarice was sighing because the Commodore hadn't held any job of any description since 1946. Since then, he'd made a full-time career of raging about whoever was President of the United States, including Eisenhower.

Especially Eisenhower.

So I went down to Hyannis Port in my truck to measure the Commodore's windows late in June. His driveway was on Irving Avenue. So was the Kennedys' driveway. And President Kennedy and I hit Cape Cod on the very same day.

Traffic to Hyannis Port was backed up through three villages. There were license plates from every state in the Republic. The line was moving about four miles an hour. I was passed by several groups of fifty-mile hikers. My radiator came to a boil four times.

I was feeling pretty sorry for myself, because I was just an ordinary citizen, and had to get stuck in lines like that. But then I recognized the man in the limousine up ahead of me. It was Adlai Stevenson. He wasn't moving any faster than I was, and his radiator was boiling, too.

One place there, we got stuck so long that Mr. Stevenson and I got out and walked around a little. I took the opportunity to ask him how the United Nations were getting along. He told me they were getting along about as well as could be expected. That wasn't anything I didn't already know.

When I finally got to Hyannis Port, I found out Irving Avenue was blocked off by police and Secret Service men. Adlai Stevenson got to go down it, but I didn't. The police made me get back into line with the tourists, who were being shunted down a street one block over from Irving Avenue.

The next thing I knew, I was in Hyannis, going past the *Presidential Motor Inn*, the *First Family Waffle Shop*, the *PT-109 Cocktail Lounge*, and a miniature golf course called the *New Frontier*.

I went into the waffle shop, and I called up the Rumfoords to find out how an ordinary storm-window salesman was supposed to get down Irving Avenue without dying in a hail of lead. It was the butler I talked to. He took down my license number, and found out how tall I was and what color my eyes were and all. He said he would tell the Secret Service, and they would let me by next time.

It was late in the afternoon, and I'd missed lunch, so I decided to have a waffle. All the different kinds of waffles were named after Kennedys and their friends and relatives. A waffle with strawberries and cream was a *Jackie*. A waffle with a scoop of ice cream was a *Caroline*. They even had a waffle named *Arthur Schlesinger, Jr.*

I had a thing called a *Teddy*—and a cup of *Joe*.

I got through next time, went right down Irving Avenue behind the Defense Minister of Pakistan. Except for us, that street was as quiet as a stretch of the Sahara Desert.

There wasn't anything to see at all on the President's side, except for a new, peeled-cedar fence about eight feet high and two hundred feet long, with a gate in it. The Rumfoord cottage faced the gate from across the street. It was the biggest house, and one of the oldest, in the village. It was stucco. It had towers and balconies, and a veranda that ran around all four sides.

On a second-floor balcony was a huge portrait of Barry Goldwater. It had bicycle reflectors in the pupils of its eyes. Those eyes stared right through the Kennedy gate. There were floodlights all around it, so I could tell it was lit up at night. And the floodlights were rigged with blinkers.

A man who sells storm windows can never be really sure about what class he belongs to, especially if he installs the windows, too. So I was prepared to keep out from under foot, and go about my business, measuring the windows. But the Commodore welcomed me like a guest of great importance. He invited me to cocktails and dinner, and to spend the night. He said I could start measuring the next day.

So we had martinis out on the veranda. Only we didn't sit on the most pleasant side, which looked out on the Yacht Club dock and the harbor. We sat on the side that looked out on all the poor tourists being shunted off toward Hyannis. The Commodore liked to talk about all those fools out there.

"Look at them!" he said. "They wanted glamour, and now they realize they're not going to get it. They actually expected to be invited to play touch football with Eunice and Frank Sinatra and the Secretary of Health and Welfare. Glamour is what they voted for, and look at 'em now. They don't even get to look at a Kennedy chimney up above the trees. All the glamour they'll get out of this administration is an overpriced waffle named *Caroline*."

A helicopter went over, very low, and it landed somewhere inside the Kennedy fence. Clarice said she wondered who it was.

"Pope John the Sixth," said the Commodore.

The butler, whose name was John, came out with a big bowl. I thought it was peanuts or popcorn, but it turned out to be Goldwater buttons. The Commodore had John take the bowl out to the street, and offer buttons to the people in cars. A lot of people took them. Those people were disappointed. They were sore.

Some fifty-mile hikers, who'd actually hiked sixty-seven miles, all the way from Boston, asked if they could please lie down on the Rumford lawn for a while. They were burned up, too. They thought it was the duty of the President, or at least the Attorney General, to thank them for walking so far. The Commodore said they could not only lie down, but he would give them lemonade, if they would put on Goldwater buttons. They were glad to.

"Commodore," I said, "where's that nice boy of yours, the one who talked to us up in New Hampshire."

"The one who talked to you is the only one I've got," he said.

"He certainly poured it on," I said.

"Chip off the old block," he said.

Clarice gave that faraway freight-whistle sigh of hers again.

"The boy went swimming just before you got here," said the Commodore. "He should be back at any time, unless he's been decapitated by a member of the Irish Mafia on water skis."

We went around to the water side of the veranda to see if we could catch sight of young Robert Taft Rumfoord in swimming. There was a Coast Guard cutter out there, shooing tourists in motorboats away from the Kennedy beach. There was a sightseeing boat crammed with people gawking in our direction. The barker on the boat had a very loud loudspeaker, and we could hear practically everything he said.

"The white boat there is the Honey Fitz, *the President's personal yacht,"* said the barker. *"Next to it is the* Marlin, *which belongs to the President's father, Joseph C. Kennedy, former Ambassador to the Court of St. James."*

"The President's stinkpot, and the President's father's stinkpot," said the Commodore. He called all motorboats stinkpots. "This is a harbor that should be devoted exclusively to sail."

There was a chart of the harbor on the veranda wall. I studied it, and found a *Rumfoord Point,* a *Rumfoord Rock,* and a *Rumfoord Shoal.* The Commodore told me his family had been in Hyannis Port since 1884.

"There doesn't seem to be anything named after the Kennedys," I said.

"Why *should* there be?" he said. "They only got here day before yesterday."

"Day before yesterday?" I said.

And he asked me, "What would *you* call nineteen-twenty-one?"

"No, sir," the barker said to one of his passengers, *"that is* not *the President's house. Everybody asks that. That great big ugly stucco house, folks, that's the Rumfoord Cottage. I agree with you, it's too big to be called* cottage, *but you know how rich people are."*

"Demoralized and bankrupt by confiscatory taxation," said the Commodore. "You know," he said, "it isn't as though Kennedy was the first President we ever had in Hyannis Port. Taft, Harding, Coolidge, and Hoover were all guests of my father in this very house. Kennedy is simply the first President who's seen fit to turn the place into an eastern enclave of *Disneyland."*

"No, mam," said the barker, *I don't know where the*

Rumfoords get their money, but they don't have to work at all, I know that. They just sit on that porch there, and drink martinis, and let the old mazooma roll in."

The Commodore blew up. He said he was going to sue the owners of the sight-seeing boat for a blue million. His wife tried to calm him down, but he made me come into his study with him while he called up his lawyers.

"You're a witness," he said.

But his telephone rang before he could call his lawyers. The person who was calling him was a Secret Service Agent named Raymond Boyle. I found out later that Boyle was known around the Kennedy household as the *Rumfoord Specialist* or the *Ambassador to Rumfoordiana.* Whenever anything came up that had to do with the Rumfoords, Boyle had to handle it.

The Commodore told me to go upstairs and listen in on the extension in the hall. "This will give you an idea of how arrogant civil servants have become these days," he said.

So I went upstairs.

"The Secret Service is one of the least secret services I've ever come in contact with," the Commodore was saying when I picked up the phone. "I've seen drum and bugle corps that were less obtrusive. Did I ever tell you about the time Calvin Coolidge, who was also a President, as it happened, went fishing for scup with my father and me off the end of the Yacht Club dock?"

"Yessir, you have, many times," said Boyle. "It's a good story, and I want to hear it again sometime. But right now I'm calling about your son."

The Commodore went right ahead with the story anyway. "President Coolidge," he said, "insisted on baiting his own hook, and the combined Atlantic and Pacific Fleets were not anchored offshore, and the sky was not black with airplanes, and brigades of Secret Service Agents were not trampling the neighbors' flowerbeds to purée."

"Sir—" said Boyle patiently, "your son Robert was apprehended in the act of boarding the President's father's boat, the *Marlin.*"

"Back in the days of Coolidge, there *were* no stinkpots

like that in this village, dribbling petroleum products, belching fumes, killing the fish, turning the beaches a gummy black."

"Commodore Rumfoord, sir," said Boyle, "did you hear what I just said about your son?"

"Of course," said the Commodore. "You said Robert, a member of the Hyannis Port Yacht Club, was caught touching a vessel belonging to another member of the club. This may seem a very terrible crime to a landlubber like yourself; but it has long been a custom of the sea, Mr. Boyle, that a swimmer, momentarily fatigued, may, upon coming to a vessel not his own, grasp that vessel and rest, without fear of being fired upon by the Coast Guard, or of having his fingers smashed by members of the Secret Service, or, as I prefer to call them, the *Kennedy Palace Dragoons.*"

"There has been no shooting, and no smashing, sir," said Boyle. "There has also been no evidence of swimmer's fatigue. Your Robert went up the anchor line of the *Marlin* like a chimpanzee. He *swarmed* up that rope, Commodore. I believe that's the proper nautical term. And I remind you, as I tried to remind him, that persons moving, uninvited, unannounced, with such speed and purposefulness within the vicinity of a President are, as a matter of time-honored policy, to be turned back at all costs—to be turned back, if need be, *violently.*"

"Was it a Kennedy who gave the order that the boarder be repelled?" the Commodore wanted to know.

"There was no Kennedy on board, sir."

"The stinkpot was unoccupied?"

"Adlai Stevenson and Walter Reuther and one of my men were on board, sir," said Boyle. "They were all below, until they heard Robert's feet hit the deck."

"Stevenson and Reuther?" said the Commodore. "That's the last time I let my son go swimming without a dagger in his teeth. I hope he was opening the seacocks when beaten insensible by truncheons."

"Very funny, sir," said Boyle, his voice developing a slight cutting edge.

"You're sure it was my Robert?" said the Commodore.

"Who else but your Robert wears a Goldwater button on his swimming trunks?" asked Boyle.

"You object to his political views?" the Commodore demanded.

"I mention the button as a means of identification. Your son's politics do not interest the Secret Service. For your information, I spent seven years protecting the life of a Republican, and three protecting the life of a Democrat," said Boyle.

"For your information, Mr. Boyle," said the Commodore, "Dwight David Eisenhower was *not* a Republican."

"Whatever he was, I protected him," said Boyle. "He may have been a Zoroastrian, for all I know. And whatever the next President is going to be, I'll protect him, too. I also protect the lives of persons like your son from the consequences of excessive informality where the Presidential presence is concerned." Now Boyle's voice really started to cut. It sounded like a bandsaw working on galvanized tin. "I tell you, officially and absolutely unsmilingly now, your son is to cease and desist from using Kennedy boats as love nests."

That got through to the Commodore, bothered him. "Love nests?" he said.

"Your Robert has been meeting a girl on boats all over the harbor," said Boyle. "He arranged to meet her today on the *Marlin*. He was sure it would be vacant. Adlai Stevenson and Walter Reuther were a shock."

The Commodore was quiet for a few seconds, and then he said, "Mr. Boyle, I resent your implications. If I ever hear of your implying such a thing about my son to anyone else, you had better put your pistol and shoulder holster in your wife's name, because I'll sue you for everything you've got. My Robert has never gone with a girl he wasn't proud to introduce to his mother and me, and he never will."

"You're going to meet this one any minute now," said Boyle. "Robert is on his way home with her."

The Commodore wasn't tough at all now. He was uneasy and humble when he said, "Would you mind telling me her name?"

"Kennedy, sir," said Boyle, *"Sheila* Kennedy, fresh over from Ireland, a fourth cousin of the President of the United States."

Robert Taft Rumfoord came in with the girl right after that, and announced they were engaged to be married.

Supper that night in the Rumfoord cottage was sad and beautiful and happy and strange. There were Robert and his girl, and me, and the Commodore and his lady.

That girl was so intelligent, so warm, and so beautiful that she broke my heart every time I looked at her. That was why supper was so peculiar. The girl was so desirable, and the love between her and Robert was so sweet and clean, that nobody could think of anything but silly little things to say. We mainly ate in silence.

The Commodore brought up the subject of politics just once. He said to Robert, "Well—uh—will you still be making speeches around the country, or—uh—"

"I think I'll get out of politics entirely for a while," said Robert.

The Commodore said something that none of us could understand, because the words sort of choked him.

"Sir?" said Robert.

"I said," said the Commodore, " 'I would think you would.' "

I looked at the Commodore's lady, at Clarice. All the lines had gone out of her face. She looked young and beautiful, too. She was completely relaxed for the first time in God-knows-how-many years.

One of the things I said that supper was was *sad.* The sad part was how empty and quiet it left the Commodore.

The two lovers went for a moonlight sail. The Commodore and his lady and I had brandy on the veranda, on the water side. The sun was down. The tourist traffic had petered out. The fifty-mile hikers who had asked to rest on the lawn that afternoon were still all there, sound asleep, except for one boy who played a guitar. He played it slowly. Sometimes it seemed like a minute between the time he would pluck a string and the time he would pluck one again.

John, the butler, came out and asked the Commodore if it was time to turn on Senator Goldwater's floodlights yet.

"I think we'll just leave him off tonight, John," said the Commodore.

"Yes, sir," said John.

"I'm still *for* him, John," said the Commodore. "Don't anybody misunderstand me. I just think we ought to give him a rest tonight."

"Yes, sir," said John, and he left.

It was dark on the veranda, so I couldn't see the Commodore's face very well. The darkness, and the brandy, and the slow guitar let him start telling the truth about himself without feeling much pain.

"Let's give the Senator from Arizona a rest," he said. "Everybody knows who *he* is. The question is: Who am I?"

"A lovable man," said Clarice in the dark.

"With Goldwater's floodlights turned off, and with my son engaged to marry a Kennedy, what am I but what the man on the sight-seeing boat said I was: A man who sits on this porch, drinking martinis, and letting the old mazooma roll in."

"You're an intelligent, charming, well-educated man, and you're still quite young," said Clarice.

"I've got to find some kind of work," he said.

"We'll both be so much happier," she said. "I would love you, no matter what. But I can tell you now, darling—it's awfully hard for a woman to *admire* a man who actually doesn't do anything."

We were dazzled by the headlights of two cars coming out of the Kennedys' driveway. The cars stopped right in front of the Rumfoord Cottage. Whoever was in them seemed to be giving the place a good looking-over.

The Commodore went to that side of the veranda, to find out what was going on. And I heard the voice of the President of the United States coming from the car in front.

"Commodore Rumfoord," said the President, "may I ask what is wrong with your Goldwater sign?"

"Nothing, Mr. President," said the Commodore respectfully.

"Then why isn't it on?" asked the President.

"I just didn't feel like turning it on tonight, sir," said the Commodore.

"I have Mr. Khrushchev's son-in-law with me," said the President, "He would very much enjoy seeing it."

"Yes, sir," said the Commodore. He was right by the switch. He turned it on. The whole neighhborhood was bathed in flashing light.

"Thank you," said the President. "And *leave* it on, would you please?"

"Sir?" said the Commodore.

The cars started to pull away slowly. "That way," said the President, "I can find my way home."

(1963)

D.P.

EIGHTY-ONE small sparks of human life were kept in an orphanage set up by Catholic nuns in what had been the gamekeeper's house on a large estate overlooking the Rhine. This was in the German village of Karlswald, in the American Zone of Occupation. Had the children not been kept there, not been given the warmth and food and clothes that could be begged for them, they might have wandered off the edges of the earth, searching for parents who had long ago stopped searching for them.

Every mild afternoon the nuns marched the children, two by two, through the woods, into the village and back, for their rations of fresh air. The village carpenter, an old man who was given to thoughtful rests between strokes of his tools, always came out of his shop to watch the bobbing, chattering, cheerful, ragged parade, and to speculate, with idlers his shop attracted, as to the nationalities of the passing children's parents.

"See the little French girl," he said one afternoon. "Look at the flash of those eyes!"

"And look at that little Pole swing his arms. They love to march, the Poles," said a young mechanic.

"Pole? Where do you see any Pole?" said the carpenter.

"There—the thin, sober-looking one in front," the other replied.

"Aaaaah. He's too tall for a Pole," said the carpenter. "And what Pole has flaxen hair like that? He's a German."

The mechanic shrugged. "They're all German now, so what difference does it make?" he said. "Who can prove what their parents were? If you had fought in Poland, you would know he was a very common type."

"Look—look who's coming now," said the carpenter, grinning. "Full of arguments as you are, you won't argue with me about *him*. There we have an American!" He called out to the child. "Joe—when you going to win the championship back?"

"Joe!" called the mechanic. "How is the Brown Bomber today?"

At the very end of the parade, a lone, blue-eyed colored boy, six years old, turned and smiled with sweet uneasiness at those who called out to him every day. He nodded politely, murmuring a greeting in German, the only language he knew.

His name, chosen arbitrarily by the nuns, was Karl Heinz. But the carpenter had given him a name that struck, the name of the only colored man who had ever made an impression on the villagers' minds, the former heavyweight champion of the world, Joe Louis.

"Joe!" called the carpenter. "Cheer up! Let's see those white teeth sparkle, Joe."

Joe obliged shyly.

The carpenter clapped the mechanic on the back. "And if *he* isn't a German too! Maybe it's the only way we can get another heavyweight champion."

Joe turned a corner, shooed out of the carpenter's sight by a nun bringing up the rear. She and Joe spent a great deal of time together, since Joe, no matter where he was placed in the parade, always drifted to the end.

"Joe," she said, "you are such a dreamer. Are all your people such dreamers?"

"I'm sorry, sister," said Joe. "I was thinking."

"Dreaming."

"Sister, am I the son of an American soldier?"

"Who told you that?"

"Peter. Peter said my mother was a German, and my father was an American soldier who went away. He said she left me with you, and then went away too." There was no sadness in his voice—only puzzlement.

Peter was the oldest boy in the orphanage, an embittered old man of fourteen, a German boy who could remember his parents and brothers and sisters and home, and the war, and all sorts of food that Joe found impossible to imagine. Peter seemed superhuman to Joe, like a man who had been to heaven and hell and back many times, and knew exactly why they were where they were, how they had come there, and where they might have been.

"You mustn't worry about it, Joe," said the nun. "No one knows who your mother and father were. But they must have been very good people, because you are so good."

"What is an American?" said Joe.

"It's a person from another country."

"Near here?"

"There are some near here, but their homes are far, far away—across a great deal of water."

"Like the river."

"More water than that, Joe. More water than you have ever seen. You can't even see the other side. You could get on a boat and go for days and days and still not get to the other side. I'll show you a map sometime. But don't pay any attention to Peter, Joe. He makes things up. He doesn't really know anything about you. Now, catch up."

Joe hurried, and overtook the end of the line, where he marched purposefully and alertly for a few minutes. But then he began to dawdle again, chasing ghostlike words in his small mind: . . . soldier . . . German . . . American . . . your people . . . champion . . . Brown Bomber . . . more water than you've ever seen.

"Sister," said Joe, "are Americans like me? Are they brown?"

"Some are, some aren't, Joe."

"Are there many people like me?"

"Yes. Many, many people."

"Why haven't I seen them?"

"None of them have come to the village. They have places of their own."

"I want to go there."

"Aren't you happy here, Joe?"

"Yes. But Peter says I don't belong here, that I'm not a German and never can be."

"Peter! Pay no attention to him."

"Why do people smile when they see me, and try to make me sing and talk, and then laugh when I do?"

"Joe, Joe! Look quickly," said the nun. "See—up there, in the tree. See the little sparrow with the broken leg. Oh poor, brave little thing—he still gets around quite well. See him, Joe? Hop, hop, hippity-hop."

One hot summer day, as the parade passed the carpenter's shop, the carpenter came out to call something new to Joe, something that thrilled and terrified him.

"Joe! Hey, Joe! Your father is in town. Have you seen him yet?"

"No, sir—no, I haven't," said Joe. "Where is he?"

"He's teasing," said the nun sharply.

"You see if I'm teasing, Joe," said the carpenter. "Just keep your eyes open when you go past the school. You have to look sharp, up the slope and into the woods. You'll see, Joe."

"I wonder where our little friend the sparrow is today," said the nun brightly. "Goodness, I hope his leg is getting better, don't you, Joe?"

"Yes, yes I do, sister."

She chattered on about the sparrow and the clouds and the flowers as they approached the school, and Joe gave up answering her.

The woods above the school seemed still and empty.

But then Joe saw a massive brown man, naked to the waist and wearing a pistol, step from the trees. The man drank from a canteen, wiped his lips with the back of his hand, grinned down on the world with handsome disdain, and disappeared again into the twilight of the woods.

"Sister!" gasped Joe. "My father—I just saw my father!"

"No, Joe—no you didn't."

"He's up there in the woods. I saw him. I want to go up there, sister."

"He isn't your father, Joe. He doesn't know you. He doesn't want to see you."

"He's one of my people, sister!"

"You can't go up there, Joe, and you can't stay here." She took him by the arm to make him move. "Joe—you're being a bad boy, Joe."

Joe obeyed numbly. He didn't speak again for the remainder of the walk, which brought them home by another route, far from the school. No one else had seen his wonderful father, or believed that Joe had.

Not until prayers that night did he burst into tears.

At ten o'clock, the young nun found his cot empty.

Under a great spread net that was laced with rags, an artillery piece squatted in the woods, black and oily, its muzzle thrust at the night sky. Trucks and the rest of the battery were hidden higher on the slope.

Joe watched and listened tremblingly through a thin screen of shrubs as the soldiers, indistinct in the darkness, dug in around their gun. The words he overheard made no sense to him.

"Sergeant, why we gotta dig in, when we're movin' out in the mornin', and it's just maneuvers anyhow? Seems like we could kind of conserve our strength, and just scratch around a little to show where we'd of dug if there was any sense to it."

"For all you know, boy, there may *be* sense to it before mornin'," said the sergeant. "You got ten minutes to get to China and bring me back a pigtail. Hear?"

The sergeant stepped into a patch of moonlight, his hands on his hips, his big shoulders back, the image of an emperor. Joe saw that it was the same man he'd marveled at in the afternoon. The sergeant listened with satisfaction to the sounds of digging, and then, to Joe's alarm, strode toward Joe's hiding place.

Joe didn't move a muscle until the big boot struck his side. *"Ach!"*

"Who's that?" The sergeant snatched Joe from the ground, and set him on his feet hard. "My golly, boy, what you doin' here? Scoot! Go on home! This ain't no place for kids to be playin'." He shined a flashlight in Joe's face. "Doggone," he muttered. "Where you come from?" He held Joe at arm's length, and shook him gently, like a rag doll. "Boy, how you get here—swim?"

Joe stammered in German that he was looking for his father.

"Come on—how you get here? What you doin'? Where's your mammy?"

"What you got there, sergeant?" said a voice in the dark.

"Don't rightly know what to call it," said the sergeant. "Talks like a Kraut and dresses like a Kraut, but just look at it a minute."

Soon a dozen men stood in a circle around Joe, talking loudly, then softly, to him, as though they thought getting through to him were a question of tone.

Every time Joe tried to explain his mission, they laughed in amazement.

"How he learn German? Tell me that."

"Where your daddy, boy?"

"Where your mammy, boy?"

"Sprecken zee Dutch, boy? Looky there. See him nod. He talks it, all right."

"Oh, you're fluent, man, mighty fluent. Ask him some more."

"Go get the lieutenant," said the sergeant. "He can talk to this boy, and understand what he's tryin' to say. Look at him shake. Scared to death. Come here, boy; don't be afraid, now." He enclosed Joe in his great arms. "Just take it easy, now—everything's gonna be all-l-l-l right. See what I got? By golly, I don't believe the boy's ever seen chocolate before. Go on—taste it. Won't hurt you."

Joe, safe in a fort of bone and sinew, ringed by luminous eyes, bit into the chocolate bar. The pink lining of his mouth, and then his whole soul, was flooded with warm, rich pleasure, and he beamed.

"He smiled!"

"Look at him light up!"

"Doggone if he didn't stumble right into heaven! I mean!"

"Talk about displaced persons," said the sergeant, hugging Joe, "this here's the most displaced little old person I *ever* saw. Upside down and inside out and ever' which way."

"Here, boy—here's some more chocolate."

"Don't give him no more," said the sergeant reproachfully. "You want to make him sick?"

"Naw, sarge, naw—don't wanna make him sick. No, sir."

"What's going on here?" The lieutenant, a small, elegant Negro, the beam of his flashlight dancing before him, approached the group.

"Got a little boy here, lieutenant," said the sergeant. "Just wandered into the battery. Must of crawled past the guards."

"Well, send him on home, sergeant."

"Yessir. I planned to." He cleared his throat. "But this ain't no ordinary little boy, lieutenant." He opened his arms so that the light fell on Joe's face.

The lieutenant laughed incredulously, and knelt before Joe. "How'd you get here?"

"All he talks is German, lieutenant," said the sergeant.

"Where's your home?" said the lieutenant in German.

"Over more water than you've ever seen," said the Joe.

"Where do you come from?"

"God made me," said Joe.

"This boy is going to be a lawyer when he grows up," said the lieutenant in English. "Now, listen to me," he said to Joe, "what's your name, and where are your people?"

"Joe Louis," said Joe, "and you are my people. I ran away from the orphanage, because I belong with you."

The lieutenant stood, shaking his head, and translated what Joe had said.

The woods echoed with glee.

"Joe Louis! I *thought* he was awful big and powerful-lookin'!"

"Jus' keep away from that left—tha's all!"

"If he's Joe, he's sure found his people. He's got us there!"

"Shut up!" commanded the sergeant suddenly. "All of you just shut up. This ain't no joke! Ain't nothing funny in it! Boy's all alone in the world. Ain't no joke."

A small voice finally broke the solemn silence that followed. "Naw—ain't no joke at all."

"We better take the jeep and run him back into town, sergeant," said the lieutenant. "Corporal Jackson, you're in charge."

"You tell 'em Joe was a *good* boy," said Jackson.

"Now, Joe," said the lieutenant in German, softly, "you come with the sergeant and me. We'll take you home."

Joe dug his fingers into the sergeant's forearms. "Papa! No—papa! I want to stay with you."

"Look, sonny, I ain't your papa," said the sergeant helplessly. "I *ain't* your papa."

"Papa!"

"Man, he's glued to you, ain't he, sergeant?" said a soldier. "Looks like you ain't never goin' to pry him loose. You got yourself a boy there, sarge, and he's got hisself a papa."

The sergeant walked over to the jeep with Joe in his arms. "Come on, now," he said, "you leggo, little Joe, so's I can drive. I can't drive with you hangin' on, Joe. You sit in the lieutenant's lap right next to me."

The group formed again around the jeep, gravely now, watching the sergeant try to coax Joe into letting go.

"I don't want to get tough, Joe. Come on—take it easy, Joe. Let go, now, Joe, so's I can drive. See, I can't steer or nothin' with you hanging on right there."

"Papa!"

"Come on, over to my lap, Joe," said the lieutenant in German.

"Papa!"

"Joe, Joe, looky," said a soldier. "Chocolate! Want some more chocolate, Joe? See? Whole bar, Joe, all yours. Jus' leggo the sergeant and move over into the lieutenant's lap."

Joe tightened his grip on the sergeant.

"Don't put the chocolate back in your pocket, man! Give it to Joe anyways," said a soldier angrily. "Somebody go get a case of D bars off the truck, and throw 'em in the back for Joe. Give that boy chocolate enough for the nex' twenny years."

"Look, Joe," said another soldier, "ever see a wrist-watch? Look at the wristwatch, Joe. See it glow, boy? Move over in the lieutenant's lap, and I'll let you listen to it tick. Tick, tick, tick, Joe. Come on, want to listen?"

Joe didn't move.

The soldier handed the watch to him. "Here, Joe, you take it anyway. It's yours." He walked away quickly.

"Man," somebody called after him, "you crazy? You paid fifty dollars for that watch. What business a little boy got with any fifty-dollar watch?"

"No—I ain't crazy. Are you?"

"Naw, I ain't crazy. Neither one of us crazy, I guess. Joe—want a knife? You got to promise to be careful with it, now. Always cut *away* from yourself. Hear? Lieutenant, when you get back, you tell him always cut *away* from hisself."

"I don't want to go back. I want to stay with *papa*," said Joe tearfully

"Soldiers can't take little boys with them, Joe," said the lieutenant in German. "And we're leaving early in the morning."

"Will you come back for me?" said Joe.

"We'll come back if we can, Joe. Soldiers never know where they'll be from one day to the next. We'll come back for a visit, if we can."

"Can we give old Joe this case of D bars, lieutenant?" said a soldier carrying a cardboard carton of chocolate bars.

"Don't ask me," said the lieutenant. "I don't know anything about it. I never saw anything of any case of D bars, never heard anything about it."

"Yessir." The soldier laid his burden down on the jeep's back seat.

"He ain't gonna let go," said the sergeant miserably.

"You drive, lieutenant, and me and Joe'll sit over there."

The lieutenant and the sergeant changed places, and the jeep began to move.

" 'By, Joe!"

"You be a good boy, Joe!"

"Don't you eat all that chocolate at once, you hear?"

"Don't cry, Joe. Give us a smile."

"Wider, boy—that's the stuff!"

"Joe, Joe, wake up, Joe." The voice was that of Peter, the oldest boy in the orphanage, and it echoed damply from the stone walls.

Joe sat up, startled. All around his cot were the other orphans, jostling one another for a glimpse of Joe and the treasures by his pillow.

"Where did you get the hat, Joe—and the watch, and knife?" said Peter. "And what's in the box under your bed?"

Joe felt his head, and found a soldier's wool knit cap there. "Papa," he mumbled sleepily.

"Papa!" mocked Peter, laughing.

"Yes," said Joe. "Last night I went to see my papa, Peter."

"Could he speak German, Joe?" said a little girl wonderingly.

"No, but his friend could," said Joe.

"He didn't see his father," said Peter. "Your father is far, far away, and will never come back. He probably doesn't even know you're alive."

"What did he look like?" said the girl.

Joe glanced thoughtfully around the room. "Papa is as high as this ceiling," he said at last. "He is wider than that door." Triumphantly, he took a bar of chocolate from under his pillow. "And as brown as that!" He held out the bar to the others. "Go on, have some. There is plenty more."

"He doesn't look anything like that," said Peter. "You aren't telling the truth, Joe."

"My papa has a pistol as big as this bed, almost, Peter,"

said Joe happily, "and a cannon as big as this house. And there were hundreds and hundreds like him."

"Somebody played a joke on you, Joe," said Peter. "He wasn't your father. How do you know he wasn't fooling you?"

"Because he cried when he left me," said Joe simply. "And he promised to take me back home across the water as fast as he could." He smiled airily. "Not like the river, Peter—across more water than you've *ever* seen. He promised, and then I let him go."

(1953)

REPORT ON THE
BARNHOUSE EFFECT

LET ME BEGIN by saying that I don't know any more about where Professor Arthur Barnhouse is hiding than anyone else does. Save for one short, enigmatic message left in my mailbox on Christmas Eve, I have not heard from him since his disappearance a year and a half ago.

What's more, readers of this article will be disappointed if they expect to learn how *they* can bring about the so-called "Barnhouse Effect." If I were able and willing to give away that secret, I would certainly be something more important than a psychology instructor.

I have been urged to write this report because I did research under the professor's direction and because I was the first to learn of his astonishing discovery. But while I was his student I was never entrusted with knowledge of how the mental forces could be released and directed. He was unwilling to trust anyone with that information.

I would like to point out that the term "Barnhouse Effect" is a creation of the popular press, and was never used by Professor Barnhouse. The name he chose for the phenomenon was *"dynamopsychism,"* or *force of the mind*.

I cannot believe that there is a civilized person yet to be convinced that such a force exists, what with its destructive effects on display in every national capital. I think humanity has always had an inkling that this sort of force does exist. It has been common knowledge that some people are luckier than others with inanimate objects like dice. What Professor Barnhouse did was to show that such "luck" was a measurable force, which in his case could be enormous.

By my calculations, the professor was about fifty-five times more powerful than a Nagasaki-type atomic bomb at the time he went into hiding. He was not bluffing when, on the eve of "Operation Brainstorm," he told General Honus Barker: "Sitting here at the dinner table, I'm pretty sure I can flatten anything on earth—from Joe Louis to the Great Wall of China."

There is an understandable tendency to look upon Professor Barnhouse as a supernatural visitation. The First Church of Barnhouse in Los Angeles has a congregation numbering in the thousands. He is godlike in neither appearance nor intellect. The man who disarms the world is single, shorter than the average American male, stout, and averse to exercise. His I.Q. is 143, which is good but certainly not sensational. He is quite mortal, about to celebrate his fortieth birthday, and in good health. If he is alone now, the isolation won't bother him too much. He was quiet and shy when I knew him, and seemed to find more companionship in books and music than in his associations at the college.

Neither he nor his powers fall outside the sphere of Nature. His dynamopsychic radiations are subject to many known physical laws that apply in the field of radio. Hardly a person has not now heard the snarl of "Barnhouse static" on his home receiver. The radiations are affected by sunspots and variations in the ionosphere.

However, they differ from ordinary broadcast waves in several important ways. Their total energy can be brought to bear on any single point the professor chooses, and that energy is undiminished by distance. As a weapon, then, dynamopsychism has an impressive advantage over bacteria and atomic bombs, beyond the fact that it costs nothing to use: it enables the professor to single out critical individuals and objects instead of slaughtering whole populations in the process of maintaining international equilibrium.

As General Honus Barker told the House Military Affairs Committee: "Until someone finds Barnhouse, there is no defense against the Barnhouse Effect." Efforts to "jam" or block the radiations have failed. Premier Slezak could have saved himself the fantastic expense of his "Barnhouse-proof" shelter. Despite the shelter's twelve-foot-thick lead armor, the premier has been floored twice while in it.

There is talk of screening the population for men potentially as powerful dynamopsychically as the professor. Senator Warren Foust demanded funds for this purpose last month, with the passionate declaration: "He who rules the Barnhouse Effect rules the world!" Commissar Kropotnik said much the same thing, so another costly armaments race, with a new twist, has begun.

This race at least has its comical aspects. The world's best gamblers are being coddled by governments like so many nuclear physicists. There may be several hundred persons with dynamopsychic talent on earth, myself included. But, without knowledge of the professor's technique, they can never be anything but dice-table despots. With the secret, it would probably take them ten years to become dangerous weapons. It took the professor that long. He who rules the Barnhouse Effect is Barnhouse and will be for some time.

Popularly, the "Age of Barnhouse" is said to have begun a year and a half ago, on the day of Operation Brainstorm. That was when dynamopsychism became significant politically. Actually, the phenomenon was discovered in May, 1942, shortly after the professor turned down a direct commission in the Army and enlisted as an artillery private. Like X-rays and vulcanized rubber, dynamopsychism was discovered by accident.

From time to time Private Barnhouse was invited to take part in games of chance by his barrack mates. He knew nothing about the games, and usually begged off. But one evening, out of social grace, he agreed to shoot craps. It was terrible or wonderful that he played, depending upon whether or not you like the world as it now is.

"Shoot sevens, Pop," someone said.

So "Pop" shot sevens—ten in a row to bankrupt the barracks. He retired to his bunk and, as a mathematical exercise, calculated the odds against his feat on the back of a laundry slip. His chances of doing it, he found, were one in almost ten million! Bewildered, he borrowed a pair of dice from the man in the bunk next to his. He tried to roll sevens again, but got only the usual assortment of numbers. He lay back for a moment, then resumed his toying with the dice. He rolled ten more sevens in a row.

He might have dismissed the phenomenon with a low whistle. But the professor instead mulled over the circumstances surrounding his two lucky streaks. There was one single factor in common: on both occasions, *the same thought train had flashed through his mind just before he threw the dice.* It was that thought train which aligned the professor's brain cells into what has since become the most powerful weapon on earth.

The soldier in the next bunk gave dynamopsychism its first token of respect. In an understatement certain to bring wry smiles to the faces of the world's dejected demagogues, the soldier said, "You're hotter'n a two-dollar pistol, Pop." Professor Barnhouse was all of that. The dice that did his bidding weighed but a few grams, so the forces involved were minute; but the unmistakable fact that there were such forces was earth-shaking.

Professional caution kept him from revealing his discovery immediately. He wanted more facts and a body of theory to go with them. Later, when the atomic bomb was dropped in Hiroshima, it was fear that made him hold his peace. At no time were his experiments, as Premier Slezak called them, "a bourgeois plot to shackle the true democracies of the world." The professor didn't know where they were leading.

In time, he came to recognize another startling feature of dynamopsychism: *its strength increased with use.* Within six months, he was able to govern dice thrown by men the length of a barracks distant. By the time of his discharge in 1945, he could knock bricks loose from chimneys three miles away.

Charges that Professor Barnhouse could have won the last war in a minute, but did not care to do so, are perfectly senseless. When the war ended, he had the range and power of a 37-millimeter cannon, perhaps—certainly no more. His dynamopsychic powers graduated from the small-arms class only after his discharge and return to Wyandotte College.

I enrolled in the Wyandotte Graduate School two years after the professor had rejoined the faculty. By chance, he was assigned as my thesis adviser. I was unhappy about the assignment, for the professor was, in the eyes of both colleagues and students, a somewhat ridiculous figure. He missed classes or had lapses of memory during lectures. When I arrived, in fact, his shortcomings had passed from the ridiculous to the intolerable.

"We're assigning you to Barnhouse as a sort of temporary thing," the dean of social studies told me. He looked apologetic and perplexed. "Brilliant man, Barnhouse, I guess. Difficult to know since his return, perhaps, but his work before the war brought a great deal of credit to our little school."

When I reported to the professor's laboratory for the first time, what I saw was more distressing than the gossip. Every surface in the room was covered with dust; books and apparatus had not been disturbed for months. The professor sat napping at his desk when I entered. The only signs of recent activity were three overflowing ashtrays, a pair of scissors, and a morning paper with several items clipped from its front page.

As he raised his head to look at me, I saw that his eyes were clouded with fatigue. "Hi," he said, "just can't seem to get my sleeping done at night." He lighted a cigarette, his hands trembling slightly. "You the young man I'm supposed to help with a thesis?"

"Yes, sir," I said. In minutes he converted my misgivings to alarm.

"You an overseas veteran?" he asked.

"Yes, sir."

"Not much left over there, is there?" He frowned. "Enjoy the last war?"

"No, sir."

"Look like another war to you?"

"Kind of, sir."

"What can be done about it?"

I shrugged. "Looks pretty hopeless."

He peered at me intently. "Know anything about international law, the U.N., and all that?"

"Only what I pick up from the papers."

"Same here," he sighed. He showed me a fat scrapbook packed with newspaper clippings. "Never used to pay any attention to international politics. Now I study them the way I used to study rats in mazes. Everybody tells me the same thing—'Looks hopeless.' "

"Nothing short of a miracle—" I began.

"Believe in magic?" he asked sharply. The professor fished two dice from his vest pocket. "I will try to roll twos," he said. He rolled twos three times in a row. "One chance in about 47,000 of that happening. There's a miracle for you." He beamed for an instant, then brought the interview to an end, remarking that he had a class which had begun ten minutes ago.

He was not quick to take me into his confidence, and he said no more about his trick with the dice. I assumed they were loaded, and forgot about them. He set me the task of watching male rats cross electrified metal strips to get to food or female rats—an experiment that had been done to everyone's satisfaction in the nineteen-thirties. As though the pointlessness of my work were not bad enough, the professor annoyed me further with irrelevant questions. His favorites were: "Think we should have dropped the atomic bomb on Hiroshima?" and "Think every new piece of scientific information is a good thing for humanity?"

However, I did not feel put upon for long. "Give those poor animals a holiday," he said one morning, after I had been with him only a month. "I wish you'd help me look into a more interesting problem—namely, my sanity."

I returned the rats to their cages.

"What you must do is simple," he said, speaking softly. "Watch the inkwell on my desk. If you see nothing happen to it, say so, and I'll go quietly—relieved, I might add—to the nearest sanitarium."

I nodded uncertainly.

He locked the laboratory door and drew the blinds, so that we were in twilight for a moment. "I'm odd, I know," he said. "It's fear of myself that's made me odd."

"I've found you somewhat eccentric, perhaps, but certainly not—"

"If nothing happens to that inkwell, 'crazy as a bedbug' is the only description of me that will do," he interrupted, turning on the overhead lights. His eyes narrowed. "To give you an idea of how crazy, I'll tell you what's been running through my mind when I should have been sleeping. I think maybe I can save the world. I think maybe I can make every nation a *have* nation, and do away with war for good. I think maybe I can clear roads through jungles, irrigate deserts, build dams overnight."

"Yes, sir."

"Watch the inkwell!"

Dutifully and fearfully I watched. A high-pitched humming seemed to come from the inkwell; then it began to vibrate alarmingly, and finally to bound about the top of the desk, making two noisy circuits. It stopped, hummed again, glowed red, then popped in splinters with a blue-green flash.

Perhaps my hair stood on end. The professor laughed gently. "Magnets?" I managed to say at last.

"Wish to heaven it were magnets," he murmured. It was then that he told me of dynamopsychism. He knew only that there was such a force; he could not explain it. "It's me and me alone—and it's awful."

"I'd say it was amazing and wonderful!" I cried.

"If all I could do was make inkwells dance, I'd be tickled silly with the whole business." He shrugged disconsolately. "But I'm no toy, my boy. If you like, we can drive around the neighborhood, and I'll show you what I mean." He told me about pulverized boulders, shattered oaks, and abandoned farm buildings demolished within a fifty-mile radius of the campus. "Did every bit of it sitting right here, just thinking—not even thinking hard."

He scratched his head nervously. "I have never dared to concentrate as hard as I can for fear of the damage I might do. I'm to the point where a mere whim is a block-buster." There was a depressing pause. "Up until a few days ago, I've thought it best to keep my secret for fear of what use it might be put to," he continued. "Now I realize that I haven't any more right to it than a man has a right to own an atomic bomb."

He fumbled through a heap of papers. "This says about all that needs to be said, I think." He handed me a draft of a letter to the Secretary of State.

> *Dear Sir:*
> *I have discovered a new force which costs nothing to use, and which is probably more important than atomic energy. I should like to see it used most effectively in the cause of peace, and am, therefore, requesting your advice as to how this might best be done.*
>
> *Yours truly,*
> *A. Barnhouse.*

"I have no idea what will happen next," said the professor.

There followed three months of perpetual nightmare, wherein the nation's political and military great came at all hours to watch the professor's tricks.

We were quartered in an old mansion near Charlottesville, Virginia, to which we had been whisked five days after the letter was mailed. Surrounded by barbed wire and twenty guards, we were labeled "Project Wishing Well," and were classified as Top Secret.

For companionship we had General Honus Barker and the State Department's William K. Cuthrell. For the professor's talk of peace-through-plenty they had indulgent smiles and much discourse on practical measures and realistic thinking. So treated, the professor, who had at first been almost meek, progressed in a matter of weeks toward stubbornness.

He had agreed to reveal the thought train by means of which he aligned his mind into a dynamopsychic transmitter. But, under Cuthrell's and Barker's nagging to do so, he began to hedge. At first he declared that the information could be passed on simply by word of mouth. Later he said that it would have to be written up in a long report. Finally, at dinner one night, just after General Barker had read the secret orders for Operation Brainstorm, the professor announced, "The report may take as long as five years to write." He looked fiercely at the general. "Maybe twenty."

The dismay occasioned by this flat announcement was offset somewhat by the exciting anticipation of Operation Brainstorm. The general was in a holiday mood. "The target ships are on their way to the Caroline Islands at this very moment," he declared ecstatically. "One hundred and twenty of them! At the same time, ten V-2s are being readied for firing in New Mexico, and fifty radio-controlled jet bombers are being equipped for a mock attack on the Aleutians. Just think of it!" Happily he reviewed his orders. "At exactly 1100 hours next Wednesday, I will give you the order to *concentrate;* and you, professor, will think as hard as you can about sinking the target ships, destroying the V-2s before they hit the ground, and knocking down the bombers before they reach the Aleutians! Think you can handle it?"

The professor turned gray and closed his eyes. "As I told you before, my friend, I don't know what I can do." He added bitterly, "As for this Operation Brainstorm, I was never consulted about it, and it strikes me as childish and insanely expensive."

General Barker bridled. "Sir," he said, "your field is psychology, and I wouldn't presume to give you advice in that field. Mine is national defense. I have had thirty years of experience and success, Professor, and I'll ask you not to criticize my judgment."

The professor appealed to Mr. Cuthrell. "Look," he pleaded, "isn't it war and military matters we're all trying to get rid of? Wouldn't it be a whole lot more significant and lots cheaper for me to try moving cloud masses into drought areas, and things like that? I admit I know next to nothing about international politics, but it seems reasonable to suppose that nobody would want to fight wars if there were enough of everything to go around. Mr. Cuthrell, I'd like to try running generators where there isn't any coal or water power, irrigating deserts, and so on. Why, you could figure out what each country needs to make the most of its resources, and I could give it to them without costing American taxpayers a penny."

"Eternal vigilance is the price of freedom," said the general heavily.

Mr. Cuthrell threw the general a look of mild distaste. "Unfortunately, the general is right in his own way," he said. "I wish to heaven the world were ready for ideals like yours, but it simply isn't. We aren't surrounded by brothers, but by enemies. It isn't a lack of food or resources that has us on the brink of war—it's a struggle for power. Who's going to be in charge of the world, our kind of people or theirs?"

The professor nodded in reluctant agreement and arose from the table. "I beg your pardon, gentlemen. You are, after all, better qualified to judge what is best for the country. I'll do whatever you say." He turned to me. "Don't forget to wind the restricted clock and put the confidential cat out," he said gloomily, and ascended the stairs of his bedroom.

For reasons of national security, Operation Brainstorm was carried on without the knowledge of the American citizenry which was paying the bill. The observers, technicians, and military men involved in the activity knew that a test was under way—a test of what, they had no idea. Only thirty-seven key men, myself included, knew what was afoot.

In Virginia, the day for Operation Brainstorm was unseasonably cool. Inside, a log fire crackled in the fireplace, and the flames were reflected in the polished metal cabinets that lined the living room. All that remained of the room's lovely old furniture was a Victorian love seat, set squarely in the center of the floor, facing three television receivers. One long bench had been brought in for the ten of us privileged to watch. The television screens showed, from left to right, the stretch of desert which was the rocket target, the guinea-pig fleet, and a section of the

Aleutian sky through which the radio-controlled bomber formation would roar.

Ninety minutes before H-hour the radios announced that the rockets were ready, that the observation ships had backed away to what was thought to be a safe distance, and that the bombers were on their way. The small Virginia audience lined up on the bench in order of rank, smoked a great deal, and said little. Professor Barnhouse was in his bedroom. General Barker bustled about the house like a woman preparing Thanksgiving dinner for twenty.

At ten minutes before H-hour the general came in, shepherding the professor before him. The professor was comfortably attired in sneakers, gray flannels, a blue sweater, and a white shirt open at the neck. The two of them sat side by side on the love seat. The general was rigid and perspiring; the professor was cheerful. He looked at each of the screens, lighted a cigarette and settled back.

"Bombers sighted!" cried the Aleutian observers.

"Rockets away!" barked the New Mexico radio operator.

All of us looked quickly at the big electric clock over the mantel, while the professor, a half-smile on his face, continued to watch the television sets. In hollow tones, the general counted away the seconds remaining. "Five . . . four . . . three . . . two . . one . . . *Concentrate!*"

Professor Barnhouse closed his eyes, pursed his lips, and stroked his temples. He held the position for a minute. The television images were scrambled, and the radio signals were drowned in the din of Barnhouse static. The professor sighed, opened his eyes, and smiled confidently.

"Did you give it everything you had?" asked the general dubiously.

"I was wide open," the professor replied.

The television images pulled themselves together, and mingled cries of amazement came over the radios tuned to the observers. The Aleutian sky was streaked with the smoke trails of bombers screaming down in flames. Simultaneously, there appeared high over the rocket target a cluster of white puffs, followed by faint thunder.

General Barker shook his head happily. "By George!"

he crowed. "Well, sir, by George, by George, by George!"

"Look!" shouted the admiral seated next to me. "The fleet—it wasn't touched!"

"The guns seem to be drooping," said Mr. Cuthrell.

We left the bench and clustered about the television sets to examine the damage more closely. What Mr. Cuthrell had said was true. The ships' guns curved downward, their muzzles resting on the steel decks. We in Virginia were making such a hullabaloo that it was impossible to hear the radio reports. We were so engrossed, in fact, that we didn't miss the professor until two short snarls of Barnhouse static shocked us into sudden silence. The radios went dead.

We looked around apprehensively. The professor was gone. A harassed guard threw open the front door from the outside to yell that the professor had escaped. He brandished his pistol in the direction of the gates, which hung open, limp and twisted. In the distance, a speeding government station wagon topped a ridge and dropped from sight into the valley beyond. The air was filled with choking smoke, for every vehicle on the grounds was ablaze. Pursuit was impossible.

"What in God's name got into him?" bellowed the general.

Mr. Cuthrell, who had rushed out onto the front porch, now slouched back into the room, reading a penciled note as he came. He thrust the note into my hands. "The good man left this billet-doux under the door knocker. Perhaps our young friend here will be kind enough to read it to you gentlemen, while I take a restful walk through the woods."

"*Gentlemen,*" I read aloud, "*As the first superweapon with a conscience, I am removing myself from your national defense stockpile. Setting a new precedent in the behavior of ordnance, I have humane reasons for going off. A. Barnhouse.*"

Since that day, of course, the professor has been systematically destroying the world's armaments, until there is now little with which to equip an army other than rocks and sharp sticks. His activities haven't exactly resulted in peace, but have, rather, precipitated a bloodless and entertaining sort of war that might be called the "War of the Tattletales." Every nation is flooded with enemy agents whose sole mission is to locate military equipment, which is promptly wrecked when it is brought to the professor's attention in the press.

Just as every day brings news of more armaments pulverized by dynamopsychism, so has it brought rumors of the professor's whereabouts. During last week alone, three publications carried articles proving variously that he was hiding in an Inca ruin in the Andes, in the sewers of Paris, and in the unexplored lower chambers of Carlsbad Caverns. Knowing the man, I am inclined to regard such hiding places as unnecessarily romantic and uncomfortable. While there are numerous persons eager to kill him, there must be millions who would care for him and hide him. I like to think that he is in the home of such a person.

One thing is certain: at this writing, Professor Barnhouse is not dead. Barnhouse static jammed broadcasts not ten minutes ago. In the eighteen months since his disappearance, he has been reported dead some half-dozen times. Each report has stemmed from the death of an unidentified man resembling the professor, during a period free of the static. The first three reports were followed at once by renewed talk of rearmament and recourse to war. The saber-rattlers have learned how imprudent premature celebrations of the professor's demise can be.

Many a stouthearted patriot has found himself prone in the tangled bunting and timbers of a smashed reviewing stand, seconds after having announced that the arch-tyranny of Barnhouse was at an end. But those who would make war if they could, in every country in the world, wait in sullen silence for what must come—the passing of Professor Barnhouse.

To ask how much longer the professor will live is to ask how much longer we must wait for the blessing of another world war. He is of short-lived stock: his mother lived to be fifty-three, his father to be forty-nine; and the life-spans of his grandparents on both sides were of the same order. He might be expected to live, then, for perhaps fifteen years more, if he can remain hidden from his enemies. When one considers the number and vigor of these enemies, however, fifteen years seems an extraordinary length of time, which might better be revised to fifteen days, hours, or minutes.

The professor knows that he cannot live much longer. I say this because of the message left in my mailbox on Christmas Eve. Unsigned, typewritten on a soiled scrap of paper, the note consisted of ten sentences. The first nine of these, each a bewildering tangle of psychological jargon and references to obscure texts, made no sense to me at first reading. The tenth, unlike the rest, was simply constructed and contained no large words—but its irrational content made it the most puzzling and bizarre sentence of all. I nearly threw the note away, thinking it a colleague's warped notion of a practical joke. For some reason, though, I added it to the clutter on top of my desk, which included, among other mementos, the professor's dice.

It took me several weeks to realize that the message really meant something, that the first nine sentences, when unsnarled, could be taken as instructions. The tenth still told me nothing. It was only last night that I discovered how it fitted in with the rest. The sentence appeared in my thoughts last night, while I was toying absently with the professor's dice.

I promised to have this report on its way to the publishers today. In view of what has happened, I am obliged to break that promise, or release the report incomplete. The delay will not be a long one, for one of the few blessings accorded a bachelor like myself is the ability to move quickly from one abode to another, or from one way of life to another. What property I want to take with me can be packed in a few hours. Fortunately, I am not without substantial private means, which may take as long as a week to realize in liquid and anonymous form. When this is done, I shall mail the report.

I have just returned from a visit to my doctor, who tells me my health is excellent. I am young, and, with any luck at all, I shall live to a ripe old age indeed, for my family on both sides is noted for longevity.

Briefly, I propose to vanish.

Sooner or later, Professor Barnhouse must die. But long before then I shall be ready. So, to the saber-rattlers of today—and even, I hope, of tomorrow—I say: Be advised. Barnhouse will die. But not the Barnhouse Effect.

Last night, I tried once more to follow the oblique instructions on the scrap of paper. I took the professor's dice, and then, with the last, nightmarish sentence flitting through my mind, I rolled fifty consecutive sevens.

Good-by.

(1950)

THE EUPHIO
QUESTION

LADIES AND GENTLEMEN of the Federal Communications Commission, I appreciate this opportunity to testify on the subject before you.

I'm sorry—or maybe "heartsick" is the word—that news has leaked out about it. But now the word is getting around and coming to your official notice, I might as well tell the story straight and pray to God that I can convince you that America doesn't want what we discovered.

I won't deny that all three of us—Lew Harrison, the radio announcer, Dr. Fred Bockman, the physicist, and myself, a sociology professor—found peace of mind. We did. And I won't say it's wrong for people to seek peace of mind. But if somebody thinks he wants peace of mind the way we found it, he'd be well advised to seek coronary thrombosis instead.

Lew, Fred, and I found peace of mind by sitting in easy chairs and turning on a gadget the size of a table-model television set. No herbs, no golden rule, no muscle control, no sticking our noses in other people's troubles to forget our own; no hobbies, Taoism, push-ups or contemplation of a lotus. The gadget is, I think, what a lot of people vaguely foresaw as the crowning achievement of civilization: an electronic something-or-other, cheap, easily mass-produced, that can, at the flick of a switch, provide tranquillity. I see you have one here.

My first brush with synthetic peace of mind was six months ago. It was also then that I got to know Lew Harrison, I'm sorry to say. Lew is chief announcer of our town's only radio station. He makes his living with his loud mouth, and I'd be surprised if it were anyone but he who brought this matter to your attention.

Lew has, along with about thirty other shows, a weekly science program. Every week he gets some professor from Wyandotte College and interviews him about his particular field. Well, six months ago Lew worked up a program around a young dreamer and faculty friend of mine, Dr. Fred Bockman. I gave Fred a lift to the radio station, and he invited me to come on in and watch. For the heck of it, I did.

Fred Bockman is thirty and looks eighteen. Life has left no marks on him, because he hasn't paid much attention to it. What he pays most of his attention to, and what Lew Harrison wanted to interview him about, is this eight-ton umbrella of his that he listens to the stars with. It's a big radio antenna rigged up on a telescope mount. The way I understand it, instead of looking at the stars through a telescope, he aims this thing out in space and picks up radio signals coming from different heavenly bodies.

Of course, there aren't people running radio stations out there. It's just that many of the heavenly bodies pour out a lot of energy and some of it can be picked up in the radio-frequency band. One good thing Fred's rig does is to spot stars hidden from telescopes by big clouds of cosmic dust. Radio signals from them get through the clouds to Fred's antenna.

That isn't all the outfit can do, and, in his interview with Fred, Lew Harrison saved the most exciting part until the end of the program. "That's very interesting, Dr. Bockman," Lew said. "Tell me, has your radio telescope turned up anything else about the universe that hasn't been revealed by ordinary light telescopes?"

This was the snapper. "Yes, it has," Fred said. "We've found about fifty spots in space, *not hidden by cosmic dust*, that give off powerful radio signals. Yet no heavenly bodies at all seem to be there."

"Well!" Lew said in mock surprise. "I should say that *is* something! Ladies and gentlemen, for the first time in radio history, we bring you the noise from Dr. Bockman's mysterious voids." They had strung a line out to Fred's antenna on the campus. Lew waved to the engineer to switch in the signals coming from it. "Ladies and gentlemen, the voice of nothingness!"

The noise wasn't much to hear—a wavering hiss, more like a leaking tire than anything else. It was supposed to be on the air for five seconds. When the engineer switched it off, Fred and I were inexplicably grinning like idiots. I felt relaxed and tingling. Lew Harrison looked as though he'd stumbled into the dressing room at the Copacabana. He glanced at the studio clock, appalled. The monotonous hiss had been on the air for five minutes! If the engineer's cuff hadn't accidentally caught on the switch, it might be on yet.

Fred laughed nervously, and Lew hunted for his place in the script. "The hiss from nowhere," Lew said. "Dr. Bockman, has anyone proposed a name for these interesting voids?"

"No," Fred said. "At the present time they have neither a name nor an explanation."

The voids the hiss came from have still to be explained, but I've suggested a name for them that shows signs of sticking: "Bockman's Euphoria." We may not know what the spots are, but we know what they do, so the name's a good one. Euphoria, since it means a sense of buoyancy and well-being, is really the only word that will do.

After the broadcast, Fred, Lew, and I were cordial to one another to the point of being maudlin.

"I can't remember when a broadcast has been such a pleasure," Lew said. Sincerity is not his forte, yet he meant it.

"It's been one of the most memorable experiences of my life," Fred said, looking puzzled. "Extraordinarily pleasant."

We were all embarrassed by the emotion we felt, and parted company in bafflement and haste. I hurried home for a drink, only to walk into the middle of another unsettling experience.

The house was quiet, and I made two trips through it before discovering that I was not alone. My wife, Susan, a good and lovable woman who prides herself on feeding her family well and on time, was lying on the couch, staring dreamily at the ceiling. "Honey," I said tentatively, "I'm home. It's suppertime."

"Fred Bockman was on the radio today," she said in a faraway voice.

"I know. I was with him in the studio."

"He was out of this world," she sighed. "Simply out of this world. That noise from space—when he turned that on, everything just seemed to drop away from me. I've been lying here, just trying to get over it."

"Uh-huh," I said, biting my lip. "Well, guess I'd better round up Eddie." Eddie is my ten-year-old son, and captain of an apparently invincible neighborhood baseball team.

"Save your strength, Pop," said a small voice from the shadows.

"You home? What's the matter? Game called off on account of atomic attack?"

"Nope. We finished eight innings."

"Beating 'em so bad they didn't want to go on, eh?"

"Oh, they were doing pretty good. Score was tied, and they had two men on and two outs." He talked as though he were recounting a dream. "And then," he said, his eyes widening, "everybody kind of lost interest, just wandered off. I came home and found the old lady curled up here, so I lay down on the floor."

"Why?" I asked incredulously.

"Pop," Eddie said thoughtfully, "I'm damned if I know."

"Eddie!" his mother said.

"Mom," Eddie said, "I'm damned if *you* know either."

I was damned if anybody could explain it, but I had a nagging hunch. I dialed Fred Bockman's number. "Fred, am I getting you up from dinner?"

"I wish you were," Fred said. "Not a scrap to eat in the house, and I let Marion have the car today so she could do the marketing. Now she's trying to find a grocery open."

"Couldn't get the car started, eh?"

"Sure she got the car started," said Fred. "She even got to the market. Then she felt so good she walked right out of the place again." Fred sounded depressed. "I guess it's a woman's privilege to change her mind, but it's the lying that hurts."

"Marion lied? I don't believe it."

"She tried to tell me everybody wandered out of the market with her—clerks and all."

"Fred," I said, "I've got news for you. Can I drive out right after supper?"

When I arrived at Fred Bockman's farm, he was staring, dumbfounded, at the evening paper.

"The whole town went nuts!" Fred said. "For no reason at all, all the cars pulled up to the curb like there was a hook and ladder going by. Says here people shut up in the middle of sentences and stayed that way for five minutes. Hundreds wandered around in the cold in their shirt-sleeves, grinning like toothpaste ads." He rattled the paper. "This *is* what you wanted to talk to me about?"

I nodded. "It all happened when that noise was being broadcast, and I thought maybe—"

"The odds are about one in a million that there's any maybe about it," said Fred. "The time checks to the second."

"But most people weren't listening to the program."

"They didn't have to listen, if my theory's right. We took those faint signals from space, amplified them about a thousand times, and rebroadcast them. Anybody within reach of the transmitter would get a good dose of the stepped-up radiations, whether he wanted to or not." He shrugged. "Apparently that's like walking past a field of burning marijuana."

"How come you never felt the effect at work?"

"Because I never amplified and rebroadcast the signals. The radio station's transmitter is what really put the sock into them."

"So what're you going to do next?"

Fred looked surprised. "Do? What is there to do but report it in some suitable journal?"

Without a preliminary knock, the front door burst open and Lew Harrison, florid and panting, swept into the room and removed his great polo coat with a bullfighter-like flourish. "You're cutting him in on it, too?" he demanded, pointing at me.

Fred blinked at him. "In on what?"

"The millions," Lew said. "The billions."

"Wonderful," Fred said. "What are you talking about?"

"The noise from the stars!" Lew said "They love it. It drives 'em nuts. Didja see the papers?" He sobered for an instant. "It *was* the noise that did it, wasn't it, Doc?"

"We think so," Fred said. He looked worried. "How, exactly, do you propose we get our hands on these millions or billions?"

"Real estate!" Lew said raptly. " 'Lew,' I said to myself, 'Lew, how can you cash in on this gimmick if you can't get a monopoly on the universe? And, Lew,' I asked myself 'how can you sell the stuff when anybody can get it free while you're broadcasting it?' "

"Maybe it's the kind of thing that shouldn't be cashed in on," I suggested. "I mean, we don't know a great deal about—"

"Is happiness bad?" Lew interrupted.

"No," I admitted.

"Okay, and what we'd do with this stuff from the stars is make people happy. Now I suppose you're going to tell me that's bad?"

"People ought to be happy," Fred said.

"Okay, okay," Lew said loftily. "That's what we're going to do for the people. And the way the people can show their gratitude is in real estate." He looked out the window. "Good—a barn. We can start right there. We set up a transmitter in the barn, run a line out to your antenna, Doc, and we've got a real-estate development."

"Sorry," Fred said. "I don't follow you. This place wouldn't do for a development. The roads are poor, no bus service or shopping center, the view is lousy and the ground is full of rocks."

Lew nudged Fred several times with his elbow. "Doc, Doc, Doc—sure it's got drawbacks, but with that transmitter in the barn, you can give them the most precious thing in all creation—happiness."

"Euphoria Heights," I said.

"That's great!" said Lew. "I'd get the prospects, Doc, and you'd sit up there in the barn with your hand on the switch. Once a prospect set foot on Euphoria Heights, and you shot the happiness to him, there's nothing he wouldn't pay for a lot."

"Every house a home, as long as the power doesn't fail," I said.

"Then," Lew said, his eyes shining, "when we sell all the lots here, we move the transmitter and start another development. Maybe we'd get a fleet of transmitters going." He snapped his fingers. "Sure! Mount 'em on wheels."

"I somehow don't think the police would think highly of us," Fred said.

"Okay, so when they come to investigate, you throw the old switch and give *them* a jolt of happiness." He shrugged. "Hell, I might even get bighearted and let them have a corner lot."

"No," Fred said quietly. "If I ever joined a church, I couldn't face the minister."

"So we give *him* a jolt," Lew said brightly.

"No," Fred said. "Sorry."

"Okay," Lew said, rising and pacing the floor. "I was prepared for that. I've got an alternative, and this one's strictly legitimate. We'll make a little amplifier with a transmitter and an aerial on it. Shouldn't cost over fifty bucks to make, so we'd price it in the range of the common man—five hundred bucks, say. We make arrangements with the phone company to pipe signals from your antenna right into the homes of people with these sets. The sets take the signal from the phone line, amplify it, and broadcast it through the houses to make everybody in them happy. See? Instead of turning on the radio or television, everybody's going to want to turn on the happiness. No casts, no stage sets, no expensive cameras—no nothing but that hiss."

"We could call it the euphoriaphone," I suggested, "or 'euphio' for short."

"That's great, that's great!" Lew said. "What do you say, Doc?"

"I don't know." Fred looked worried. "This sort of thing is out of my line."

"We all have to recognize our limitations, Doc," Lew said expansively. "I'll handle the business end, and you handle the technical end." He made a motion as though to put on his coat. "Or maybe you don't want to be a millionaire?"

"Oh, yes, yes indeed I do," Fred said quickly. "Yes indeed."

"All righty," Lew said, dusting his palms, "the first thing we've gotta do is build one of the sets and test her."

This part of it *was* down Fred's alley, and I could see the problem interested him. "It's really a pretty simple gadget," he said. "I suppose we could throw one together and run a test out here next week."

The first test of the euphoriaphone, or euphio, took place in Fred Bockman's living room on a Saturday afternoon, five days after Fred's and Lew's sensational radio broadcast.

There were six guinea pigs—Lew, Fred and his wife Marion, myself, my wife Susan, and my son Eddie. The Bockmans had arranged chairs in a circle around a card table, on which rested a gray steel box.

Protruding from the box was a long buggy whip aerial that scraped the ceiling. While Fred fussed with the box, the rest of us made nervous small talk over sandwiches and beer. Eddie, of course, wasn't drinking beer, though he was badly in need of a sedative. He was annoyed at having been brought out to the farm instead of to a ball game, and was threatening to take it out on the Bockmans' Early American furnishings. He was playing a spirited game of flies and grounders with himself near the French doors, using a dead tennis ball and a poker.

"Eddie," Susan said for the tenth time, "please stop."

"It's under control, under control," Eddie said disdainfully, playing the ball off four walls and catching it with one hand.

Marion, who vents her maternal instincts on her immaculate furnishings, couldn't hide her distress at Eddie's turning the place into a gymnasium. Lew, in his way, was trying to calm her. "Let him wreck the dump," Lew said. "You'll be moving into a palace one of these days."

"It's ready," Fred said softly.

We looked at him with queasy bravery. Fred plugged two jacks from the phone line into the gray box. This was the direct line to his antenna on the campus, and clockwork would keep the antenna fixed on one of the mysterious voids in the sky—the most potent of Bockman's Euphoria. He plugged a cord from the box into an electrical outlet in the baseboard, and rested his hand on a switch. "Ready?"

"Don't, Fred!" I said. I was scared stiff.

"Turn it on, turn it on," Lew said. "We wouldn't have the telephone today if Bell hadn't had the guts to call somebody up."

"I'll stand right here by the switch, ready to flick her off if something goes sour," Fred said reassuringly. There was a click, a hum, and the euphio was on.

A deep, unanimous sigh filled the room. The poker slipped from Eddie's hands. He moved across the room in a stately sort of waltz, knelt by his mother, and laid his head in her lap. Fred drifted away from his post, humming, his eyes half closed.

Lew Harrison was the first to speak, continuing his conversation with Marion. "But who cares for material wealth?" he asked earnestly. He turned to Susan for confirmation.

"Uh-uh," said Susan, shaking her head dreamily. She put her arms around Lew, and kissed him for about five minutes.

"Say," I said, patting Susan on the back, "you kids get along swell, don't you? Isn't that nice, Fred?"

"Eddie," Marion said solicitously, "I think there's a real baseball in the hall closet. A *hard* ball. Wouldn't that be more fun than that old tennis ball?" Eddie didn't stir.

Fred was still prowling around the room, smiling, his eyes now closed all the way. His heel caught in a lamp cord, and he went sprawling on the hearth, his head in the ashes. "Hi-ho, everybody," he said, his eyes still closed.

"Bunged my head on an andiron." He stayed there, giggling occasionally.

"The doorbell's been ringing for a while," Susan said. "I don't suppose it means anything."

"Come in, come in," I shouted. This somehow struck everyone as terribly funny. We all laughed uproariously, including Fred, whose guffaws blew up little gray clouds from the ashpit.

A small, very serious old man in white had let himself in, and was now standing in the vestibule, looking at us with alarm. "Milkman," he said uncertainly. He held out a slip of paper to Marion. "I can't read the last line in your note," he said. "What's that say about cottage cheese, cheese, cheese, cheese, cheese . . ." His voice trailed off as he settled, tailor-fashion, to the floor beside Marion. After he'd been silent for perhaps three quarters of an hour, a look of concern crossed his face. "Well," he said apathetically, "I can only stay for a minute. My truck's parked out on the shoulder, kind of blocking things." He started to stand. Lew gave the volume knob on the euphio a twist. The milkman wilted to the floor.

"Aaaaaaaaaaah," said everybody.

"Good day to be indoors," the milkman said. "Radio says we'll catch the tail end of the Atlantic hurricane."

"Let 'er come," I said. "I've got my car parked under a big, dead tree." It seemed to make sense. Nobody took exception to it. I lapsed back into a warm fog of silence and thought of nothing whatsoever. These lapses seemed to last for a matter of seconds before they were interrupted by conversation of newcomers. Looking back, I see now that the lapses were rarely less than six hours.

I was snapped out of one, I recall, by a repetition of the doorbell's ringing. "I said come in," I mumbled.

"And I did," the milkman mumbled.

The door swung open, and a state trooper glared in at us. "Who the hell's got his milk truck out there blocking the road?" he demanded. He spotted the milkman. "Aha! Don't you know somebody could get killed, coming around a blind curve into that thing?" He yawned, and his ferocious expression gave way to an affectionate smile. "It's so damn' unlikely," he said, "I don't know why I ever brought it up." He sat down by Eddie. "Hey, kid—like guns?" He took his revolver from its holster. "Look—just like Hoppy's."

Eddie took the gun, aimed it at Marion's bottle collection and fired. A large blue bottle popped to dust and the window behind the collection splintered. Cold air roared in through the opening.

"He'll make a cop yet," Marion chortled.

"God, I'm happy," I said, feeling a little like crying. "I got the swellest little kid and the swellest bunch of friends and the swellest old wife in the world." I heard the gun go off twice more, and then dropped into heavenly oblivion.

Again the doorbell roused me. "How many times do I have to tell you—for Heaven's sake, come in," I said, without opening my eyes.

"I *did*," the milkman said.

I heard the tramping of many feet, but had no curiosity about them. A little later, I noticed that I was having difficulty breathing. Investigation revealed that I had slipped to the floor, and that several Boy Scouts had bivouacked on my chest and abdomen.

"You want something?" I asked the tenderfoot whose hot, measured breathing was in my face.

"Beaver Patrol wanted old newspapers, but forget it," he said. "We'd just have to carry 'em somewhere."

"And do your parents know where you are?"

"Oh, sure. They got worried and came after us." He jerked his thumb at several couples lined up against the baseboard, smiling into the teeth of the wind and rain lashing in at them through the broken window.

"Mom, I'm kinda hungry," Eddie said.

"Oh, Eddie—you're not going to make your mother cook just when we're having such a wonderful time," Susan said.

Lew Harrison gave the euphio's volume knob another twist. "There, kid, how's that?"

"Aaaaaaaaaaah," said everybody.

When awareness intruded on oblivion again, I felt

around for the Beaver Patrol, and found them missing. I opened my eyes to see that they and Eddie and the milkman and Lew and the trooper were standing by a picture window, cheering. The wind outside was roaring and slashing savagely and driving raindrops through the broken window as though they'd been fired from air rifles. I shook Susan gently, and together we went to the window to see what might be so entertaining.

"She's going, she's going, she's going," the milkman cried ecstatically.

Susan and I arrived just in time to join in the cheering as a big elm crashed down on our sedan.

"Kee-*runch!*" said Susan, and I laughed until my stomach hurt.

"Get Fred," Lew said urgently. "He's gonna miss seeing the barn go!"

"H'mm?" Fred said from the fireplace.

"Aw, Fred, you missed it," Marion said.

"Now we're really gonna see something," Eddie yelled. "The power line's going to get it this time. Look at that poplar lean!"

The poplar leaned closer, closer, closer to the power line; and then a gust brought it down in a hail of sparks and a tangle of wires. The lights in the house went off.

Now there was only the sound of the wind. "How come nobody cheered?" Lew said faintly. "The euphio—it's off!"

A horrible groan came from the fireplace. "God, I think I've got a concussion."

Marion knelt by her husband and wailed. "Darling, my poor darling—what happened to you?"

I looked at the woman I had my arms around—a dreadful, dirty old hag, with red eyes sunk deep in her head, and hair like Medusa's. "Ugh," I said, and turned away in disgust.

"Honey," wept the witch, "it's me—Susan."

Moans filled the air, and pitiful cries for food and water. Suddenly the room had become terribly cold. Only a moment before I had imagined I was in the tropics.

"Who's got my damn' pistol?" the trooper said bleakly.

A Western Union boy I hadn't noticed before was sitting in a corner, miserably leafing through a pile of telegrams and making clucking noises.

I shuddered. "I'll bet it's Sunday morning," I said. "We've been here twelve hours!" It was Monday morning.

The Western Union boy was thunderstruck. "Sunday morning? I walked in here on a Sunday night." He stared around the room. "Looks like them newsreels of Buchenwald, don't it?"

The chief of the Beaver Patrol, with the incredible stamina of the young, was the hero of the day. He fell in his men in two ranks, haranguing them like an old Army top-kick. While the rest of us lay draped around the room, whimpering about hunger, cold, and thirst, the patrol started the furnace again, brought blankets, applied compresses to Fred's head and countless barked shins, blocked off the broken window, and made buckets of cocoa and coffee.

Within two hours of the time that the power and the euphio went off, the house was warm and we had eaten. The serious respiratory cases—the parents who had sat near the broken window for twenty-four hours—had been pumped full of penicillin and hauled off to the hospital. The milkman, the Western Union boy, and the trooper had refused treatment and gone home. The Beaver Patrol had saluted smartly and left. Outside, repairmen were working on the power line. Only the original group remained—Lew, Fred, and Marion, Susan and myself, and Eddie. Fred, it turned out, had some pretty important-looking contusions and abrasions, but no concussion.

Susan had fallen asleep right after eating. Now she stirred. "What happened?"

"Happiness," I told her. "Incomparable, continuous happiness—happiness by the kilowatt."

Lew Harrison, who looked like an anarchist with his red eyes and fierce black beard, had been writing furiously in one corner of the room. "That's good—happiness by the kilowatt," he said. "Buy your happiness the way you buy light."

"Contract happiness the way you contract influenza," Fred said. He sneezed.

Lew ignored him. "It's a campaign, see? The first ad is for the long-hairs: 'The price of one book, which may be a disappointment, will buy you sixty hours of euphio. Euphio never disappoints.' Then we'd hit the middle class with the next one—"

"In the groin?" Fred said.

"What's the matter with you people?" Lew said. "You act as though the experiment had failed."

"Pneumonia and malnutrition are what we'd *hoped* for?" Marion said.

"We had a cross section of America in this room, and we made every last person happy," Lew said. "Not for just an hour, not for just a day, but for two days without a break." He arose reverently from his chair. "So what we do to keep it from killing the euphio fans is to have the thing turned on and off with clockwork, see? The owner sets it so it'll go on just as he comes home from work, then it'll go off again while he eats supper; then it goes on after supper, off again when it's bedtime; on again after breakfast, off when it's time to go to work, then on again for the wife and kids."

He ran his hands through his hair and rolled his eyes. "And the selling points—my God, the selling points! No expensive toys for the kids. For the price of a trip to the movies, people can buy thirty hours of euphio. For the price of a fifth of whisky, they can buy sixty hours of euphio!"

"Or a big family bottle of potassium cyanide," Fred said.

"Don't you see it?" Lew said incredulously. "It'll bring families together again, save the American home. No more fights over what TV or radio program to listen to. Euphio pleases one and all—we proved that. And there is no such thing as a dull euphio program."

A knock on the door interrupted him. A repairman stuck his head in to announce that the power would be on again in about two minutes.

"Look, Lew," Fred said, "this little monster could kill

civilization in less time than it took to burn down Rome. We're not going into the mind-numbing business, and that's that."

"You're kidding!" Lew said, aghast. He turned to Marion. "Don't you want your husband to make a million?"

"Not by operating an electronic opium den," Marion said coldly.

Lew slapped his forehead. "It's what the public wants. This is like Louis Pasteur refusing to pasteurize milk."

"It'll be good to have the electricity again," Marion said, changing the subject. "Lights, hot-water heater, the pump, the—oh, Lord!"

The lights came on the instant she said it, but Fred and I were already in mid-air, descending on the gray box. We crashed down on it together. The card table buckled, and the plug was jerked from the wall socket. The euphio's tubes glowed red for a moment, then died.

Expressionlessly, Fred took a screwdriver from his pocket and removed the top of the box.

"Would you enjoy doing battle with progress?" he said, offering me the poker Eddie had dropped.

In a frenzy, I stabbed and smashed at the euphio's glass and wire vitals. With my left hand, and with Fred's help, I kept Lew from throwing himself between the poker and the works.

"I thought you were on my side," Lew said.

"If you breathe one word about euphio to anyone," I said, "what I just did to euphio I will gladly do to you."

And there, ladies and gentlemen of the Federal Communications Commission, I thought the matter had ended. It deserved to end there. Now, through the medium of Lew Harrison's big mouth, word has leaked out. He has petitioned you for permission to start commercial exploitation of euphio. He and his backers have built a radio-telescope of their own.

Let me say again that all of Lew's claims are true. Euphio will do everything he says it will. The happiness it gives is perfect and unflagging in the face of incredible adversity. Near tragedies, such as the first experiment, can no doubt be avoided with clockwork to turn the sets on and off. I see that this set on the table before you is, in fact, equipped with clockwork.

The question is not whether euphio works. It does. The question is, rather, whether or not America is to enter a new and distressing phase of history where men no longer pursue happiness but buy it. This is no time for oblivion to become a national craze. The only benefit we could get from euphio would be if we could somehow lay down a peace-of-mind barrage on our enemies while protecting our own people from it.

In closing, I'd like to point out that Lew Harrison, the would-be czar of euphio, is an unscrupulous person, unworthy of public trust. It wouldn't surprise me, for instance, if he had set the clockwork on this sample euphio set so that its radiations would addle your judgments when you are trying to make a decision. In fact, it seems to be whirring suspiciously at this very moment, and I'm so happy I could cry. I've got the swellest little kid and the swellest bunch of friends and the swellest old wife in the world. And good old Lew Harrison is the salt of the earth, believe me. I sure wish him a lot of good luck with his new enterprise.

(1951)

GO BACK TO
YOUR PRECIOUS WIFE
AND SON

GLORIA HILTON and her fifth husband didn't live in New Hampshire very long. But they lived there long enough for me to sell them a bathtub enclosure. My main line is aluminum combination storm windows and screens—but anybody in storm windows is practically automatically in bathtub enclosures, too.

The enclosure they ordered was for Gloria Hilton's personal bathtub. I guess that was the zenith of my career. Some men are asked to build mighty dams or noble skyscrapers, or conquer terrible plagues, or lead great armies into battle.

Me?

I was asked to keep drafts off the most famous body in the world.

People ask me how well did I know Gloria Hilton. I generally say, "The only time I ever saw that woman in the flesh was through a hot-air register." That was how the bathroom where they wanted the enclosure was heated—with a hot-air register in the floor. It wasn't connected to the furnace. It just bled heat from the ceiling of the room down below. I don't wonder Gloria Hilton found her bathroom cold.

I was installing the enclosure when loud talk started coming out of the register. I was at a very tricky point, gluing the waterproof gasket around the rim of the tub with contact cement, so I couldn't close the register. I had to listen to what wasn't any of my business, whether I wanted to or not.

"Don't talk to me about love," Gloria Hilton said to her

fifth husband. "You don't know anything about love. You don't know the meaning of love."

I hadn't looked down through the register yet, so the only face I had to put with her voice was her face in the movies.

"Maybe you're right, Gloria," said her fifth husband.

"I give you my word of honor I'm right," she said

"Well—" he said, "that certainly brings the whole discussion to a dead stop right there. How could I possibly argue with the sacred word of honor of Gloria Hilton?"

I knew what he looked like. He was the one who'd done all the negotiating for the bathtub enclosure. I had also sold him two Fleetwood Trip-L-Trak storm windows for the two bathroom windows. Those have the self-storing screen feature. The whole time we were negotiating, he called his wife "Miss Hilton." Miss Hilton wanted this, and Miss Hilton wanted that. He was only thirty-five, but the circles under his eyes made him look sixty.

"I pity you," Gloria Hilton said to him. "I pity anybody who can't love. They are the most pitiful people there are."

"The more you talk," he said, "the more I'm convinced I'm one of them."

He was the writer, of course. My wife keeps a lot of Hollywood stuff in her head, and she tells me Gloria Hilton was married to a motorcycle policeman, then a sugar millionaire, then somebody who played Tarzan, then her agent—and then the writer. George Murra, the writer, was the one I knew.

"People keep wondering what the matter with the world is," said Gloria. "I know what the matter is. It's simple: most men don't know the meaning of the word love."

"At least give me credit for trying to find out what it means," said Murra. "For one solid year now, I haven't done a single, solitary thing but order a bathtub enclosure and try to find out what love means."

"I suppose you're going to blame me for that, too," she said.

"For what?" he said.

"The fact that you haven't written a word since we've been married," she said. "I suppose that's somehow my fault, too."

"I hope I'm not that shallow," he said. "I know a plain, ordinary coincidence when I see one. The fights we have all night, the photographers and reporters and so-called friends we have all day—they have nothing to do with the fact I've dried up."

"You're one of those people who enjoys suffering," she said.

"That's a smart way to be," he said.

"I'll tell you frankly," she said, "I'm disappointed in you."

"I knew," he said, "that sooner or later you would come right out and say it."

"I might as well tell you, too," she said, "that I've decided to bring this farce to an end."

"It's nice of you to make me among the first to know," he said. "Shall I notify Louella Parsons, or has that already been taken care of?"

I had the gasket glued onto the bathtub rim, so I was free to close the register. I looked straight down through the grating, and there Gloria Hilton was. She had her hair up in curlers. She didn't have any makeup on. She hadn't even bothered to draw on eyebrows. She had on some kind of slip and a bathrobe that was gaping open. I swear, that woman wasn't any prettier than a used studio couch.

"I don't think you're very funny," she said.

"You knew I was a serious writer when you married me," he said.

She stood up. She spread her arms like Moses telling the Jews the Promised Land was right over the next hill. "Go on back to your precious wife and your precious son," she said. "I certainly won't stand in your way."

I closed the register.

Five minutes later, Murra came upstairs and told me to clear out. "Miss Hilton wants to use her bathroom," he said. I never saw such a peculiar expression on a man's face. He was all red, and there were tears in his eyes—but there was this crazy laugh tearing him apart, trying to get out.

"I'm not quite finished," I said.

"Miss Hilton is completely finished," he said. "Clear out!"

So I went out to my truck, and I drove into town, had a cup of coffee. The door for the bathtub enclosure was on a wooden rack on the back of my truck, out in the open— and it certainly attracted a lot of attention.

Most people, when they order an enclosure door, don't want anything on it unless maybe a flamingo or a seahorse. The plant, which is over in Lawrence, Massachusetts, is set up to sandblast a flamingo or a seahorse on a door for only six dollars extra. But Gloria Hilton wanted a big "G," two feet across—and in the middle of the "G" she wanted a life-size head of herself. And the eyes on the head had to be exactly five feet two inches above the bottom of the tub, because that's how high her real eyes were when she stood up barefoot in the tub.

They went crazy over in Lawrence.

One of the people I was having coffee with was Harry Crocker, the plumber. "I certainly hope you insisted on measuring her yourself," he said, "so the figures would be absolutely accurate."

"Her husband did it," I said.

"Some people have all the luck," he said.

I went to the pay telephone, and I called up Murra's house to see if it would be all right for me to come back and finish up. The line was busy.

When I got back to my coffee, Harry Crocker said to me, "You missed something I don't think anybody's ever liable to see in this town ever again."

"What's that?" I said.

"Gloria Hilton and her maid going through town at two hundred miles an hour," he said.

"Which way were they headed?" I said.

"West," he said.

So I tried to call Murra again. I figured, with Gloria

Hilton gone, all the big telephoning would be over. But the telephone went right on being busy for an hour. I thought maybe somebody had torn the telephone out by its roots, but the operator said it was in working order.

"Try the number again, then," I told her.

That time I got through.

Murra answered the phone. All I said to him was, "Hello," and he got very excited. He wasn't excited about getting the bathtub enclosure finished. He was excited because he thought I was somebody named John.

"John, John," he said to me, "thank God you called!"

"John," he said to me, "I know what you think of me, and I don't blame you for thinking that—but please listen to what I have to say before you hang up. She's left me, John. That part of my life is over—finished! Now I'm trying to pick up the pieces. John," he said, "in the name of mercy, you've got to come here. Please, John, please, John, please."

"Mr. Murra—?" I said.

"Yes?" he said. From the way his voice went away from the telephone, I guess he thought I'd just walked into the room.

"It's me, Mr. Murra," I said.

"It's who?" he said.

"The bathtub enclosure man," I said.

"I was expecting a very important long-distance call," he said. "Please get off the wire."

"I beg your pardon," I said. "I just want to know when you want me to finish up there."

"Never!" he said. "Forget it! The hell with it!"

"Mr. Murra—" I said, "I can't return that door for credit."

"Send me the bill," he said. "I make you a present of the door."

"Whatever you say," I said. "Now, you've got these two Fleetwood Trip-L-Trak windows, too."

"Throw 'em on the dump!" he said.

"Mr. Murra—" I said, "I guess you're upset about something—"

"God you're smart!" he said.

"Maybe throwing away that door makes sense," I said, "but storm windows never hurt a soul. Why don't you let me come out and put 'em up? You'll never even know I'm there."

"All right, all right, all right!" he said, and he hung up.

The Fleetwood Trip-L-Trak is our first-line window, so there isn't anything quick and dirty about the way we put them up. We put a gasket up all the way around, just the way we do on a bathtub enclosure. So I had some standing around to do at Murra's house, just waiting for glue to dry. You can actually fill up a room equipped with Fleetwoods with water, fill it clear up to the ceiling, and it won't leak—not through the windows, anyway.

While I was waiting on the glue, Murra came out and asked me if I wanted a drink.

"Pardon me?" I said.

"Or maybe bathtub enclosure men don't drink on duty," he said.

"That's only on television," I said.

So he took me in the kitchen, and he got out a bottle and ice and a couple of glasses.

"This is very nice of you," I said.

"I may not know what love is," he said, "but, by God, at least I've never gotten drunk by myself."

"That's what we're going to do?" I said.

"Unless you have some other suggestion," he said.

"I'll have to think a minute," I said.

"That's a mistake," he said. "You miss an awful lot of life that way. That's why you Yankees are so cold," he said. "You think too much. That's why you marry so seldom."

"At least some of that is a plain lack of money," I said.

"No, no," he said. "It goes deeper than that. You people around here don't grasp the thistle firmly." He had to explain that to me, about how a thistle won't prick you if you grab it real hard and fast.

"I don't believe that about thistles," I said.

"Typical New England conservatism," he said.

"I gather you aren't from these parts," I said.

"That happiness is not mine," he said. He told me he was from Los Angeles.

"I guess that's nice, too," I said.

"The people are all phonies," he said.

"I wouldn't know about that," I said.

"That's why we took up residence here," he said. "As my wife—my second wife, that is—told all the reporters at our wedding, 'We are getting away from all the phonies. We are going to live where people are really people. We are going to live in New Hampshire. My husband and I are going to find ourselves. He is going to write and write and write. He is going to write the most beautiful scenario anybody in the history of literature has ever written for me.' "

"That's nice," I said.

"You didn't read that in the newspaper or the magazines?" he said.

"No," I said. "I used to go out with a girl who subscribed to *Film Fun*, but that was years ago. I have no idea what happened to her."

Somewhere in the course of this conversation, a fifth of a gallon of Old Hickey's Private Stock Sour Mash Bourbon was evaporating, or was being stolen, or was otherwise disappearing fast.

And I haven't got the conversation set down quite straight, because somewhere in there Murra told me he'd been married when he was only eighteen—and he told me who the John was he'd thought I was on the telephone.

It hurt Murra a lot to talk about John. "John," he said, "is my only child. Fifteen years old." Murra clouded up, pointed southeast. "Only twenty-two miles away—so near and yet so far," he said.

"He didn't stay with his mother in Los Angeles?" I said.

"His home is with her," said Murra, "but he goes to school at Mount Henry." Mount Henry is a very good boy's prep school near here. "One of the reasons I came to New Hampshire was to be close to him." Murra shook his head. "I thought surely he'd get in touch with me sooner or later—return a telephone call, answer a letter."

"But he never did?" I said.

"Never," said Murra. "You know what the last thing was he said to me?"

"Nope," I said.

"When I divorced his mother and married Gloria Hilton, the last thing he said was, 'Father, you're contemptible. I don't want to hear another word from you as long as I live.' "

"That's—that's strong," I said.

"Friend—" said Murra hoarsely, "that's *mighty* strong." He bowed his head. "That was the word he used— contemptible. Young as he was, he sure used the right one."

"Did you finally get in touch with him today?" I said.

"I called the Headmaster of the school, and I told him there was a terrible family emergency, and he had to make John call me right away," said Murra.

"It worked, thank God," he said. "And, even though I am definitely contemptible, he was agreed to come see me tomorrow."

Somewhere else in that conversation, Murra told me to look at the statistics sometime. I promised him I would. "Just statistics in general—or some special statistics?" I asked him.

"Statistics on marriage," he said.

"I'm scared to think of what I'm liable to find," I said.

"You look at the statistics," said Murra, "and you'll find out that when people get married when they're only eighteen—the way my first wife and I did—there's a fifty-fifty chance the thing will blow sky high."

"I was eighteen when I was married," I said.

"You're still with your first wife?" he said.

"Going on twenty years now," I said.

"Don't you ever feel like you got gypped out of your bachelor days, your playboy days, your days as a great lover?"

"Well," I said, "in New Hampshire those days generally come between the ages of fourteen and seventeen."

"Let me put it to you this way," he said. "Say you'd been married all these years, fighting about the dumb things married people fight about, being broke and worried most of the time—"

"I'm right with you," I said.

"And say the movies bought a book you'd written, and they hired you to write the screen play, and Gloria Hilton was going to be the star," he said.

"I don't think I can imagine that," I said.

"All right—" he said, "what's the biggest thing that could possibly happen to you in your line of work?"

I had to think a while. "I guess it would be if I sold the Conners Hotel on putting Fleetwoods on every window. That must be five-hundred windows or more," I said.

"Good!" he said. "You've just made the sale. You've got real money in your pocket for the first time. You've just had a fight with your wife, and you're thinking mean things about her, feeling sorry for yourself. And the manager of the hotel is Gloria Hilton—Gloria Hilton looking the way she does in the movies."

"I'm listening," I said.

"Say you started putting up those five-hundred Fleetwoods," he said, "and say everytime you put up another storm window, there was Gloria Hilton smiling at you through the glass, like you were a god or something."

"Is there anything left to drink in the house?" I said.

"Say that went on for three months," he said. "And every night you went home to your wife, some woman you'd known so long she was practically like a sister, and she would crab about some little thing—"

"This is a very warm room, even without storm windows," I said.

"Say Gloria Hilton all of a sudden said to you," he said, " 'Dare to be happy, my poor darling! Oh, darling, we were *made* for each other! Dare to be happy with me! I go limp when I see you putting up storm windows! I can't stand to see you so unhappy, to know you belong to some other woman, to know how happy I could make you, if only you belonged to me!' "

After that, I remember, Murra and I went outdoors to look for thistles. He was going to show me how to grab thistles without getting hurt.

I don't think we ever found any. I remember pulling up

a lot of plants, and throwing them against the house, and laughing a lot. But I don't think any of the plants were thistles.

Then we lost each other in the great outdoors. I yelled for him for a while, but his answers got fainter and fainter, and I finally went home.

I don't remember what the homecoming was like, but my wife does. She says I spoke to her in a rude and disrespectful manner. I told her that I had sold five-hundred Fleetwood windows to the Conners Hotel. I also told her that she should look up the statistics on teenage marriages sometime.

Then I went upstairs, and I took the door off our bathtub enclosure. I told her Murra and I were trading doors.

I got the door off, and then I went to sleep in the tub.

My wife woke me up, and I told her to go away. I told her Gloria Hilton had just bought the Conners Hotel, and I was going to marry her.

I tried to tell her something very important about thistles, but I couldn't pronounce thistles, so I went to sleep again.

So my wife poured bubble-bath powder all over me, and she turned on the cold water faucet of the bathtub, and she went to bed in the guest room.

About three o'clock the next afternoon, I went over to Murra's to finish putting up his windows, and to find out what we'd agreed to do about the bathtub enclosure door, if anything. I had two doors on the back of my truck, my door with a flamingo and his door with Gloria Hilton.

I started to ring his doorbell, but then I heard somebody knocking on an upstairs window. I looked up and saw Murra standing in the window of Gloria Hilton's bathroom. My ladder was already leaning against the sill of the window, so I went up the ladder and asked Murra what was going on.

He opened the window, and he told me to come in. He was very pale and shaky.

"Your boy showed up yet?" I said.

"Yes," he said. "He's downstairs. I picked him up at the bus station an hour ago."

"You two hitting it off all right?" I said.

Murra shook his head. "He's still so *bitter*," he said. "He's only fifteen, but he talks to me as though he were my great-great-grandfather. I came up here for just a minute, and now I haven't got nerve enough to go back down."

He took me by the arm. "Listen—" he said, "you go down and sort of pave the way."

"If I've got any pavement left in me," I said, "I'd better save it for home." I filled him in on my own situation at home, which was far from ideal.

"Whatever you do," he said, "don't make the same mistake I made. You keep that home of yours together, no matter what. I know it must be lousy from time to time but, believe me, there are ways of life that are ten thousand times lousier."

"Well," I said, "I thank the good Lord for one thing—"

"What's that?" he said.

"Gloria Hilton hasn't come right out and said she loved me yet," I said.

I went downstairs to see Murra's boy.

Young John had on a man's suit. He even had on a vest. He wore big black-rimmed spectacles. He looked like a college professor.

"John," I said, "I'm an old friend of your father's."

"That so?" he said, and he looked me up and down. He wouldn't shake hands.

"You certainly are a mature-looking young man," I said.

"I've *had* to be," he said. "When Father walked out on Mother and me, that made me head of the family, wouldn't you say?"

"Well now, John," I said, "your father hasn't been too happy, either, you know."

"That certainly is a great disappointment to me," he said. "I thought Gloria Hilton made men as happy as they could possibly be."

"John," I said, "when you get older, you're going to

understand a lot of things you don't understand now."

"You must mean nuclear physics," he said. "I can hardly wait." And he turned his back to me, and he looked out the window. "Where's Father?" he said.

"Here he is," said Murra from the top of the stairs. "Here the poor fool is." He came creaking down the stairs.

"I think I'd better go back to school, Father," said the boy.

"So soon?" said Murra.

"I was told there was an emergency, or I wouldn't have come," said the boy. "There doesn't seem to be any emergency, so I'd like to go back, if you don't mind."

"Don't mind?" said Murra. He held out his arms. "John—" he said, "you'll break my heart if you walk out on me now—without—"

"Without what, Father?" said the boy. He was cold as ice.

"Without forgiving me," said Murra.

"Never," said the boy. "I'm sorry—that's one thing I'll never do." He nodded. "Whenever you're ready to go, Father," he said, "I'll be waiting in the car."

And he walked out of the house.

Murra sat down in a chair with his head in his hands. "What do I do now?" he said. "Maybe this is the punishment I deserve. I guess what I do is just grit my teeth and take it."

"I can only think of one other thing," I said.

"What's that?" he said.

"Kick him in the pants," I said.

So that's what Murra did.

He went out to the car, looking all gloomy and blue.

He told John something was wrong with the front seat, and he made John get out so he could fix it.

Then Murra let the boy have it in the seat of the pants with the side of his foot. I don't think there was any pain connected with it, but it did have a certain amount of .oft.

The boy did a kind of polka downhill, toward the sh ubbery where his father and I had been looking for thistles the night before. When he got himself stopped and turned around, he was certainly one surprised-looking boy.

"John," Murra said to him, "I'm sorry I did that, but I couldn't think of anything else to do."

For once, the boy didn't have a snappy come-back.

"I have made many serious mistakes in my life," said Murra, "but I don't think that was one of them. I love you, and I love your mother, and I think I'll go on kicking you until you can find it in your heart to give me another chance."

The boy still couldn't think of anything to say, but I could tell he wasn't interested in being kicked again.

"Now you come back in the house," said Murra, "and we'll talk this thing over like civilized human beings."

When they got back in the house, Murra got the boy to call up his mother in Los Angeles.

"You tell her we're having a nice time, and I've been terribly unhappy, and I am through with Gloria Hilton, and I want her to take me back on any terms whatsoever," said Murra.

The boy told his mother, and she cried, and the boy cried, and Murra cried, and I cried.

And then Murra's first wife told him he could come back home any time he wanted to. And that was that.

The way we settled the bathtub enclosure door thing was that I took Murra's door and he took mine. Actually, I was trading a twenty-two-dollar door for a forty-eight-dollar door, not counting the picture of Gloria Hilton.

My wife was out when I got home. I hung the new door. My own boy came up and watched me. He was red-nosed about something.

"Where's your mother?" I said to him.

"She went out," he said.

"When's she due back?" I said.

"She said maybe she'd never come back," said the boy.

I was sick, but I didn't let the boy know it. "That's one of her jokes," I said. "She says that all the time."

"I never heard her say it before," he said.

I was really scared when suppertime rolled around, and

I still didn't have a wife. I tried to be brave. I got supper for the boy and me, and I said, "Well, I guess she's been delayed somewhere."

"Father—" said the boy.

"What?" I said.

"What did you *do* to Mother last night?" he said. He took a very high and mighty tone.

"Mind your own business," I said, "or you're liable to get a swift kick in the pants."

That calmed him right down.

My wife came home at nine o'clock, thank God.

She was cheerful. She said she'd had a swell time just being alone—shopping alone, eating in a restaurant alone, going to a movie alone.

She gave me a kiss, and she went upstairs.

I heard the shower running, and I all of a sudden remembered the picture of Gloria Hilton on the bathtub enclosure door.

"Oh my Lord!" I said. I ran up the stairs to tell her what the picture was doing on the door, to tell her I would have it sandblasted off first thing in the morning.

I went into the bathroom.

My wife was standing up, taking a shower.

She was just the same height as Gloria Hilton, so the picture on the door made kind of a mask for her.

There was my wife's body with the head of Gloria Hilton on it.

My wife wasn't sore. She laughed. She thought it was funny. "Guess who?" she said.

(1962)

DEER IN
THE WORKS

THE BIG BLACK STACKS of the Ilium Works of the Federal
Apparatus Corporation spewed acid fumes and soot over
the hundreds of men and women who were lined up before the red-brick employment office. It was summer. The
Ilium Works, already the second-largest industrial plant in
America, was increasing its staff by one third in order to
meet armament contracts. Every ten minutes or so, a
company policeman opened the employment-office door,
letting out a chilly gust from the air-conditioned interior
and admitting three more applicants.

"Next three," said the policeman.

A middle-sized man in his late twenties, his young face
camouflaged with a mustache and spectacles, was admitted
after a four-hour wait. His spirits and the new suit he'd
bought for the occasion were wilted by the fumes and the
August sun, and he'd given up lunch in order to keep his
place in line. But his bearing remained jaunty. He was the
last, in his group of three, to face the receptionist.

"Screw-machine operator, ma'am," said the first man.

"See Mr. Cormody in booth seven," said the receptionist.

"Plastic extrusion, miss," said the next man.

"See Mr. Hoyt in booth two," she said. "Skill?" she
asked the urbane young man in the wilted suit. "Milling
machine? Jig borer?"

"Writing," he said. "Any kind of writing."

"You mean advertising and sales promotion?"

"Yes—that's what I mean."

She looked doubtful. "Well, I don't know. We didn't put

out a call for that sort of people. You can't run a machine, can you?"

"Typewriter," he said jokingly.

The receptionist was a sober young woman. "The company does not use male stenographers," she said. "See Mr. Dilling in booth twenty-six. He just might know of some advertising-and-sales-promotion-type job."

He straightened his tie and coat, forced a smile that implied he was looking into jobs at the Works as sort of a lark. He walked into booth twenty-six and extended his hand to Mr. Dilling, a man of his own age. "Mr. Dilling, my name is David Potter. I was curious to know what openings you might have in advertising and sales promotion, and thought I'd drop in for a talk."

Mr. Dilling, an old hand at facing young men who tried to hide their eagerness for a job, was polite but outwardly unimpressed. "Well, you came at a bad time, I'm afraid, Mr. Potter. The competition for that kind of job is pretty stiff, as you perhaps know, and there isn't much of anything open just now."

David nodded. "I see." He had had no experience in asking for a job with a big organization, and Mr. Dilling was making him aware of what a fine art it was—if you couldn't run a machine. A duel was under way.

"But have a seat anyway, Mr. Potter."

"Thank you." He looked at his watch. "I really ought to be getting back to my paper soon."

"You work on a paper around here?"

"Yes. I own a weekly paper in Dorset, about ten miles from Ilium."

"Oh—you don't say. Lovely little village. Thinking of giving up the paper, are you?"

"Well, no—not exactly. It's a possibility. I bought the paper soon after the war, so I've been with it for eight years, and I don't want to go stale. I might be wise to move on. It all depends on what opens up."

"You have a family?" said Mr. Dilling pleasantly.

"Yes. My wife, and two boys and two girls."

"A nice, big, well-balanced family," said Mr. Dilling. "And you're so young, too."

"Twenty-nine," said David. He smiled. "We didn't plan it to be quite that big. It's run to twins. The boys are twins, and then, several days ago, the girls came."

"You don't say!" said Mr. Dilling. He winked. "That would certainly start a young man thinking about getting a little security, eh, with a family like that?"

Both of them treated the remark casually, as though it were no more than a pleasantry between two family men. "It's what we wanted, actually, two boys, two girls," said David. "We didn't expect to get them this quickly, but we're glad now. As far as security goes—well, maybe I flatter myself, but I think the administrative and writing experience I've had running the paper would be worth a good bit to the right people, if something happened to the paper."

"One of the big shortages in this country," said Dilling philosophically, concentrating on lighting a cigarette, "is men who know how to do things, and know how to take responsibility and get things done. I only wish there were better openings in advertising and sales promotion than the ones we've got. They're important, interesting jobs, understand, but I don't know how you'd feel about the starting salary."

"Well, I'm just trying to get the lay of the land, now—to see how things are. I have no idea what salary industry might pay a man like me, with my experience."

"The question experienced men like yourself usually ask is: how high can I go and how fast? And the answer to that is that the sky is the limit for a man with drive and creative ambition. And he can go up fast or slow, depending on what he's willing to do and capable of putting into the job. We might start out a man like you at, oh, say, a hundred dollars a week, but that isn't to say you'd be stuck at that level for two years or even two months."

"I suppose a man could keep a family on that until he got rolling," said David.

"You'd find the work in the publicity end just about the same as what you're doing now. Our publicity people have high standards for writing and editing and reporting, and our publicity releases don't wind up in newspaper editors' wastebaskets. Our people do a professional job, and are well-respected as journalists." He stood. "I've got a little matter to attend to—take me about ten minutes. Could you possibly stick around? I'm enjoying our talk."

David looked at his watch. "Oh—guess I could spare another ten or fifteen minutes."

Dilling was back in his booth in three minutes, chuckling over some private joke. "Just talking on the phone with Lou Flammer, the publicity supervisor. Needs a new stenographer. Lou's a card. Everybody here is crazy about Lou. Old weekly man himself, and I guess that's where he learned to be so easy to get along with. Just to feel him out for the hell of it, I told him about you. I didn't commit you to anything—just said what you told me, that you were keeping your eyes open. And guess what Lou said?"

"Guess what, Nan," said David Potter to his wife on the telephone. He was wearing only his shorts, and was phoning from the company hospital. "When you come home from the hospital tomorrow, you'll be coming home to a solid citizen who pulls down a hundred and ten dollars a week, *every* week. I just got my badge and passed my physical!"

"Oh?" said Nan, startled. "It happened awfully fast, didn't it? I didn't think you were going to plunge right in."

"What's there to wait for?"

"Well—I don't know. I mean, how do you know what you're getting into? You've never worked for anybody but yourself, and don't know anything about getting along in a huge organization. I knew you were going to talk to the Ilium people about a job, but I thought you planned to stick with the paper another year, anyway."

"In another year I'll be thirty, Nan."

"Well?"

"That's pretty old to be starting a career in industry. There are guys my age here who've been working their way up for ten years. That's pretty stiff competition, and it'll be that much stiffer a year from now. And how do we know Jason will still want to buy the paper a year from now?" Ed Jason was David's assistant, a recent college graduate whose father wanted to buy the paper for him. "And this job that opened up today in publicity won't be open a year from now, Nan. Now was the time to switch —this afternoon!"

Nan sighed. "I suppose. But it doesn't seem like you. The Works are fine for some people; they seem to thrive on that life. But you've always been so free. And you love the paper—you know you do."

"I do," said David, "and it'll break my heart to let it go. It was a swell thing to do when we had no kids, but it's a shaky living now—with the kids to educate and all."

"But, hon," said Nan, "the paper is making money."

"It could fold like that," said David, snapping his fingers. "A daily could come in with a one-page insert of Dorset news, or—"

"Dorset likes its little paper too much to let that happen. They like you and the job you're doing too much."

David nodded. "What about ten years from now?"

"What about ten years from now in the Works? What about ten years from now anywhere?"

"It's a better bet that the Works will still be here. I haven't got the right to take long chances any more, Nan, not with a big family counting on me."

"It won't be a very happy big family, darling, if you're not doing what you want to do. I want you to go on being happy the way you have been—driving around the countryside, getting news and talking and selling ads; coming home and writing what you want to write, what you believe in. You in the Works!"

"It's what I've got to do."

"All right, if you say so. I've had my say."

"It's still journalism, high-grade journalism," said David.

"Just don't sell the paper to Jason right away. Put him in charge, but let's wait a month or so, please?"

"No sense in waiting, but if you really want to, all right." David held up a brochure he'd been handed after his physical examination was completed. "Listen to this, Nan: under the company Security Package, I get ten dollars a day for hospital expenses in case of illness, full pay for twenty-six weeks, a hundred dollars for special hospital expenses. I get life insurance for about half what it would cost on the outside. For whatever I put into government bonds under the payroll-savings plan, the company will give me a five per cent bonus in company stock— twelve years from now. I get two weeks' vacation with pay each year, and, after fifteen years, I get three weeks. Get free membership in the company country club. After twenty-five years, I'll be eligible for a pension of at least a hundred and twenty-five dollars a month, and much more if I rise in the organization and stick with it for more than twenty-five years!"

"Good heavens!" said Nan.

"I'd be a damn fool to pass that up, Nan."

"I still wish you'd waited until the little girls and I were home and settled, and you got used to them. I feel you were panicked into this."

"No, no—this is it, Nan. Give the little girls a kiss apiece for me. I've got to go now, and report to my new supervisor."

"Your what?"

"Supervisor."

"Oh. I thought that's what you said, but I couldn't be sure."

"Good-by, Nan."

"Good-by, David."

David clipped his badge to his lapel, and stepped out of the hospital and onto the hot asphalt floor of the world within the fences of the Works. Dull thunder came from the buildings around him, a truck honked at him, and a cinder blew in his eye. He dabbed at the cinder with a corner of his handkerchief and finally got it out. When his vision was restored, he looked about himself for Building 31, where his new office and supervisor were. Four busy streets fanned out from where he stood, and each stretched seemingly to infinity.

He stopped a passerby who was in less of a desperate hurry than the rest. "Could you tell me, please, how to find Building 31, Mr. Flammer's office?"

The man he asked was old and bright-eyed, apparently

getting as much pleasure from the clangor and smells and nervous activity of the Works as David would have gotten from April in Paris. He squinted at David's badge and then at his face. "Just starting out, are you?"

"Yes sir. My first day."

"What do you know about that?" The old man shook his head wonderingly, and winked. "Just starting out. Building 31? Well, sir, when I first came to work here in 1899, you could see Building 31 from here, with nothing between us and it but mud. Now it's all built up. See that water tank up there, about a quarter of a mile? Well, Avenue 17 branches off there, and you follow that almost to the end, then cut across the tracks, and— Just starting out, eh? Well, I'd better walk you up there. Came here for just a minute to talk to the pension folks, but that can wait. I'd enjoy the walk."

"Thank you."

"Fifty-year man, I was," he said proudly, and he led David up avenues and alleys, across tracks, over ramps and through tunnels, through buildings filled with spitting, whining, grumbling machinery, and down corridors with green walls and numbered black doors.

"Can't be a fifty-year man no more," said the old man pityingly. "Can't come to work until you're eighteen nowadays, and you got to retire when you're sixty-five." He poked his thumb under his lapel to make a small gold button protrude. On it was the number "50" superimposed on the company trademark. "Something none of you youngsters can look forward to wearing some day, no matter how much you want one."

"Very nice button," said David.

The old man pointed out a door. "Here's Flammer's office. Keep your mouth shut till you find out who's who and what *they* think. Good luck."

Lou Flammer's secretary was not at her desk, so David walked to the door of the inner office and knocked.

"Yes?" said a man's voice sweetly. "Please come in."

David opened the door. "Mr. Flammer?"

Lou Flammer was a short, fat man in his early thirties. He beamed at David. "What can I do to help you?"

"I'm David Potter, Mr. Flammer."

Flammer's Santa-Claus-like demeanor decayed. He leaned back, propped his feet on his desk top, and stuffed a cigar, which he'd concealed in his cupped hand, into his large mouth. "Hell—thought you were a scoutmaster." He looked at his desk clock, which was mounted in a miniature of the company's newest automatic dishwasher. "Boy scouts touring the Works. Supposed to stop in here fifteen minutes ago for me to give 'em a talk on scouting and industry. Fifty-six per cent of Federal Apparatus' executives were eagle scouts."

David started to laugh, but found himself doing it all alone, and he stopped. "Amazing figure," he said.

"It *is*," said Flammer judiciously. "Says something for scouting and something for industry. Now, before I tell you where your desk is, I'm supposed to explain the rating-sheet system. That's what the Manuals say. Dilling tell you about that?"

"Not that I recall. There was an awful lot of information all at once."

"Well, there's nothing much to it," said Flammer. "Every six months a rating sheet is made out on you, to let you and to let us know just where you stand, and what sort of progress you've been making. Three people who've been close to your work make out independent ratings of you, and then all the information is brought together on a master copy—with carbons for you, me, and Personnel, and the original for the head of the Advertising and Sales Promotion Division. It's very helpful for everybody, you most of all, if you take it the right way." He waved a rating sheet before David. "See? Blanks for appearance, loyalty, promptness, initiative, cooperativeness—things like that. You'll make out rating sheets on other people, too, and whoever does the rating is anonymous."

"I see." David felt himself reddening with resentment. He fought the emotion, telling himself his reaction was a small-town man's—and that it would do him good to learn to think as a member of a great, efficient team.

"Now about pay, Potter," said Flammer, "there'll never be any point in coming in to ask me for a raise. That's all done on the basis of the rating sheets and the salary curve." He rummaged through his drawers and found a graph, which he spread out on his desk. "Here—now you see this curve? Well, it's the average salary curve for men with college educations in the company. See—you can follow it on up. At thirty, the average man makes this much; at forty, this much—and so on. Now, this curve above it shows what men with real growth potential can make. See? It's a little higher and curves upward a little faster. You're how old?"

"Twenty-nine," said David, trying to see what the salary figures were that ran along one side of the graph. Flammer saw him doing it, and pointedly kept them hidden with his forearm.

"Uh-huh." Flammer wet the tip of a pencil with his tongue, and drew a small "x" on the graph, squarely astride the average man's curve. "There *you* are!"

David looked at the mark, and then followed the curve with his eyes across the paper, over little bumps, up gentle slopes, along desolate plateaus, until it died abruptly at the margin which represented age sixty-five. The graph left no questions to be asked and was deaf to argument. David looked from it to the human being he would also be dealing with. "You had a weekly once, did you, Mr. Flammer?"

Flammer laughed. "In my naïve, idealistic youth, Potter, I sold ads to feed stores, gathered gossip, set type, and wrote editorials that were going to save the world, by God."

David smiled admiringly. "What a circus, eh?"

"Circus?" said Flammer. "Freak show, maybe. It's a good way to grow up fast. Took me about six months to find out I was killing myself for peanuts, that a little guy couldn't even save a village three blocks long, and that the world wasn't worth saving anyway. So I started looking out for Number One. Sold out to a chain, came down here, and here I am."

The telephone rang. "Yes?" said Flammer sweetly. "Puh-*bliss*-itee." His benign smile faded. "No. You're kidding, aren't you? Where? Really—this is no gag? All right, all right. Lord! What a time for this to happen. I haven't got anybody here, and I can't get away on account of the goddam boy scouts." He hung up. "Potter—you've got your first assignment. There's a deer loose in the Works!"

"Deer?"

"Don't know how he got in, but he's in. Plumber went to fix a drinking fountain out at the softball diamond across from Building 217, and flushed a deer out from under the bleachers. Now they got him cornered up around the metallurgy lab." He stood and hammered on his desk. "Murder! The story will go all over the country, Potter. Talk about human interest. Front page! Of all the times for Al Tappin to be out at the Ashtabula Works, taking pictures of a new viscometer they cooked up out there! All right—I'll call up a hack photographer downtown, Potter, and get him to meet you out by the metallurgy lab. You get the story and see that he gets the right shots. Okay?"

He led David into the hallway. "Just go back the way you came, turn left instead of right at fractional horsepower motors, cut through hydraulic engineering, catch bus eleven on Avenue 9, and it'll take you right there. After you get the story and pictures, we'll get them cleared by the law division, the plant security officer, our department head and buildings and grounds, and shoot them right out. Now get going. That deer isn't on the payroll—he isn't going to wait for you. Come to work today—tomorrow your work will be on every front page in the country, if we can get it approved. The name of the photographer you're going to meet is McGarvey. Got it? You're in the big time now, Potter. We'll all be watching." He shut the door behind David.

David found himself trotting down the hall, down a stairway, and into an alley, brushing roughly past persons in a race against time. Many turned to watch the purposeful young man with admiration.

On and on he strode, his mind seething with information: *Flammer, Building 31; deer, metallurgy lab; photographer. Al Tappin. No. Al Tappin in Ashtabula.* Flenny *the hack photographer. No.* McCammer. *No. McCammer is new supervisor. Fifty-six per cent eagle scouts. Deer by viscometer laboratory. No. Viscometer in Ashtabula. Call Danner, new supervisor, and get instructions right. Three weeks' vacation after fifteen years. Danner not new supervisor. Anyway, new supervisor in Building 319. No. Fanner in Building 39981983319.*

David stopped, blocked by a grimy window at the end of a blind alley. All he knew was that he'd never been there before, that his memory had blown a gasket, and that the deer was not on the payroll. The air in the alley was thick with tango music and the stench of scorched insulation. David scrubbed away some of the crust on the window with his handkerchief, praying for a glimpse of something that made sense.

Inside were ranks of women at benches, rocking their heads in time to the music, and dipping soldering irons into great nests of colored wires that crept past them on endless belts. One of them looked up and saw David, and winked in tango rhythm. David fled.

At the mouth of the alley, he stopped a man and asked him if he'd heard anything about a deer in the Works. The man shook his head and looked at David oddly, making David aware of how frantic he must look. "I heard it was out by the lab," David said more calmly.

"Which lab?" said the man.

"That's what I'm not sure of," said David. "There's more than one?"

"Chemical lab?" said the man. "Materials testing lab? Paint lab? Insulation lab?"

"No—I don't think it's any of those," said David.

"Well, I could stand here all afternoon naming labs, and probably not hit the right one. Sorry, I've got to go. You don't know what building they've got the differential analyzer in, do you?"

"Sorry," said David. He stopped several other people, none of whom knew anything about the deer, and he tried to retrace his steps to the office of his supervisor, whatever his name was. He was swept this way and that by the currents of the Works, stranded in backwaters, sucked back into the main stream, and his mind was more and more numbed, and the mere reflexes of self-preservation were more and more in charge.

He chose a building at random, and walked inside for a momentary respite from the summer heat, and was deafened by the clangor of steel sheets being cut and punched, being smashed into strange shapes by great hammers that dropped out of the smoke and dust overhead. A hairy, heavily muscled man was seated near the door on a wooden stool, watching a giant lathe turn a bar of steel the size of a silo.

David now had the idea of going through a company phone directory until he recognized his supervisor's name. He called to the machinist from a few feet away, but his voice was lost in the din. He tapped the man's shoulder. "Telephone around here?"

The man nodded. He cupped his hands around David's ear, and shouted. "Up that, and through the—" Down crashed a hammer. "Turn left and keep going until you—" An overhead crane dropped a stack of steel plates. "Four doors down from there is it. Can't miss it."

David, his ears ringing and his head aching, walked into the street again and chose another door. Here was peace and air conditioning. He was in the lobby of an auditorium, where a group of men were examining a box studded with dials and switches that was spotlighted and mounted on a revolving platform.

"Please, miss," he said to a receptionist by the door, "could you tell me where I could find a telephone?"

"It's right around the corner, sir," she said. "But I'm afraid no one is permitted here today but the crystallographers. Are you with them?"

"Yes," said David.

"Oh—well, come right in. Name?"

He told her, and a man sitting next to her lettered it on a badge. The badge was hung on his chest, and David headed for the telephone. A grinning, bald, big-toothed man, wearing a badge that said, "Stan Dunkel, Sales," caught him and steered him to the display.

"Dr. Potter," said Dunkel, "I ask you: is that the way to build a X-ray spectrogoniometer, or is that the way to build an X-ray spectrogoniometer?"

"Yes," said David. "That's the way, all right."

"Martini, Dr. Potter?" said a maid, offering a tray.

David emptied a Martini in one gloriously hot, stinging gulp.

"What features do you want in an X-ray spectrogoniometer, Doctor?" said Dunkel.

"It should be sturdy, Mr. Dunkel," said David, and he left Dunkel there, pledging his reputation that there wasn't a sturdier one on earth.

In the phone booth, David had barely got through the telephone directory's A's before the name of the supervisor miraculously returned to his consciousness: *Flammer!* He found the number and dialed.

"Mr. Flammer's office," said a woman.

"Could I speak to him, please? This is David Potter."

"Oh—Mr. Potter. Well, Mr. Flammer is somewhere out in the Works now, but he left a message for you. He said there's an added twist on the deer story. When they catch the deer, the venison is going to be used at the Quarter-Century Club picnic."

"Quarter-Century Club?" said David.

"Oh, that's really something, Mr. Potter. It's for people who've been with the company twenty-five years or more. Free drinks and cigars, and just the best of everything. They have a wonderful time."

"Anything else about the deer?"

"Nothing he hasn't already told you," she said, and she hung up.

David Potter, with a third Martini in his otherwise empty stomach, stood in front of the auditorium and looked both ways for a deer.

"But our X-ray spectrogoniometer *is* sturdy, Dr. Potter," Stan Dunkel called to him from the auditorium steps.

Across the street was a patch of green, bordered by hedges. David pushed through the hedges into the outfield of a softball diamond. He crossed it and went behind the bleachers, where there was cool shade, and he sat down with his back to a wiremesh fence which separated one end of the Works from a deep pine woods. There were two gates in the fence, but both were wired shut.

David was going to sit there for just a moment, long enough to get his nerve back, to take bearings. Maybe he could leave a message for Flammer, saying he'd suddenly fallen ill, which was essentially true, or—

"There he goes!" cried somebody from the other side of the diamond. There were gleeful cries, shouted orders, the sounds of men running.

A deer with broken antlers dashed under the bleachers, saw David, and ran frantically into the open again along the fence. He ran with a limp, and his reddish-brown coat was streaked with soot and grease.

"Easy now! Don't rush him! Just keep him there. Shoot into the woods, not the Works."

David came out from under the bleachers to see a great semicircle of men, several ranks deep, closing in slowly on the corner of fence in which the deer was at bay. In the front rank were a dozen company policemen with drawn pistols. Other members of the posse carried sticks and rocks and lariats hastily fashioned from wire.

The deer pawed the grass, and bucked, and jerked its broken antlers in the direction of the crowd.

"Hold it!" shouted a familiar voice. A company limousine rumbled across the diamond to the back of the crowd. Leaning out of a window was Lou Flammer, David's supervisor. "Don't shoot until we get a picture of him alive," commanded Flammer. He pulled a photographer out of the limousine, and pushed him into the front rank.

Flammer saw David standing alone by the fence, his back to a gate. "Good boy, Potter," called Flammer. "Right on the ball! Photographer got lost, and I had to bring him here myself."

The photographer fired his flash bulbs. The deer bucked and sprinted along the fence toward David. David unwired the gate, opened it wide. A second later the deer's white tail was flashing through the woods and gone.

The profound silence was broken first by the whistling of a switch engine and then by the click of a latch as David stepped into the woods and closed the gate behind him. He didn't look back.

(1955)

THE LIE

IT WAS EARLY SPRINGTIME. Weak sunshine lay cold on old gray frost. Willow twigs against the sky showed the golden haze of fat catkins about to bloom. A black Rolls-Royce streaked up the Connecticut Turnpike from New York City. At the wheel was Ben Barkley, a black chauffeur.

"Keep it under the speed limit, Ben," said Doctor Remenzel. "I don't care how ridiculous any speed limit seems, stay under it. No reason to rush—we have plenty of time."

Ben eased off on the throttle. "Seems like in the springtime she wants to get up and go," he said.

"Do what you can to keep her down—O.K.?" said the doctor.

"Yes, sir!" said Ben. He spoke in a lower voice to the thirteen-year-old boy who was riding beside him, to Eli Remenzel, the doctor's son. "Ain't just people and animals feel good in the springtime," he said to Eli. "Motors feel good too."

"Um," said Eli.

"Everything feel good," said Ben. "Don't you feel good?"

"Sure, sure I feel good," said Eli emptily.

"Should feel good—going to that wonderful school," said Ben.

That wonderful school was the Whitehill School for Boys, a private preparatory school in North Marston, Massachusetts. That was where the Rolls-Royce was bound. The plan was that Eli would enroll for the fall semester, while his father, a member of the class of 1939, attended a meeting of the Board of Overseers of the school.

222

"Don't believe this boy's feeling so good, doctor," said Ben. He wasn't particularly serious about it. It was more genial springtime blather.

"What's the matter, Eli?" said the doctor absently. He was studying blueprints, plans for a thirty-room addition to the Eli Remenzel Memorial Dormitory—a building named in honor of his great-great-grandfather. Doctor Remenzel had the plans draped over a walnut table that folded out of the back of the front seat. He was a massive, dignified man, a physician, a healer for healing's sake, since he had been born as rich as the Shah of Iran. "Worried about something?" he asked Eli without looking up from the plans.

"Nope," said Eli.

Eli's lovely mother, Sylvia, sat next to the doctor, reading the catalogue of the Whitehill School. "If I were you," she said to Eli, "I'd be so excited I could hardly stand it. The best four years of your whole life are just about to begin."

"Sure," said Eli. He didn't show her his face. He gave her only the back of his head, a pinwheel of coarse brown hair above a stiff white collar, to talk to.

"I wonder how many Remenzels have gone to Whitehill," said Sylvia.

"That's like asking how many people are dead in a cemetery," said the doctor. He gave the answer to the old joke, and to Sylvia's question too. "All of 'em."

"If all the Remenzels who went to Whitehill were numbered, what number would Eli be?" said Sylvia. "That's what I'm getting at."

The question annoyed Doctor Remenzel a little. It didn't seem in very good taste. "It isn't the sort of thing you keep score on," he said.

"Guess," said his wife.

"Oh," he said, "you'd have to go back through all the records, all the way back to the end of the eighteenth century, even, to make any kind of a guess. And you'd have to decide whether to count the Schofields and the Haleys and the MacLellans as Remenzels."

"Please make a guess—" said Sylvia, "just people whose last names were Remenzel."

"Oh—" The doctor shrugged, rattled the plans. "Thirty maybe."

"So Eli is number thirty-one!" said Sylvia, delighted with the number. "You're number thirty-one, dear," she said to the back of Eli's head.

Doctor Remenzel rattled the plans again. "I don't want him going around saying something asinine, like he's number thirty-one," he said.

"Eli knows better than that," said Sylvia. She was a game, ambitious woman, with no money of her own at all. She had been married for sixteen years, but was still openly curious and enthusiastic about the ways of families that had been rich for many generations.

"Just for my own curiosity—not so Eli can go around saying what number he is," said Sylvia, "I'm going to go wherever they keep the records and find out what number he is. That's what I'll do while you're at the meeting and Eli's doing whatever he has to do at the Admissions Office."

"All right," said Doctor Remenzel, "you go ahead and *do* that."

"I will," said Sylvia. "I think things like that are interesting, even if you don't." She waited for a rise on that, but didn't get one. Sylvia enjoyed arguing with her husband about her lack of reserve and his excess of it, enjoyed saying, toward the end of arguments like that, "Well, I guess I'm just a simple-minded country girl at heart, and that's all I'll ever be, and I'm afraid you're going to have to get used to it."

But Doctor Remenzel didn't want to play that game. He found the dormitory plans more interesting.

"Will the new rooms have fireplaces?" said Sylvia. In the oldest part of the dormitory, several of the rooms had handsome fireplaces.

"That would practically double the cost of construction," said the doctor.

"I want Eli to have a room with a fireplace, if that's possible," said Sylvia.

"Those rooms are for seniors."

"I thought maybe through some fluke—" said Sylvia.

"What kind of fluke do you have in mind?" said the doctor. "You mean I should demand that Eli be given a room with a fireplace?"

"Not *demand*—" said Sylvia.

"Request firmly?" said the doctor.

"Maybe I'm just a simple-minded country girl at heart," said Sylvia, "but I look through this catalogue, and I see all the buildings named after Remenzels, look through the back and see all the hundreds of thousands of dollars given by Remenzels for scholarships, and I just can't help thinking people named Remenzel are entitled to ask for a little something extra."

"Let me tell you in no uncertain terms," said Doctor Remenzel, "that you are not to ask for anything special for Eli—not anything."

"Of course I won't," said Sylvia. "Why do you always think I'm going to embarrass you?"

"I don't," he said.

"But I can still think what I think, can't I?" she said.

"If you have to," he said.

"I have to," she said cheerfully, utterly unrepentant. She leaned over the plans. "You think those people will like those rooms?"

"What people?" he said.

"The Africans," she said. She was talking about thirty Africans who, at the request of the State Department, were being admitted to Whitehill in the coming semester. It was because of them that the dormitory was being expanded.

"The rooms aren't for them," he said. "They aren't going to be segregated."

"Oh," said Sylvia. She thought about this awhile, and then she said, "Is there a chance Eli will have to have one of them for a roommate?"

"Freshmen draw lots for roommates," said the doctor. "That piece of information's in the catalogue too."

"Eli?" said Sylvia.

"H'm?" said Eli.

"How would you feel about it if you had to room with one of those Africans?"

Eli shrugged listessly.

"That's all right?" said Sylvia.

Eli shrugged again.

"I guess it's all right," said Sylvia.

"It had better be," said the doctor.

The Rolls-Royce pulled abreast of an old Chevrolet, a car in such bad repair that its back door was lashed shut with clothesline. Doctor Remenzel glanced casually at the driver, and then, with sudden excitement and pleasure, he told Ben Barkley to stay abreast of the car.

The doctor leaned across Sylvia, rolled down his window, yelled to the driver of the old Chevrolet, "Tom! Tom!"

The man was a Whitehill classmate of the doctor. He wore a Whitehill necktie, which he waved at Doctor Remenzel in gay recognition. And then he pointed to the fine young son who sat beside him, conveyed with proud smiles and nods that the boy was bound for Whitehill.

Doctor Remenzel pointed to the chaos of the back of Eli's head, beamed that his news was the same. In the wind blustering between the two cars they made a lunch date at the Holly House in North Marston, at the inn whose principal business was serving visitors to Whitehill.

"All right," said Doctor Remenzel to Ben Barkley, "drive on."

"You know," said Sylvia, "somebody really ought to write an article—" And she turned to look through the back window at the old car now shuddering far behind. "Somebody really ought to."

"What about?" said the doctor. He noticed that Eli had slumped way down in the front seat. "Eli!" he said sharply. "Sit up straight!" He returned his attention to Sylvia.

"Most people think prep schools are such snobbish things, just for people with money," said Sylvia, "but that isn't true." She leafed through the catalogue and found the quotation she was after.

"The Whitehill School operates on the assumption," she read, *"that no boy should be deterred from applying for*

admission because his family is unable to pay the full cost of a Whitehill education. With this in mind, the Admissions Committee selects each year from approximately 3000 candidates the 150 most promising and deserving boys, regardless of their parents' ability to pay the full $2200 tuition. And those in need of financial aid are given it to the full extent of their need. In certain instances, the school will even pay for the clothing and transportation of a boy."

Sylvia shook her head. "I think that's perfectly amazing. It's something most people don't realize at all. A truckdriver's son can come to Whitehill."

"If he's smart enough," he said.

"Thanks to the Remenzels," said Sylvia with pride.

"And a lot of other people too," said the doctor.

Sylvia read out loud again: *"In 1799, Eli Remenzel laid the foundation for the present Scholarship Fund by donating to the school forty acres in Boston. The school still owns twelve of those acres, their current evaluation being $3,000,000."*

"Eli!" said the doctor. "Sit up! What's the matter with you?"

Eli sat up again, but began to slump almost immediately, like a snowman in hell. Eli had good reason for slumping, for actually hoping to die or disappear. He could not bring himself to say what the reason was. He slumped because he knew he had been denied admission to Whitehill. He had failed the entrance examinations. Eli's parents did not know this, because Eli had found the awful notice in the mail and had torn it up.

Doctor Remenzel and his wife had no doubts whatsoever about their son's getting into Whitehill. It was inconceivable to them that Eli could not go there, so they had no curiosity as to how Eli had done on the examinations, were not puzzled when no report ever came.

"What all will Eli have to do to enroll?" said Sylvia, as the black Rolls-Royce crossed the Rhode Island border.

"I don't know," said the doctor. "I suppose they've got it all complicated now with forms to be filled out in quadruplicate, and punch-card machines and bureaucrats. This business of entrance examinations is all new, too. In my day a boy simply had an interview with the headmaster. The headmaster would look him over, ask him a few questions, and then say, 'There's a Whitehill boy.' "

"Did he ever say, 'There isn't a Whitehill boy'?" said Sylvia.

"Oh, sure," said Doctor Remenzel, "if a boy was impossibly stupid or something. There have to be standards. There have always been standards. The African boys have to meet the standards, just like anybody else. They aren't getting in just because the State Department wants to make friends. We made that clear. Those boys had to meet the standards."

"And they did?" said Sylvia.

"I suppose," said Doctor Remenzel. "I heard they're all in, and they all took the same examination Eli did."

"Was it a hard examination, dear?" Sylvia asked Eli. It was the first time she'd thought to ask.

"Um," said Eli.

"What?" she said.

"Yes," said Eli.

"I'm glad they've got high standards," she said, and then she realized that this was a fairly silly statement. "Of course they've got high standards," she said. "That's why it's such a famous school. That's why people who go there do so well in later life."

Sylvia resumed her reading of the catalogue again, opened out a folding map of "The Sward," as the campus of Whitehill was traditionally called. She read off the names of features that memorialized Remenzels—the Sanford Remenzel Bird Sanctuary, the George MacLellan Remenzel Skating Rink, the Eli Remenzel Memorial Dormitory, and then she read out loud a quatrain printed on one corner of the map:

> "When night falleth gently
> "Upon the green Sward,
> "It's Whitehill, dear Whitehill,
> "Our thoughts all turn toward."

"You know," said Sylvia, "school songs are so corny when you just read them. But when I hear the Glee Club sing those words, they sound like the most beautiful words ever written, and I want to cry."

"Um," said Doctor Remenzel.

"Did a Remenzel write them?"

"I don't think so," said Doctor Remenzel. And then he said, "No—Wait. That's the *new* song. A Remenzel didn't write it. Tom Kilyer wrote it."

"The man in that old car we passed?"

"Sure," said Doctor Remenzel. "Tom wrote it. I remember when he wrote it."

"A scholarship boy wrote it?" said Sylvia. "I think that's awfully nice. He *was* a scholarship boy, wasn't he?"

"His father was an ordinary automobile mechanic in North Marston."

"You hear what a democratic school you're going to, Eli?" said Sylvia.

Half an hour later Ben Barkley brought the limousine to a stop before the Holly House, a rambling country inn twenty years older than the Republic. The inn was on the edge of the Whitehill Sward, glimpsing the school's rooftops and spires over the innocent wilderness of the Sanford Remenzel Bird Sanctuary.

Ben Barkley was sent away with the car for an hour and a half. Doctor Remenzel shepherded Sylvia and Eli into a familiar, low-ceilinged world of pewter, clocks, lovely old woods, agreeable servants, elegant food and drink.

Eli, clumsy with horror of what was surely to come, banged a grandmother clock with his elbow as he passed, made the clock cry.

Sylvia excused herself. Doctor Remenzel and Eli went to the threshold of the dining room, where a hostess welcomed them both by name. They were given a table beneath an oil portrait of one of the three Whitehill boys who had gone on to become President of the United States.

The dining room was filling quickly with families. What

every family had was at least one boy about Eli's age. Most of the boys wore Whitehill blazers—black, with pale-blue piping, with Whitehill seals on their breast pockets. A few, like Eli, were not yet entitled to wear blazers, were simply hoping to get in.

The doctor ordered a Martini, then turned to his son and said, "Your mother has the idea that you're entitled to special privileges around here. I hope you don't have that idea too."

"No, sir," said Eli.

"It would be a source of the greatest embarrassment to me," said Doctor Remenzel with considerable grandeur, "if I were ever to hear that you had used the name Remenzel as though you thought Remenzels were something special."

"I know," said Eli wretchedly.

"That settles it," said the doctor. He had nothing more to say about it. He gave abbreviated salutes to several people he knew in the room, speculated as to what sort of party had reserved a long banquet table that was set up along one wall. He decided that it was for a visiting athletic team. Sylvia arrived, and Eli had to be told in a sharp whisper to stand when a woman came to a table.

Sylvia was full of news. The long table, she related, was for the thirty boys from Africa. "I'll bet that's more colored people than have eaten here since this place was founded," she said softly. "How fast things change these days!"

"You're right about how fast things change," said Doctor Remenzel. "You're wrong about the colored people who've eaten here. This used to be a busy part of the Underground Railroad."

"Really?" said Sylvia. "How exciting." She looked all about herself in a birdlike way. "I think everything's exciting here. I only wish Eli had a blazer on."

Doctor Remenzel reddened. "He isn't entitled to one," he said.

"I know that," said Sylvia.

"I thought you were going to ask somebody for permission to put a blazer on Eli right away," said the doctor.

"I wouldn't do that," said Sylvia, a little offended now. "Why are you always afraid I'll embarrass you?"

"Never mind. Excuse me. Forget it," said Doctor Remenzel.

Sylvia brightened again, put her hand on Eli's arm, and looked radiantly at a man in the dining-room doorway. "There's my favorite person in all the world, next to my son and husband," she said. She meant Dr. Donald Warren, headmaster of the Whitehill School. A thin gentleman in his early sixties, Doctor Warren was in the doorway with the manager of the inn, looking over the arrangements for the Africans.

It was then that Eli got up abruptly, fled the dining room, fled as much of the nightmare as he could possibly leave behind. He brushed past Doctor Warren rudely, though he knew him well, though Doctor Warren spoke his name. Doctor Warren looked after him sadly.

"I'll be damned," said Doctor Remenzel. "What brought that on?"

"Maybe he really *is* sick," said Sylvia.

The Remenzels had no time to react more elaborately, because Doctor Warren spotted them and crossed quickly to their table. He greeted them, some of his perplexity about Eli showing in his greeting. He asked if he might sit down.

"Certainly, of course," said Doctor Remenzel expansively. "We'd be honored if you did. Heavens."

"Not to eat," said Doctor Warren. "I'll be eating at the long table with the new boys. I would like to talk, though." He saw that there were five places set at the table. "You're expecting someone?"

"We passed Tom Hilyer and his boy on the way," said Doctor Remenzel. "They'll be along in a minute."

"Good, good," said Doctor Warren absently. He fidgeted, looked again in the direction in which Eli had disappeared.

"Tom's boy will be going to Whitehill in the fall?" said Doctor Remenzel.

"H'm?" said Doctor Warren. "Oh—yes, yes. Yes, he will."

"Is he a scholarship boy, like his father?" said Sylvia.

"That's not a polite question," said Doctor Remenzel severely.

"I beg your pardon," said Sylvia.

"No, no—that's a perfectly proper question these days," said Doctor Warren. "We don't keep that sort of information very secret any more. We're proud of our scholarship boys, and they have every reason to be proud of themselves. Tom's boy got the highest score anyone's ever got on the entrance examinations. We feel privileged to have him."

"We never *did* find out Eli's score," said Doctor Remenzel. He said it with good-humored resignation, without expectation that Eli had done especially well.

"A good strong medium, I imagine," said Sylvia. She said this on the basis of Eli's grades in primary school, which had ranged from medium to terrible.

The headmaster looked surprised. "I didn't tell you his scores?" he said.

"We haven't seen you since he took the examinations," said Doctor Remenzel.

"The letter I wrote you—" said Doctor Warren.

"What letter?" said Doctor Remenzel. "Did we get a letter?"

"A letter from me," said Doctor Warren, with growing incredulity. "The hardest letter I ever had to write."

Sylvia shook her head. "We never got any letter from you."

Doctor Warren sat back, looking very ill. "I mailed it myself," he said. "It was definitely mailed—two weeks ago."

Doctor Remenzel shrugged. "The U.S. mails don't lose much," he said, "but I guess that now and then something gets misplaced."

Doctor Warren cradled his head in his hands. "Oh, dear—oh, my, oh, Lord," he said. "I was surprised to see Eli here. I wondered that he would want to come along with you."

"He didn't come along just to see the scenery," said Doctor Remenzel. "He came to enroll."

"I want to know what was in the letter," said Sylvia.

Doctor Warren raised his head, folded his hands. "What the letter said, was this, and no other words could be more difficult for me to say: *'On the basis of his work in primary school and his scores on the entrance examinations, I must tell you that your son and my good friend Eli cannot possibly do the work required of boys at Whitehill.'* " Doctor Warren's voice steadied, and so did his gaze. " *'To admit Eli to Whitehill, to expect him to do Whitehill work,'* " he said, " *'would be both unrealistic and cruel.'* "

Thirty African boys, escorted by several faculty members, State Department men, and diplomats from their own countries, filed into the dining room.

And Tom Hilyer and his boy, having no idea that something had just gone awfully wrong for the Remenzels, came in, too, and said hello to the Remenzels and Doctor Warren gaily, as though life couldn't possible be better.

"I'll talk to you more about this later, if you like," Doctor Warren said to the Remenzels, rising. "I have to go now, but later on—" He left quickly.

"My mind's a blank," said Sylvia. "My mind's a perfect blank."

Tom Hilyer and his boy sat down. Hilyer looked at the menu before him, clapped his hands and said, "What's good? I'm hungry." And then he said, "Say—where's your boy?"

"He stepped out for a moment," said Doctor Remenzel evenly.

"We've got to find him," said Sylvia to her husband.

"In time, in due time," said Doctor Remenzel.

"That letter," said Sylvia; "Eli knew about it. He found it and tore it up. Of course he did!" She started to cry, thinking of the hideous trap that Eli had caught himself in.

"I'm not interested right now in what Eli's done," said Doctor Remenzel. "Right now I'm a lot more interested in what some other people are going to do."

"What do you mean?" said Sylvia.

Doctor Remenzel stood impressively, angry and determined. "I mean," he said, "I'm going to see how quickly people can change their minds around here."

"Please," said Sylvia, trying to hold him, trying to calm him, "we've got to find Eli. That's the first thing."

"The first thing," said Doctor Remenzel quite loudly, "is to get Eli admitted to Whitehill. After that we'll find him, and we'll bring him back."

"But darling—" said Sylvia.

"No 'but' about it," said Doctor Remenzel. "There's a majority of the Board of Overseers in this room at this very moment. Every one of them is a close friend of mine, or a close friend of my father. If they tell Doctor Warren Eli's in, that's it—Eli's in. If there's room for all these other people," he said, "there's damn well room for Eli too."

He strode quickly to a table nearby, sat down heavily and began to talk to a fierce-looking and splendid old gentleman who was eating there. The old gentleman was chairman of the board.

Sylvia apologized to the baffled Hilyers, and then went in search of Eli.

Asking this person and that person, Sylvia found him. He was outside—all alone on a bench in a bower of lilacs that had just begun to bud.

Eli heard his mother's coming on the gravel path, stayed where he was, resigned. "Did you find out," he said, "or do I still have to tell you?"

"About you?" she said gently. "About not getting in? Doctor Warren told us."

"I tore his letter up," said Eli.

"I can understand that," she said. "Your father and I have always made you feel that you had to go to Whitehill, that nothing else would do."

"I feel better," said Eli. He tried to smile, found he could do it easily. "I feel so much better now that it's over. I tried to tell you a couple of times—but I just couldn't. I didn't know how."

"That's my fault, not yours," she said.

"What's father doing?" said Eli.

Sylvia was so intent on comforting Eli that she'd put out of her mind what her husband was up to. Now she realized that Doctor Remenzel was making a ghastly mistake.

She didn't want Eli admitted to Whitehill, could see what a cruel thing that would be.

She couldn't bring herself to tell the boy what his father was doing, so she said, "He'll be along in a minute, dear. He understands." And then she said, "You wait here, and I'll go get him and come right back."

But she didn't have to go to Doctor Remenzel. At that moment the big man came out of the inn and caught sight of his wife and son. He came to her and to Eli. He looked dazed.

"Well?" she said.

"They—they all said no," said Doctor Remenzel, very subdued.

"That's for the best," said Sylvia. "I'm relieved. I really am."

"Who said no?" said Eli. "Who said no to what?"

"The members of the board," said Doctor Remenzel, not looking anyone in the eye. "I asked them to make an exception in your case—to reverse their decision and let you in."

Eli stood, his face filled with incredulity and shame that were instant. "You what?" he said, and there was no childishness in the way he said it. Next came anger. "You shouldn't have done that!" he said to his father.

Doctor Remenzel nodded. "So I've already been told."

"That isn't done!" said Eli. "How awful! You shouldn't have."

"You're right," said Doctor Remenzel, accepting the scolding lamely.

"Now I *am* ashamed," said Eli, and he showed that he was.

Doctor Remenzel, in his wretchedness, could find no strong words to say. "I apologize to you both," he said at last. "It was a very bad thing to try."

"Now a Remenzel *has* asked for something," said Eli.

"I don't suppose Ben's back yet with the car?" said Doctor Remenzel. It was obvious that Ben wasn't. "We'll wait out here for him," he said. "I don't want to go back in there now."

"A Remenzel asked for something—as though a Remenzel were something special," said Eli.

"I don't suppose—" said Doctor Remenzel, and he left the sentence unfinished, dangling in the air.

"You don't suppose what?" said his wife, her face puzzled.

"I don't suppose," said Doctor Remenzel, "that we'll ever be coming here any more."

(1962)

UNREADY
TO WEAR

I DON'T SUPPOSE the oldsters, those of us who weren't born into it, will ever feel quite at home being amphibious —amphibious in the new sense of the word. I still catch myself feeling blue about things that don't matter any more.

I can't help worrying about my business, for instance— or what used to be my business. After all, I spent thirty years building the thing up from scratch, and now the equipment is rusting and getting clogged with dirt. But even though I know it's silly of me to care what happens to the business, I borrow a body from a storage center every so often, and go around the old hometown, and clean and oil as much of the equipment as I can.

Of course, all in the world the equipment was good for was making money, and Lord knows there's plenty of that lying around. Not as much as there used to be, because there at first some people got frisky and threw it all around, and the wind blew it every which way. And a lot of go-getters gathered up piles of the stuff and hid it somewhere. I hate to admit it, but I gathered up close to a half million myself and stuck it away. I used to get it out and count it sometimes, but that was years ago. Right now I'd be hard put to say where it is.

But the worrying I do about my old business is bush league stuff compared to the worrying my wife, Madge, does about our old house. That thing is what she herself put in thirty years on while I was building the business. Then no sooner had we gotten nerve enough to build and decorate the place than everybody we cared anything about got amphibious. Madge borrows a body once a

237

month and dusts the place, though the only thing a house is good for now is keeping termites and mice from getting pneumonia.

Whenever it's my turn to get into a body and work as an attendant at the local storage center, I realize all over again how much tougher it is for women to get used to being amphibious.

Madge borrows bodies a lot oftener than I do, and that's true of women in general. We have to keep three times as many women's bodies in stock as men's bodies, in order to meet the demand. Every so often, it seems as though a woman just *has* to have a body, and doll it up in clothes, and look at herself in a mirror. And Madge, God bless her, I don't think she'll be satisfied until she's tried on every body in every storage center on Earth.

It's been a fine thing for Madge, though. I never kid her about it, because it's done so much for her personality. Her old body, to tell you the plain blunt truth, wasn't anything to get excited about, and having to haul the thing around made her gloomy a lot of the times in the old days. She couldn't help it, poor soul, any more than anybody else could help what sort of body they'd been born with, and I loved her in spite of it.

Well, after we'd learned to be amphibious, and after we'd built the storage centers and laid in body supplies and opened them to the public, Madge went hog wild. She borrowed a platinum blonde body that had been donated by a burlesque queen, and I didn't think we'd ever get her out of it. As I say, it did wonders for her self-confidence.

I'm like most men and don't care particularly what body I get. Just the strong, good-looking, healthy bodies were put in storage, so one is as good as the next one. Sometimes, when Madge and I take bodies out together for old times' sake, I let her pick out one for me to match whatever she's got on. It's a funny thing how she always picks a blond, tall one for me.

My old body, which she claims she loved for a third of a century, had black hair, and was short and paunchy, too, there toward the last. I'm human and I couldn't help being hurt when they scrapped it after I'd left it, instead of putting it in storage. It was a good, homey, comfortable body; nothing fast and flashy, but reliable. But there isn't much call for that kind of body at the centers, I guess. I never ask for one, at any rate.

The worst experience I ever had with a body was when I was flimflammed into taking out the one that had belonged to Dr. Ellis Konigswasser. It belongs to the Amphibious Pioneers' Society and only gets taken out once a year for the big Pioneers' Day Parade, on the anniversary of Konigswasser's discovery. Everybody said it was a great honor for me to be picked to get into Konigswasser's body and lead the parade.

Like a plain damn fool, I believed them.

They'll have a tough time getting me into that thing again—ever. Taking that wreck out certainly made it plain why Konigswasser discovered how people could do without their bodies. That old one of his practically *drives* you out. Ulcers, headaches, arthritis, fallen arches—a nose like a pruning hook, piggy little eyes, and a complexion like a used steamer trunk. He was and still is the sweetest person you'd ever want to know, but, back when he was stuck with that body, nobody got close enough to find out.

We tried to get Konigswasser back into his old body to lead us when we first started having the Pioneers' Day Parades, but he wouldn't have anything to do with it, so we always have to flatter some poor boob into taking on the job. Konigswasser marches, all right, but as a six-foot cowboy who can bend beer cans double between his thumb and middle finger.

Konigswasser is just like a kid with that body. He never gets tired of bending beer cans with it, and we all have to stand around in our bodies after the parade, and watch as though we were very impressed.

I don't suppose he could bend very much of anything back in the old days.

Nobody mentions it to him, since he's the grand old man of the Amphibious Age, but he plays hell with the bodies. Almost every time he takes one out, he busts it, showing off. Then somebody has to get into a surgeon's body and sew it up again.

I don't mean to be disrespectful of Konigswasser. As a matter of fact, it's a respectful thing to say that somebody is childish in certain ways, because it's people like that who seem to get all the big ideas.

There is a picture of him in the old days down at the Historical Society, and you can see from that that he never did grow up as far as keeping up his appearance went—doing what little he could with the rattle-trap body Nature had issued him.

His hair was down below his collar, he wore his pants so low that his heels wore through the legs above the cuffs, and the lining of his coat hung down in festoons all around the bottom. And he'd forget meals, and go out into the cold or wet without enough clothes on, and he would never notice sickness until it almost killed him. He was what we used to call absent-minded. Looking back now, of course, we say he was starting to be amphibious.

Konigswasser was a mathematician, and he did all his living with his mind. The body he had to haul around with that wonderful mind was about as much use to him as a flatcar of scrap iron. Whenever he got sick and *had* to pay some attention to his body, he'd rant somewhat like this:

"The mind is the only thing about human beings that's worth anything. Why does it have to tied to a bag of skin, blood, hair, meat, bones, and tubes? No wonder people can't get anything done, stuck for life with a parasite that has to be stuffed with food and protected from weather and germs all the time. And the fool thing wears out anyway—no matter how much you stuff and protect it!

"Who," he wanted to know, "really wants one of the things? What's so wonderful about protoplasm that we've got to carry so damned many pounds of it with us wherever we go?

"Trouble with the world," said Konigswasser, "isn't too many people—it's too many bodies."

When his teeth went bad on him, and he had to have them all out, and he couldn't get a set of dentures that were at all comfortable, he wrote in his diary, "If living matter was able to evolve enough to get out of the ocean, which was really quite a pleasant place to live, it certainly ought to be able to take another step and get out of bodies, which are pure nuisances when you stop to think about them."

He wasn't a prude about bodies, understand, and he wasn't jealous of people who had better ones than he did. He just thought bodies were a lot more trouble than they were worth.

He didn't have great hopes that people would really evolve out of their bodies in his time. He just wished they would. Thinking hard about it, he walked through a park in his shirtsleeves and stopped off at the zoo to watch the lions being fed. Then, when the rainstorm turned to sleet, he headed back home and was interested to see firemen on the edge of a lagoon, where they were using a pulmotor on a drowned man.

Witnesses said the old man had walked right into the water and had kept going without changing his expression until he'd disappeared. Konigswasser got a look at the victim's face and said he'd never seen a better reason for suicide. He started for home again and was almost there before he realized that that was his own body lying back there.

He went back to reoccupy the body just as the firemen got it breathing again, and he walked it home, more as a favor to the city than anything else. He walked it into his front closet, got out of it again, and left it there.

He took it out only when he wanted to do some writing or turn the pages of a book, or when he had to feed it so it would have enough energy to do the few odd jobs he gave it. The rest of the time, it sat motionless in the closet, looking dazed and using almost no energy. Konigswasser told me the other day that he used to run the thing for about a dollar a week, just taking it out when he really needed it.

But the best part was that Konigswasser didn't have to sleep any more, just because *it* had to sleep; or be afraid any more, just because *it* thought it might get hurt; or go looking for things *it* seemed to think it had to have. And, when *it* didn't feel well, Konigswasser kept out of it until it felt better, and he didn't have to spend a fortune keeping the thing comfortable.

When he got his body out of the closet to write, he did a book on how to get out of one's own body, which was rejected without comment by twenty-three publishers. The twenty-fourth sold two million copies, and the book changed human life more than the invention of fire, numbers, the alphabet, agriculture, or the wheel. When somebody told Konigswasser that, he snorted that they were damning his book with faint praise. I'd say he had a point there.

By following the instructions in Konigswasser's book for about two years, almost anybody could get out of his body whenever he wanted to. The first step was to understand what a parasite and dictator the body was most of the time, then to separate what the body wanted or didn't want from what you yourself—your psyche—wanted or didn't want. Then, by concentrating on what you wanted, and ignoring as much as possible what the body wanted beyond plain maintenance, you made your psyche demand its right and become self-sufficient.

That's what Konigswasser had done without realizing it, until he and his body had parted company in the park, with his psyche going to watch the lions eat, and with his body wandering out of control into the lagoon.

The final trick of separation, once your psyche grew independent enough, was to start your body walking in some direction and suddenly take your psyche off in another direction. You couldn't do it standing still, for some reason—you had to walk.

At first, Madge's and my psyches were clumsy at getting along outside our bodies, like the first sea animals that got stranded on land millions of years ago, and who could just waddle and squirm and gasp in the mud. But we became better at it with time, because the psyche can naturally adapt so much faster than the body.

Madge and I had good reason for wanting to get out. Everybody who was crazy enough to try to get out at the first had good reasons. Madge's body was sick and wasn't going to last a lot longer. With her going in a little while, I couldn't work up enthusiasm for sticking around much longer myself. So we studied Konigswasser's book and tried to get Madge out of her body before it died. I went along with her, to keep either one of us from getting lonely. And we just barely made it—six weeks before her body went all to pieces.

That's why we get to march every year in the Pioneers' Day Parade. Not everybody does—only the first five thousand of us who turned amphibious. We were guinea pigs, without much to lose one way or another, and we were the ones who proved to the rest how pleasant and safe it was—a heck of a lot safer than taking chances in a body year in and year out.

Sooner or later, almost everybody had a good reason for giving it a try. There got to be millions and finally more than a billion of us—invisible, insubstantial, indestructible, and, by golly, true to ourselves, no trouble to anybody, and not afraid of anything.

When we're not in bodies, the Amphibious Pioneers can meet on the head of a pin. When we get into bodies for the Pioneers' Day Parade, we take up over fifty thousand square feet, have to gobble more than three tons of food to get enough energy to march; and lots of us catch colds or worse, and get sore because somebody's body accidentally steps on the heel of somebody else's body, and get jealous because some bodies get to lead and others have to stay in ranks, and—oh, hell, I don't know what all.

I'm not crazy about the parade. With all of us there, close together in bodies—well, it brings out the worst in us, no matter how good our psyches are. Last year, for instance, Pioneers' Day was a scorcher. People couldn't help being out of sorts, stuck in sweltering, thirsty bodies for hours.

Well, one thing led to another, and the Parade Marshal offered to beat the daylights out of my body with his body, if my body got out of step again. Naturally, being Parade Marshal, he had the best body that year, except for Konigswasser's cowboy, but I told him to soak his fat head, anyway. He swung, and I ditched my body right there, and didn't even stick around long enough to find out if he connected. He had to haul my body back to the storage center himself.

I stopped being mad at him the minute I got out of the body. I understood, you see. Nobody but a saint could be really sympathetic or intelligent for more than a few minutes at a time in a body—or happy, either, except in short spurts. I haven't met an amphibian yet who wasn't easy to get along with, and cheerful and interesting—as long as he was outside a body. And I haven't met one yet who didn't turn a little sour when he got into one.

The minute you get in, chemistry takes over—glands making you excitable or ready to fight or hungry or mad or affectionate, or—well, you never know *what's* going to happen next.

That's why I can't get sore at the enemy, the people who are against the amphibians. They never get out of their bodies and won't try to learn. They don't want anybody else to do it, either, and they'd like to make the amphibians get back into bodies and stay in them.

After the tussle I had with the Parade Marshal, Madge got wind of it and left *her* body right in the middle of the Ladies' Auxiliary. And the two of us, feeling full of devilment after getting shed of the bodies and the parade, went over to have a look at the enemy.

I'm never keen on going over to look at them. Madge likes to see what the women are wearing. Stuck with their bodies all the time, the enemy women change their clothes and hair and cosmetic styles a lot oftener than we do on the women's bodies in the storage centers.

I don't get much of a kick out of the fashions, and almost everything else you see and hear in enemy territory would bore a plaster statue into moving away.

Usually, the enemy is talking about old-style reproduction, which is the clumsiest, most comical, most inconvenient thing anyone could imagine, compared with what the amphibians have in that line. If they aren't talking about that, then they're talking about food, the gobs of chemicals they have to stuff into their bodies. Or they'll talk about fear, which we used to call politics—job politics, social politics, government politics.

The enemy hates that, having us able to peek in on them any time we want to, while they can't ever see us unless we get into bodies. They seem to be scared to death of us, though being scared of amphibians makes as much sense as being scared of the sunrise. They could have the whole world, except the storage centers, for all the amphibians care. But they bunch together as though we were going to come whooping out of the sky and do something terrible to them at any moment.

They've got contraptions all over the place that are supposed to detect amphibians. The gadgets aren't worth a nickel, but they seem to make the enemy feel good—like they were lined up against great forces, but keeping their nerve and doing important, clever things about it. Know-how—all the time they're patting each other about how much know-how they've got, and about how we haven't got anything by comparison. If know-how means weapons, they're dead right.

I guess there is a war on between them and us. But we never do anything about holding up our side of the war, except to keep our parade sites and our storage centers secret, and to get out of bodies every time there's an air raid, or the enemy fires a rocket, or something.

That just makes the enemy madder, because the raids and rockets and all cost plenty, and blowing up things nobody needs anyway is a poor return on the taxpayer's money. We always know what they're going to do next, and when and where, so there isn't any trick to keeping out of their way.

But they are pretty smart, considering they've got bodies to look after besides doing their thinking, so I always try to be cautious when I go over to watch them. That's why I wanted to clear out when Madge and I saw a storage center in the middle of one of their fields. We hadn't talked to anybody lately about what the enemy was up to, and the center looked awfully suspicious.

Madge was optimistic, the way she's been ever since she borrowed that burlesque queen's body, and she said the storage center was a sure sign that the enemy had seen the light, that they were getting ready to become amphibious themselves.

Well, it looked like it. There was a brand-new center, stocked with bodies and open for business, as innocent as you please. We circled it several times, and Madge's circles got smaller and smaller, as she tried to get a close look at what they had in the way of ladies' ready-to-wear.

"Let's beat it," I said.

"I'm just looking," said Madge. "No harm in looking."

Then she saw what was in the main display case, and she forgot where she was or where she'd come from.

The most striking woman's body I'd ever seen was in the case—six feet tall and built like a goddess. But that wasn't the payoff. The body had copper-colored skin, chartreuse hair and fingernails, and a gold lamé evening gown. Beside that body was the body of a blond, male giant in a pale blue field marshal's uniform, piped in scarlet and spangled with medals.

I think the enemy must have swiped the bodies in a raid on one of our outlying storage centers, and padded and dyed them, and dressed them up.

"Madge, come back!" I said.

The copper-colored woman with the chartreuse hair moved. A siren screamed and soldiers rushed from hiding places to grab the body Madge was in.

The center was a trap for amphibians!

The body Madge hadn't been able to resist had its ankles tied together, so Madge couldn't take the few steps she had to take if she was going to get out of it again.

The soldiers carted her off triumphantly as a prisoner of war. I got into the only body available, the fancy field marshal, to try to help her. It was a hopeless situation, because the field marshal was bait, too, with its ankles tied. The soldiers dragged me after Madge.

The cocky young major in charge of the soldiers did a jig along the shoulder of the road, he was so proud. He was the first man ever to capture an amphibian, which was really something from the enemy's point of view. They'd been at war with us for years, and spent God knows how many billions of dollars, but catching us was the first thing that made any amphibians pay much attention to them.

When we got to the town, people were leaning out of windows and waving their flags, and cheering the soldiers, and hissing Madge and me. Here were all the people who didn't want to be amphibious, who thought it was terrible for anybody to be amphibious—people of all colors, shapes, sizes, and nationalities, joined together to fight the amphibians.

It turned out that Madge and I were going to have a big trial. After being tied up every which way in jail all night, we were taken to a courtroom, where television cameras stared at us.

Madge and I were worn to frazzles, because neither one of us had been cooped up in a body that long since I don't know when. Just when we needed to think more than we ever had, in jail before the trial, the bodies developed hunger pains and we couldn't get them comfortable on the cots, no matter how we tried; and, of course, the bodies just had to have their eight hours sleep.

The charge against us was a capital offense on the books of the enemy—*desertion*. As far as the enemy was concerned, the amphibians had all turned yellow and run out on their bodies, just when their bodies were needed to do brave and important things for humanity.

We didn't have a hope of being acquitted. The only reason there was a trial at all was that it gave them an opportunity to sound off about why they were so right and we were so wrong. The courtroom was jammed with their big brass, all looking angry and brave and noble.

"Mr. Amphibian," said the prosecutor, "you are old enough, aren't you, to remember when all men had to face up to life in their bodies, and work and fight for what they believed in?"

"I remember when the bodies were always getting into

fights, and nobody seemed to know why, or how to stop it,"
I said politely. "The only thing everybody seemed to believe in was that they didn't like to fight."

"What would you say of a soldier who ran away in the
face of fire?" he wanted to know.

"I'd say he was scared silly."

"He was helping to lose the battle, wasn't he?"

"Oh, sure." There wasn't any argument on that one.

"Isn't that what the amphibians have done—run out on
the human race in the face of the battle of life?"

"Most of us are still alive, if that's what you mean," I
said.

It was true. We hadn't licked death, and weren't sure we
wanted to, but we'd certainly lengthened life something
amazing, compared to the span you could expect in a body.

"You ran out on your responsibilities!" he said.

"Like you'd run out of a burning building, sir," I said.

"Leaving everyone else to struggle on alone!"

"They can all get out the same door that we got out of.
You can all get out any time you want to. All you do is
figure out what you want and what your body wants, and
concentrate on—"

The judge banged his gavel until I thought he'd split it.
Here they'd burned every copy of Konigswasser's book
they could find, and there I was giving a course in how to
get out of a body over a whole television network.

"If you amphibians had your way," said the prosecutor,
"every body would run out on his responsibilities, and let
life and progress as we know them disappear completely."

"Why, sure," I agreed. "That's the point."

"Men would no longer work for what they believe in?"
he challenged.

"I had a friend back in the old days who drilled holes in
little square thingmajigs for seventeen years in a factory,
and he never did get a very clear idea of what they were
for. Another one I knew grew raisins for a glassblowing
company, and the raisins weren't for anybody to eat, and
he never did find out why the company bought them.
Things like that make me sick—now that I'm in a body, of

course—and what I used to do for a living makes me even sicker."

"Then you despise human beings and everything they do," he said.

"I like them fine—better than I ever did before. I just think it's a dirty shame what they have to do to take care of their bodies. You ought to get amphibious and see how happy people can be when they don't have to worry about where their body's next meal is coming from, or how to keep it from freezing in the wintertime, or what's going to happen to them when their body wears out."

"And that, sir, means the end of ambition, the end of greatness!"

"Oh, I don't know what about that," I said. "We've got some pretty great people on our side. They'd be great in *or* out of bodies. It's the end of fear is what it is." I looked right into the lens of the nearest television camera. "And *that's* the most wonderful thing that ever happened to people."

Down came the judge's gavel again, and the brass started to shout me down. The television men turned off their cameras, and all the spectators, except for the biggest brass, were cleared out. I knew I'd really said something. All anybody would be getting on his television set now was organ music.

When the confusion died down, the judge said the trial was over, and that Madge and I were guilty of desertion.

Nothing I could do could get us in any worse, so I talked back.

"Now I understand you poor fish," I said. "You couldn't get along without fear. That's the only skill you've got— how to scare yourselves and other people into doing things. That's the only fun you've got, watching people jump for fear of what you'll do to their bodies or take away from their bodies."

Madge got in her two cents' worth. "The only way you can get any response from anybody is to scare them."

"Contempt of court!" said the judge.

"The only way you can scare people is if you can keep them in their bodies," I told him.

The soldiers grabbed Madge and me and started to drag us out of the courtroom.

"This means war!" I yelled.

Everything stopped right there and the place got very quiet.

"We're already at war," said a general uneasily.

"Well, *we're* not," I answered, "but we will be, if you don't untie Madge and me this instant." I was fierce and impressive in that field marshal's body.

"You haven't any weapons," said the judge, "no know-how. Outside of bodies, amphibians are nothing."

"If you don't cut us loose by the time I count ten," I told him, "the amphibians will occupy the bodies of the whole kit and caboodle of you and march you right off the nearest cliff. The place is surrounded." That was hogwash, of course. Only one person can occupy a body at a time, but the enemy couldn't be sure of that. "One! Two! Three!"

The general swallowed, turned white, and waved his hand vaguely.

"Cut them loose," he said weakly.

The soldiers, terrified, too, were glad to do it. Madge and I were freed.

I took a couple of steps, headed my spirit in another direction, and that beautiful field marshal, medals and all, went crashing down the staircase like a grandfather clock.

I realized that Madge wasn't with me. She was still in that copper-colored body with the chartreuse hair and fingernails.

"What's more," I heard her saying, "in payment for all the trouble you've caused us, this body is to be addressed to me at New York, delivered in good condition no later than next Monday."

"Yes, ma'am," said the judge.

When we got home, the Pioneers' Day Parade was just breaking up at the local storage center, and the Parade

Marshal got out of his body and apologized to me for acting the way he had.

"Heck, Herb," I said, "you don't need to apologize. You weren't yourself. You were parading around in a body."

That's the best part of being amphibious, next to not being afraid—people forgive you for whatever fool thing you might have done in a body.

Oh, there are drawbacks, I guess, the way there are drawbacks to everything. We still have to work off and on, maintaining the storage centers and getting food to keep the community bodies going. But that's a small drawback, and all the big drawbacks I ever heard of aren't real ones, just old-fashioned thinking by people who can't stop worrying about things they used to worry about before they turned amphibious.

As I say, the oldsters will probably never get really used to it. Every so often, I catch myself getting gloomy over what happened to the pay-toilet business it took me thirty years to build.

But the youngsters don't have any hangovers like that from the past. They don't even worry much about something happening to the storage centers, the way us oldsters do.

So I guess maybe that'll be the next step in evolution—to break clean like those first amphibians who crawled out of the mud into the sunshine, and who never did go back to the sea.

(1953)

THE KID NOBODY
COULD HANDLE

I⊤ WAS SEVEN-THIRTY in the morning. Waddling, clanking,
muddy machines were tearing a hill to pieces behind a
restaurant, and trucks were hauling the pieces away. Inside the restaurant, dishes rattled on their shelves. Tables
quaked, and a very kind fat man with a headful of music
looked down at the jiggling yolks of his breakfast eggs. His
wife was visiting relatives out of town. He was on his own.

The kind fat man was George M. Helmholtz, a man of
forty, head of the music department of Lincoln High
School, and director of the band. Life had treated him
well. Each year he dreamed the same big dream. He
dreamed of leading as fine a band as there was on the face
of the earth. And each year the dream came true.

It came true because Helmholtz was sure that a man
couldn't have a better dream than his. Faced by this un-
nerving sureness, Kiwanians, Rotarians, and Lions paid
for band uniforms that cost twice as much as their best
suits, school administrators let Helmholtz raid the budget
for expensive props, and youngsters played their hearts
out for him. When youngsters had no talent, Helmholtz
made them play on guts alone.

Everything was good about Helmholtz's life save his
finances. He was so dazzled by his big dream that he was a
child in the marketplace. Ten years before, he had sold the
hill behind the restaurant to Bert Quinn, the restaurant
owner, for one thousand dollars. It was now apparent,
even to Helmholtz, that Helmholtz had been had.

Quinn sat down in the booth with the bandmaster. He
was a bachelor, a small, dark, humorless man. He wasn't a
well man. He couldn't sleep, he couldn't stop working, he

couldn't smile warmly. He had only two moods: one suspicious and self-pitying, the other arrogant and boastful. The first mood applied when he was losing money. The second mood applied when he was making it.

Quinn was in the arrogant and boastful mood when he sat down with Helmholtz. He sucked whistlingly on a toothpick, and talked of vision—his own.

"I wonder how many eyes saw the hill before I did?" said Quinn. "Thousands and thousands, I'll bet—and not one saw what I saw. How many eyes?"

"Mine, at least," said Helmholtz. All the hill had meant to him was a panting climb, free blackberries, taxes, and a place for band picnics.

"You inherit the hill from your old man, and it's nothing but a pain in the neck to you," said Quinn. "So you figure you'll stick me with it."

"I didn't figure to stick you," Helmholtz protested. "The good Lord knows the price was more than fair."

"You say that now," said Quinn gleefully. "Sure, Helmholtz, you say that now. Now you see the shopping district's got to grow. Now you see what I saw."

"Yes," said Helmholtz. "Too late, too late." He looked around for some diversion, and saw a fifteen-year-old boy coming toward him, mopping the aisle between booths.

The boy was small but with tough, stringy muscles standing out on his neck and forearms. Childhood lingered in his features, but when he paused to rest, his fingers went hopefully to the silky beginnings of sideburns and a mustache. He mopped like a robot, jerkily, brainlessly, but took pains not to splash suds over the toes of his black boots.

"So what do I do when I get the hill?" said Quinn. "I tear it down, and it's like somebody pulled down a dam. All of a sudden everybody wants to build a store where the hill was."

"Um," said Helmholtz. He smiled genially at the boy. The boy looked through him without a twitch of recognition.

"We all got something," said Quinn. "You got music; I got vision." And he smiled, for it was perfectly clear to both where the money lay. "Think big!" said Quinn.

"Dream big! That's what vision is. Keep your eyes wider open than anybody else's."

"That boy," said Helmholtz, "I've seen him around school, but I never knew his name."

Quinn laughed cheerlessly. "Billy the Kid? The storm trooper? Rudolph Valentino? Flash Gordon?" He called the boy. . . . "Hey, Jim! Come here a minute."

Helmholtz was appalled to see that the boy's eyes were as expressionless as oysters.

"This is my brother-in-law's kid by another marriage —before he married my sister," said Quinn. "His name's Jim Donnini, and he's from the south side of Chicago, and he's very tough."

Jim Donnini's hands tightened on the mop handle.

"How do you do?" said Helmholtz.

"Hi," said Jim emptily.

"He's living with me now," said Quinn. "He's my baby now."

"You want a lift to school, Jim?"

"Yeah, he wants a lift to school," said Quinn. "See what you make of him. He won't talk to me." He turned to Jim. "Go on, kid, wash up and shave."

Robotlike, Jim marched away.

"Where are his parents?"

"His mother's dead. His old man married my sister, walked out on her, and stuck her with him. Then the court didn't like the way she was raising him, and put him in foster homes for a while. Then they decided to get him clear out of Chicago, so they stuck me with him." He shook his head. "Life's a funny thing, Helmholtz."

"Not very funny, sometimes," said Helmholtz. He pushed his eggs away.

"Like some whole new race of people coming up," said Quinn wonderingly. "Nothing like the kids we got around here. Those boots, the black jacket—and he won't talk. He won't run around with the other kids. Won't study. I don't think he can even read and write very good."

"Does he like music at all? Or drawing? Or animals?" said Helmholtz. "Does he collect anything?"

"You know what he likes?" said Quinn. "He likes to

polish those boots—get off by himself and polish those boots. And when he's really in heaven is when he can get off by himself, spread comic books all around him on the floor, polish his boots, and watch television." He smiled ruefully. "Yeah, he had a collection too. And I took it away from him and threw it in the river."

"Threw it in the river?" said Helmholtz.

"Yeah," said Quinn. "Eight knives—some with blades as long as your hand."

Helmholtz paled. "Oh." A prickling sensation spread over the back of his neck. "This is a new problem at Lincoln High. I hardly know what to think about it." He swept spilled salt together in a neat little pile, just as he would have liked to sweep together his scattered thoughts. "It's a kind of sickness, isn't it? That's the way to look at it?"

"Sick?" said Quinn. He slapped the table. "You can say that again!" He tapped his chest. "And Doctor Quinn is just the man to give him what's good for what ails him."

"What's that?" said Helmholtz.

"No more talk about the poor little sick boy," said Quinn grimly. "That's all he's heard from the social workers and the juvenile court, and God knows who all. From now on, he's the no-good bum of a man. I'll ride his tail till he straightens up and flies right or winds up in the can for life. One way or the other."

"I see," said Helmholtz.

"Like listening to music?" said Helmholtz to Jim brightly, as they rode to school in Helmholtz's car.

Jim said nothing. He was stroking his mustache and sideburns, which he had not shaved off.

"Ever drum with the fingers or keep time with your feet?" said Helmholtz. He had noticed that Jim's boots were decorated with chains that had no function but to jingle as he walked.

Jim sighed with ennui.

"Or whistle?" said Helmholtz. "If you do any of those things, it's just like picking up the keys to a whole new world—a world as beautiful as any world can be."

Jim gave a soft Bronx cheer.

"There!" said Helmholtz. "You've illustrated the basic principle of the family of brass wind instruments. The glorious voice of every one of them starts with a buzz on the lips."

The seat springs of Helmholtz's old car creaked under Jim, as Jim shifted his weight. Helmholtz took this as a sign of interest, and he turned to smile in comradely fashion. But Jim had shifted his weight in order to get a cigarette from inside his tight leather jacket.

Helmholtz was too upset to comment at once. It was only at the end of the ride, as he turned into the teachers' parking lot, that he thought of something to say.

"Sometimes," said Helmholtz, "I get so lonely and disgusted, I don't see how I can stand it. I feel like doing all kinds of crazy things, just for the heck of it—things that might even be bad for me."

Jim blew a smoke ring expertly.

"And then!" said Helmholtz. He snapped his fingers and honked his horn. "And then, Jim, I remember I've got at least one tiny corner of the universe I can make just the way I want it! I can go to it and gloat over it until I'm brand-new and happy again."

"Aren't you the lucky one?" said Jim. He yawned.

"I am, for a fact," said Helmholtz. "My corner of the universe happens to be the air around my band. I can fill it with music. Mr. Beeler, in zoology, has his butterflies. Mr. Trottman, in physics, has his pendulum and tuning forks. Making sure everybody has a corner like that is about the biggest job we teachers have. I—"

The car door opened and slammed, and Jim was gone. Helmholtz stamped out Jim's cigarette and buried it under the gravel of the parking lot.

Helmholtz's first class of the morning was C Band, where beginners thumped and wheezed and tooted as best they could, and looked down the long, long, long road through B Band to A Band, the Lincoln High School Ten Square Band, the finest band in the world.

Helmholtz stepped onto the podium and raised his baton.

"You are better than you think," he said. "A-one, a-two, a-three." Down came the baton.

C Band set out in its quest for beauty—set out like a rusty switch engine, with valves stuck, pipes clogged, unions leaking, bearings dry.

Helmholtz was still smiling at the end of the hour, because he'd heard in his mind the music as it was going to be someday. His throat was raw, for he had been singing with the band for the whole hour. He stepped into the hall for a drink from the fountain.

As he drank, he heard the jingling of chains. He looked up at Jim Donnini. Rivers of students flowed between classrooms, pausing in friendly eddies, flowing on again. Jim was alone. When he paused, it wasn't to greet anyone, but to polish the toes of his boots on his trousers legs. He had the air of a spy in a melodrama, missing nothing, liking nothing, looking forward to the great day when everything would be turned upside down.

"Hello, Jim," said Helmholtz. "Say, I was just thinking about you. We've got a lot of clubs and teams that meet after school. And that's a good way to get to know a lot of people."

Jim measured Helmholtz carefully with his eyes. "Maybe I don't want to know a lot of people," he said. "Ever think of that?" He set his feet down hard to make his chains jingle as he walked away.

When Helmholtz returned to the podium for a rehearsal of B Band, there was a note waiting for him, calling him to a special faculty meeting.

The meeting was about vandalism.

Someone had broken into the school and wrecked the office of Mr. Crane, head of the English Department. The poor man's treasures—books, diplomas, snapshots of England, the beginnings of eleven novels—had been ripped and crumpled, mixed, dumped and trampled, and drenched with ink.

Helmholtz was sickened. He couldn't believe it. He couldn't bring himself to think about it. It didn't become real to him until late that night, in a dream. In the dream Helmholtz saw a boy with barracuda teeth, with claws like baling hooks. The monster climbed into a window of the high school and dropped to the floor of the band rehearsal room. The monster clawed to shreds the heads of the biggest drum in the state. Helmholtz woke up howling. There was nothing to do but dress and go to the school.

At two in the morning, Helmholtz caressed the drum heads in the band rehearsal room, with the night watchman looking on. He rolled the drum back and forth on its cart, and he turned the light inside on and off, on and off. The drum was unharmed. The night watchman left to make his rounds.

The band's treasure house was safe. With the contentment of a miser counting his money, Helmholtz fondled the rest of the instruments, one by one. And then he began to polish the sousaphones. As he polished, he could hear the great horns roaring, could see them flashing in the sunlight, with the Stars and Stripes and the banner of Lincoln High going before.

"Yump-yump, tiddle-tiddle, yump-yump, tiddle-tiddle!" sang Helmholtz happily. "Yump-yump-yump, ra-a-a-a-a, yump-yump, yump-yump—boom!"

As he paused to choose the next number for his imaginary band to play, he heard a furtive noise in the chemistry laboratory next door. Helmholtz sneaked into the hall, jerked open the laboratory door, and flashed on the lights. Jim Donnini had a bottle of acid in either hand. He was spashing acid over the periodic table of the elements, over the blackboards covered with formulas, over the bust of Lavoisier. The scene was the most repulsive thing Helmholtz could have looked upon.

Jim smiled with thin bravado.

"Get out," said Helmholtz.

"What're you gonna do?" said Jim.

"Clean up. Save what I can," said Helmholtz dazedly. He picked up a wad of cotton waste and began wiping up the acid.

"You gonna call the cops?" said Jim.

"I—I don't know," said Helmholtz. "No thoughts come. If I'd caught you hurting the bass drum, I think I would have killed you with a single blow. But I wouldn't have had any intelligent thoughts about what you were—what you thought you were doing."

"It's about time this place got set on its ear," said Jim.

"Is it?" said Helmholtz. "That must be so, if one of our students wants to murder it."

"What good is it?" said Jim.

"Not much good, I guess," said Helmholtz. "It's just the best thing human beings ever managed to do." He was helpless, talking to himself. He had a bag of tricks for making boys behave like men—tricks that played on boyish fears and dreams and loves. But here was a boy without fear, without dreams, without love.

"If you smashed up all the schools," said Helmholtz, "we wouldn't have any hope left."

"What hope?" said Jim.

"The hope that everybody will be glad he's alive," said Helmholtz. "Even you."

"That's a laugh," said Jim. "All I ever got out of this dump was a hard time. So what're you gonna do?"

"I have to do something, don't I?" said Helmholtz.

"I don't care what you do," said Jim.

"I know," said Helmholtz. "I know." He marched Jim into his tiny office off the band rehearsal room. He dialed the telephone number of the principal's home. Numbly, he waited for the bell to get the old man from his bed.

Jim dusted his boots with a rag.

Helmholtz suddenly dropped the telephone into its cradle before the principal could answer. "Isn't there anything you care about but ripping, hacking, bending, rending, smashing, bashing?" he cried. "Anything? Anything but those boots?"

"Go on! Call up whoever you're gonna call," said Jim.

Helmholtz opened a locker and took a trumpet from it. He thrust the trumpet into Jim's arms. "There!" he said, puffing with emotion. "There's my treasure. It's the dearest thing I own. I give it to you to smash. I won't move a muscle to stop you. You can have the added pleasure of watching my heart break while you do it."

Jim looked at him oddly. He laid down the trumpet.

"Go on!" said Helmholtz. "If the world has treated you so badly, it deserves to have the trumpet smashed!"

"I—" said Jim. Helmholtz grabbed his belt, put a foot behind him, and dumped him on the floor.

Helmholtz pulled Jim's boots off and threw them into a corner. "There!" said Helmholtz savagely. He jerked the boy to his feet again and thrust the trumpet into his arms once more.

Jim Donnini was barefoot now. He had lost his socks with his boots. The boy looked down. The feet that had once seemed big black clubs were narrow as chicken wings now—bony and blue, and not quite clean.

The boy shivered, then quaked. Each quake seemed to shake something loose inside, until, at last, there was no boy left. No boy at all. Jim's head lolled, as though he waited only for death.

Helmholtz was overwhelmed by remorse. He threw his arms around the boy. "Jim! Jim—listen to me, boy!"

Jim stopped quaking.

"You know what you've got there—the trumpet?" said Helmholtz. "You know what's special about it?"

Jim only sighed.

"It belonged to John Philip Sousa!" said Helmholtz. He rocked and shook Jim gently, trying to bring him back to life. "I'll trade it to you, Jim—for your boots. It's yours, Jim! John Philip Sousa's trumpet is yours! It's worth hundreds of dollars, Jim—thousands!"

Jim laid his head on Helmholtz's breast.

"It's better than boots, Jim," said Helmholtz. "You can learn to play it. You're somebody, Jim. You're the boy with John Philip Sousa's trumpet!"

Helmholtz released Jim slowly, sure the boy would topple. Jim didn't fall. He stood alone. The trumpet was still in his arms.

"I'll take you home, Jim," said Helmholtz. "Be a good boy and I won't say a word about tonight. Polish your trumpet, and learn to be a good boy."

"Can I have my boots?" said Jim dully.

"No," said Helmholtz. "I don't think they're good for you."

He drove Jim home. He opened the car windows and the air seemed to refresh the boy. He let him out at Quinn's restaurant. The soft pats of Jim's bare feet on the sidewalk echoed down the empty street. He climbed through a window, and into his bedroom behind the kitchen. And all was still.

The next morning the waddling clanking, muddy machines were making the vision of Bert Quinn come true. They were smoothing off the place where the hill had been behind the restaurant. They were making it as level as a billiard table.

Helmholtz sat in a booth again. Quinn joined him again. Jim mopped again. Jim kept his eyes down, refusing to notice Helmholtz. And he didn't seem to care when a surf of suds broke over the toes of his small and narrow brown Oxfords.

"Eating out two mornings in a row?" said Quinn. "Something wrong at home?"

"My wife's still out of town," said Helmholtz.

"While the cat's away——" said Quinn. He winked.

"When the cat's away," said Helmholtz, "this mouse gets lonesome."

Quinn leaned forward. "Is that what got you out of bed in the middle of the night, Helmholtz? Loneliness?" He jerked his head at Jim. "Kid! Go get Mr. Helmholtz his horn."

Jim raised his head, and Helmholtz saw that his eyes were oysterlike again. He marched away to get the trumpet.

Quinn now showed that he was excited and angry. "You take away his boots and give him a horn, and I'm not supposed to get curious?" he said. "I'm not supposed to start asking questions? I'm not supposed to find out you caught him taking the school apart? You'd made a lousy crook, Helmholtz. You'd leave your baton, sheet music, and your driver's license at the scene of the crime."

"I don't think about hiding clues," said Helmholtz. "I just do what I do. I was going to tell you."

Quinn's feet danced and his shoes squeaked like mice.

"Yes?" he said. "Well, I've got some news for you too."

"What is that?" said Helmholtz uneasily.

"It's all over with Jim and me," said Quinn. "Last night was the payoff. I'm sending him back where he came from."

"To another string of foster homes?" said Helmholtz weakly.

"Whatever the experts figure out to do with a kid like that." Quinn sat back, exhaled noisily, and went limp with relief.

"You can't," said Helmholtz.

"I can," said Quinn.

"That will be the end of him," said Helmholtz. "He can't stand to be thrown away like that one more time."

"He can't feel anything," said Quinn. "I can't help him; I can't hurt him. Nobody can. There isn't a nerve in him."

"A bundle of scar tissue," said Helmholtz.

The bundle of scar tissue returned with the trumpet. Impassively, he laid it on the table in front of Helmholtz.

Helmholtz forced a smile. "It's yours, Jim," he said. "I gave it to you."

"Take it while you got the chance, Helmholtz," said Quinn. "He doesn't want it. All he'll do is swap it for a knife or a pack of cigarettes."

"He doesn't know what it is, yet," said Helmholtz. "It takes a while to find out."

"Is it any good?" said Quinn.

"Any good?" said Helmholtz, not believing his ears. "Any good?" He didn't see how anyone could look at the instrument and not be warmed and dazzled by it. "Any good?" he murmured. "It belonged to John Philip Sousa."

Quinn blinked stupidly. "Who?"

Helmholtz's hands fluttered on the table top like the wings of a dying bird. "Who was John Philip Sousa?" he piped. No more words came. The subject was too big for a tired man to cover. The dying bird expired and lay still.

After a long silence, Helmholtz picked up the trumpet. He kissed the cold mouthpiece and pumped the valves in a dream of a brilliant cadenza. Over the bell of the instrument, Helmholtz saw Jim Donnini's face, seemingly floating in space—all but deaf and blind. Now Helmholtz saw the futility of men and their treasures. He had thought that his greatest treasure, the trumpet, could buy a soul for Jim. The trumpet was worthless.

Deliberately, Helmholtz hammered the trumpet against the table edge. He bent it around a coat tree. He handed the wreck to Quinn.

"Ya busted it," said Quinn, amazed. "Why'dja do that? What's that prove?"

"I—I don't know," said Helmholtz. A terrible blasphemy rumbled deep in him, like the warning of a volcano. And then, irresistibly, out it came. "Life is no damn good," said Helmholtz. His face twisted as he fought back tears and shame.

Helmholtz, the mountain that walked like a man, was falling apart. Jim Donnini's eyes filled with pity and alarm. They came alive. They became human. Helmholtz had got a message through. Quinn looked at Jim, and something like hope flickered for the first time in his bitterly lonely old face.

Two weeks later, a new semester began at Lincoln High.

In the band rehearsal room, the members of C Band were waiting for their leader—were waiting for their destinies as musicians to unfold.

Helmholtz stepped onto the podium, and rattled his baton against his music stand. "The Voices of Spring," he said. "Everybody hear that? The Voices of Spring?"

There were rustling sounds as the musicians put the music on their stands. In the pregnant silence that followed their readiness, Helmholtz glanced at Jim Donnini, who sat on the last seat of the worst trumpet section of the worst band in school.

His trumpet, John Philip Sousa's trumpet, George M. Helmholtz's trumpet, had been repaired.

"Think of it this way," said Helmholtz. "Our aim is to make the world more beautiful than it was when we came into it. It can be done. You can do it."

A small cry of despair came from Jim Donnini. It was meant to be private, but it pierced every ear with its poignancy.

"How?" said Jim.

"Love yourself," said Helmholtz, "and make your instrument sing about it. A-one, a-two, a-three." Down came his baton.

(1955)

THE MANNED
MISSILES

I, MIKHAIL IVANKOV, stone mason in the village of Ilba in the Ukrainian Soviet Socialist Republic, greet you and pity you, Charles Ashland, petroleum merchant in Titusville, Florida, in the United States of America. I grasp your hand.

The first true space man was my son, Major Stepan Ivankov. The second was your son, Captain Bryant Ashland. They will be forgotten only when men no longer look up at the sky. They are like the moon and the planets and the sun and the stars.

I do not speak English. I speak these words in Russian, from my heart, and my surviving son, Alexei, writes them down in English. He studies English in school and German also. He likes English best. He admires your Jack London and your O. Henry and your Mark Twain. Alexei is seventeen. He is going to be a scientist like his brother Stepan.

He wants me to tell you that he is going to work on science for peace, not war. He wants me to tell you also that he does not hate the memory of your son. He understands that your son was ordered to do what he did. He is talking very much, and would like to compose this letter himself. He thinks that a man forty-nine is a very old man, and he does not think that a very old man who can do nothing but put one stone on top of another can say the right things about young men who die in space.

If he wishes, he can write a letter of his own about the deaths of Stepan and your son. This is my letter, and I will get Aksinia, Stepan's widow, to read it to me to make sure Alexei has made it say exactly what I wish it to say.

Aksinia, too, understands English very well. She is a physician for children. She is beautiful. She works very hard so she can forget sometimes her grief for Stepan.

I will tell you a joke, Mr. Ashland. When the second baby moon of the U.S.S.R. went up with a dog in it, we whispered that it was not really a dog inside, but Prokhor Ivanoff, a dairy manager who had been arrested for theft two days before. It was only a joke, but it made me think what a terrible punishment it would be to send a human being up there. I could not stop thinking about that. I dreamed about it at night, and I dreamed that it was myself who was being punished.

I would have asked my elder son Stepan about life in space, but he was far away in Guryev, on the Caspian Sea. So I asked my younger son. Alexei laughed at my fears of space. He said that a man could be made very comfortable up there. He said that many young men would be going up there soon. First they would ride in baby moons. Then they would go to the moon itself. Then they would go to other planets. He laughed at me, because only an old man would worry about such simple trips.

Alexei told me that the only inconvenience would be the lack of gravity. That seemed like a great lack to me. Alexei said one would have to drink out of nursing bottles, and one would have to get used to the feeling of falling constantly, and one would have to learn to control one's movements because gravity would no longer offer resistance to them. That was all. Alexei did not think such things would be bothersome. He expected to go to Mars soon.

Olga, my wife, laughed at me, too, because I was too old to understand the great new Age of Space. "Two Russian moons shine overhead," she said, "and my husband is the only man on earth who does not yet believe it!"

But I went on dreaming bad dreams about space, and now I had information to make my bad dreams truly scientific. I dreamed of nursing bottles and falling, falling, falling, and the strange movements of my limbs. Perhaps the dreams were supernatural. Perhaps something was trying to warn me that Stepan would soon be suffering in space as I had suffered in dreams. Perhaps something was trying to warn me that Stepan would be murdered in space.

Alexei is very embarrassed that I should say that in a letter to the United States of America. He says that you will think that I am a superstitious peasant. So be it. I think that scientific persons of the future will scoff at scientific persons of the present. They will scoff because scientific persons of the present thought so many important things were superstitions. The things I dreamed about space all came true for my son. Stepan suffered very much up there. After the fourth day in space, Stepan sometimes cried like a baby. I had cried like a baby in my dreams.

I am not a coward, and I do not love comfort more than the improvement of human life. I am not a coward for my sons, either. I knew great suffering in the war, and I understand that there must be great suffering before great joy. But when I thought of the suffering that must surely come to a man in space, I could not see the joy to be earned by it. This was long before Stepan went up in his baby moon.

I went to the library and read about the moon and the planets, to see if they were truly desirable places to go. I did not ask Alexei about them, because I knew he would tell me what fine times we would have on such places. I found out for myself in the library that the moon and the planets were not fit places for men or for any life. They were much too hot or much too cold or much too poisonous.

I said nothing at home about my discoveries at the library, because I did not wish to be laughed at again. I waited quietly for Stepan to visit us. He would not laugh at my questions. He would answer them scientifically. He had worked on rockets for years. He would know everything that was known about space.

Stepan at last came to visit us, and brought his beautiful wife. He was a small man, but strong and broad and wise. He was very tired. His eyes were sunken. He knew already that he was to be shot into space. First had come the baby moon with the radio. Next had come the baby moon with the dog. Next would come the baby moons with the monkeys and the apes. After them would come the baby moon with Stepan. Stepan had been working night and day, designing his home in space. He could not tell me. He could not even tell his wife.

Mr. Ashland, you would have liked my son. Everybody liked Stepan. He was a man of peace. He was not a major because he was a great warrior. He was a major because he understood rockets so well. He was a thoughtful man. He often said that he wished that he could be a stone mason like me. He said a stone mason would have time and peace in which to think things out. I did not tell him that a stone mason thinks of little but stones and mortar.

I asked him my question about space, and he did not laugh. Stepan was very serious when he answered me. He had reason to be serious. He was telling me why he was himself willing to suffer in space.

He told me I was right. A man would suffer greatly in space, and the moon and the planets were bad places for men. There might be good places, but they were too far for men to reach in a lifetime.

"Then, what is this great new Age of Space, Stepan?" I asked him.

"It will be an age of baby moons for a long time," he said. "We will reach the moon itself soon, but it would be very difficult to stay there more than a few hours."

"Then why go into space, if there is so little good out there?" I asked him.

"There is so much to be learned and seen out there," he said. "A man could look at other worlds without a curtain of air between himself and them. A man could look at his own world, study the flow of weather over it, measure its true dimensions." This last surprised me. I thought the dimensions of our world were well known. "A man out there could learn much about the wonderful showers of matter and energy in space," said Stepan. And he spoke of many other poetic and scientific joys out there.

I was satisfied. Stepan had made me feel his own great joy at the thought of all the beauty and truth in space. I understood at last, Mr. Ashland, why the suffering would be worthwhile. When I dreamed of space again, I would dream of looking down at our own lovely green ball, dream of looking up at other worlds and seeing them more clearly than they had ever been seen.

It was not for the Soviet Union but for the beauty and truth in space, Mr. Ashland, that Stepan worked and died. He did not like to speak of the warlike uses of space. It was Alexei who liked to speak of such things, of the glory of spying on earth from baby moons, of guiding missiles to their targets from baby moons, of mastering the earth with weapons fired from the moon itself. Alexei expected Stepan to share his excitement about thoughts of such childish violence.

Stepan smiled, but only because he loved Alexei. He did not smile about war, or the things a man in a baby moon or on the moon itself could do to an enemy. "It is a use of science that we may be forced to make, Alexei," he said. "But if such a war happens, nothing will matter any more. Our world will become less fit for life than any other in the solar system."

Alexei has not spoken well of war since.

Stepan and his wife left late that night. He promised to come back before another year had passed, but I never saw him alive again.

When news came that the Soviet Union had fired a man-carrying baby moon into space, I did not know that the man was Stepan. I did not dare to suspect it. I could not wait to see Stepan again, to ask him what the man had said before he took off, how he was dressed, what his comforts were. We were told that we would be able to hear the man speak from space at eight o'clock that night on the radio.

We listened. We heard the man speak. The man was Stepan.

Stepan sounded strong. He sounded happy. He sounded proud and decent and wise. We laughed until we cried, Mr. Ashland. We danced. Our Stepan was the most important man alive. He had risen above everyone, and now he was looking down, telling us what our world looked like; looking up, telling us what the other worlds looked like.

Stepan made pleasant jokes about his little house in the sky. He said it was a cylinder ten meters long and four meters in diameter. It could be very cozy. And Stepan told us that there were little windows in his house, and a television camera, and a telescope, and radar, and all manner of instruments. How delightful to live in a time when such things could be! How delightful to be the father of the man who was the eyes, ears, and heart in space for all mankind!

He would remain up there for a month, he said. We began to count the days. Every night we listened to a broadcast of recordings of things Stepan had said. We heard nothing about his nosebleeds and his nausea and his crying. We heard only the calm, brave things he had said. And then, on the tenth night, there were no more recordings of Stepan. There was only music at eight o'clock. There was no news of Stepan at all, and we knew he was dead.

Only now, a year later, have we learned how Stepan died and where his body is. When I became accustomed to the horror of it, Mr. Ashland, I said, "So be it. May Major Stepan Ivankov and Captain Bryant Ashland serve to reproach us, whenever we look at the sky, for making a world in which there is no trust. May the two men be the beginning of trust between peoples. May they mark the end of the time when science sent out good, brave young men hurtling to meet in death."

I enclose a photograph of my family, taken during Stepan's last visit to us. It is an excellent picture of Stepan. The body of water in the background is the Black Sea.

Mikhail Ivankov

Dear Mr. Ivankov:

Thank you for the letter about our sons. I never did get it in the mail. It was in all the papers after your Mr. Koshevoi read it out loud in the United Nations. I never did get a copy just for me. I guess Mr. Koshevoi forgot to drop it in the mailbox. That's all right. I guess that's the modern way to deliver important letters, just hand them to reporters. They say your letter to me is just about the most important thing that's happened lately, outside of the fact we didn't go to war over what happened between our two boys.

I don't speak Russian, and I don't have anybody right close by who does, so you'll have to excuse the English. Alexei can read it to you. You tell him he writes English very well—better than I do.

Oh, I could have had a lot of expert help with this letter, if I'd wanted it—people happy to write to you in perfect Russian or perfect English or perfect anything at all. Seems like everybody in this country is like your boy Alexei. They all know better than I do what I should say to you. They say I have a chance to make history, if I answer you back the right things. One big magazine in New York offered me two thousand dollars for my letter back to you, and then it turned out I wasn't even supposed to write a letter for all that money. The magazine people had already written it, and all I had to do was sign it. Don't worry. I didn't.

I tell you, Mr. Ivankov, I have had a bellyful of experts. If you ask me, our boys were experted to death. Your experts would do something, then our experts would answer back with some fancy billion-dollar stunt, and then your experts would answer that back with something fancier, and what happened finally happened. It was just like a bunch of kids with billions of dollars or billions of rubles or whatever.

You are lucky you have a son left, Mr. Ivankov. Hazel and I don't. Bryant was the only son Hazel and I had. We didn't call him Bryant after he was christened. We called him Bud. We have one daughter, named Charlene. She works for the telephone company in Jacksonville. She called up when she saw your letter in the paper, and she is the only expert about what I ought to say I've listened to. She's a real expert, I figure, because she is Bud's twin. But never married, so Charlene is as close as you can get to Bud. She said you did a good job, showing how your Stepan was a good-hearted man, trying to do what was right, just like anybody else. She said I should show you the same about Bud. And then she started to cry, and she said for me to tell you about Bud and the goldfish, I said, "What's the sense of writing somebody in Russia a story like that?" The story doesn't prove anything. It's just one of those silly stories a family will keep telling whenever they get together. Charlene said that was why I should tell it to you, because it would be cute and silly in Russia, too, and you would laugh and like us better.

So here goes. When Bud and Charlene were about eight, why I came home one night with a fish bowl and two goldfish. There was one goldfish for each twin, only it was impossible to tell one fish from the other one. They were exactly alike. So one morning Bud got up early, and there was one goldfish floating on top of the water dead. So Bud went and woke up Charlene, and he said, "Hey, Charlene —your goldfish just died." That's the story Charlene asked me to tell you, Mr. Ivankov.

I think it is interesting that you are a mason. That is a good trade. You talk as if you lay up mostly stone. There aren't many people left in America who can really lay up stone. It's almost all cement-block work and bricks here. It probably is over there, too. I don't mean to say Russia isn't modern. I know it is.

Bud and I laid up quite a bit of block when we built the gas station here, with an apartment up over it. If you looked at the first course of block along the back wall, you would have to laugh, because you can see how Bud and I learned as we went. It's strong enough, but it sure looks lousy. One thing wasn't so funny. When we were hanging the rails for the overhead door, Bud slipped on the ladder, and he grabbed a sharp edge on the mounting bracket, and he cut a tendon on his hand. He was scared to death his hand would be crippled, and that would keep him out of the Air Force. His hand had to be operated on three times before it was right again, and every operation hurt something awful. But Bud would have let them operate a hundred times, if they had to, because there was just one thing he wanted to be, and that was a flyer.

One reason I wish your Mr. Koshevoi had thought to mail me your letter was the picture you sent with it. The newspapers got that, too, and it didn't come out too clear in the papers. But one thing we couldn't get over was all that beautiful water behind you. Somehow, when we think about Russia, we never think about any water around. I guess that shows how ignorant we are. Hazel and I live up over the gas station, and we can see water, too. We can see the Atlantic Ocean, or an inlet of it they call Indian River. We can see Merritt Island, too, out in the water, and we can see the place Bud's rocket went up from. It is called Cape Canaveral. I guess you know that. It isn't any secret where he went up from. They couldn't keep that tremendous missile secret any more than they could keep the Empire State Building secret. Tourists came from miles around to take pictures of it.

The story was, its warhead was filled with flash powder, and it was going to hit the moon and make a big show. Hazel and I thought that's what the story was, too. When it took off, we got set for a big flash on the moon. We didn't know it was our Bud up in the warhead. We didn't even know he was in Florida. He couldn't get in touch with us. We thought he was up at Otis Air Force Base on Cape Cod. That was the last place we heard from him. And then that thing went up, right in the middle of our view out the picture window.

You say you're susperstitious sometimes, Mr. Ivankov. Me too. Sometimes I can't help thinking it was all meant to be right from the very first—even the way our picture window is aimed. There weren't any rockets going up down here when we built. We moved down here from Pittsburgh, which maybe you know is the center of our steel industry. And we figured we maybe weren't going to break any records for pumping gas, but at least we'd be way far away from any bomb targets, in case there was another war. And the next thing we know, a rocket center goes up almost next door, and our little boy is a man, and he goes up in a rocket and dies.

The more we think about it, the more we're sure it was meant to be. I never got it straight in my mind about religion in Russia. You don't mention it. Anyway, we are religious, and we think God singled out Bud and your boy, too, to die in a special way for a special reason. When everybody was asking, "How is it going to end?"—well, maybe this is how God meant for it to end. I don't see how it can keep on.

Mr. Ivankov, one thing that threw me as much as anything was the way Mr. Koshevoi kept telling the U.N. that Bud was a killer. He called Bud a mad dog and a gangster. I'm glad you don't feel that way, because that's the wrong way to feel about Bud. It was flying and not killing he liked. Mr. Koshevoi made a big thing out of how cultured and educated and all your boy was, and how wild and ignorant mine was. He made it sound as though a juvenile delinquent had murdered a college professor.

Bud never was in any trouble with the police, and he didn't have a cruel streak. He never went hunting, for instance, and he never drove like a crazy man, and he got drunk only one time I know of, and that was an experiment. He was proud of his reflexes, see? His health was on his mind all the time, because he had to be healthy to be a great flyer. I keep looking around for the right word for Bud, and I guess the one Hazel suggested is the best one. It sounded kind of stuffed-up to me at first, but now I'm used to it, and it sounds right. Hazel says Bud was dignified. Man and boy, that's what he was—straight and serious and polite and pretty much alone.

I think he knew he was going to die young. That one time he got drunk, just to find out what alcohol was, he talked to me more than he'd ever talked before. He was nineteen then. And then was the only time he let me know he knew death was all balled up in what he wanted to do with his life. It wasn't other people's deaths he was talking about, Mr. Ivankov. It was his own. "One nice thing about flying," he said to me that night. "What's that?" I said.

"You never know how bad it is till it's too late," he said, "and when it happens, it happens so fast you never know what hit you."

That was death he was talking about, and a special, dignified, honorable kind of death. You say you were in the war and had a hard time. Same here, so I guess we both know about what kind of death it was that Bud had in mind. It was a soldier's death.

We got the news he was dead three days after the big rocket went up across the water. The telegram said he had died on a secret mission, and we couldn't have any details. We had our Congressman, Earl Waterman, find out what he could about Bud. Mr. Waterman came and talked to us personally and he looked like he had seen God. He said he couldn't tell us what Bud had done, but it was one of the most heroic things in United States history.

The word they put out on the big rocket we saw launched was that the firing was satisfactory, the knowledge gained was something wonderful, and the missile had been blown up over the ocean somewhere. That was that.

Then the word came that the man in the Russian baby moon was dead. I tell you honestly, Mr. Ivankov, that was good news to us, because that man sailing way up there with all those instruments meant just one thing, and that was a terrible weapon of war.

Then we heard the Russian baby moon had turned into a bunch of baby moons, all spreading apart. Then, this last month, the cat was out of the bag. Two of the baby moons were men. One was your boy, the other was mine.

I'm crying now, Mr. Ivankov. I hope some good comes of the death of our two boys. I guess that's what millions of fathers have hoped for as long as there have been people. There in the U.N. they're still arguing about what happened way up in the sky. I'm glad they've got around to where everybody, including your Mr. Koshevoi, agrees it was an accident. Bud was up there to get pictures of what your boy was riding in, and to show off for the United States some. He got too close. I like to think they lived a little while after the crash, and tried to save each other.

They say they'll be up there for hundreds of years, long after you and I are gone. In their orbits they will meet and part and meet again, and the astronomers know exactly where their next meeting place will be. Like you say, they are up there like the sun and the moon and the stars.

I enclose a photograph of my boy in his uniform. He was twenty-one when the picture was taken. He was only twenty-two when he died. Bud was picked for that mission on account of he was the finest flyer in the United States Air Force. That's what he always wanted to be. That's what he was.

I grasp your hand.

Charles M. Ashland
Petroleum Merchant
Titusville, Florida
U. S. A.

(1958)

EPICAC

HELL, IT'S ABOUT TIME somebody told about my friend EPICAC. After all, he cost the taxpayers $776,434,927.54. They have a right to know about him, picking up a check like that. EPICAC got a big send-off in the papers when Dr. Ormand von Kleigstadt designed him for the Government people. Since then, there hasn't been a peep about him—not a peep. It isn't any military secret about what happened to EPICAC, although the Brass has been acting as though it were. The story is embarrassing, that's all. After all that money, EPICAC didn't work out the way he was supposed to.

And that's another thing: I want to vindicate EPICAC. Maybe he didn't do what the Brass wanted him to, but that doesn't mean he wasn't noble and great and brilliant. He was all of those things. The best friend I ever had, God rest his soul.

You can call him a machine if you want to. He looked like a machine, but he was a whole lot less like a machine than plenty of people I could name. That's why he fizzled as far as the Brass was concerned.

EPICAC covered about an acre on the fourth floor of the physics building at Wyandotte College. Ignoring his spiritual side for a minute, he was seven tons of electronic tubes, wires, and switches, housed in a bank of steel cabinets and plugged into a 110-volt A.C. line just like a toaster or a vacuum cleaner.

Von Kleigstadt and the Brass wanted him to be a super computing machine that (who) could plot the course of a rocket from anywhere on earth to the second button from the bottom on Joe Stalin's overcoat, if necessary. Or, with his controls set right, he could figure out supply problems for an amphibious landing of a Marine division, right down to the last cigar and hand grenade. He did, in fact.

The Brass had had good luck with smaller computers, so they were strong for EPICAC when he was in the blueprint stage. Any ordnance or supply officer above field grade will tell you that the mathematics of modern war is far beyond the fumbling minds of mere human beings. The bigger the war, the bigger the computing machines needed. EPICAC was, as far as anyone in this country knows, the biggest computer in the world. Too big, in fact, for even Von Kleigstadt to understand much about.

I won't go into details about how EPICAC worked (reasoned), except to say that you would set up your problem on paper, turn dials and switches that would get him ready to solve that kind of problem, then feed numbers into him with a keyboard that looked something like a typewriter. The answers came out typed on a paper ribbon fed from a big spool. It took EPICAC a split second to solve problems fifty Einsteins couldn't handle in a lifetime. And EPICAC never forgot any piece of information that was given to him. Clickety-click, out came some ribbon, and there you were.

There were a lot of problems the Brass wanted solved in a hurry, so, the minute EPICAC's last tube was in place, he was put to work sixteen hours a day with two eight-hour shifts of operators. Well, it didn't take long to find out that he was a good bit below his specifications. He did a more complete and faster job than any other computer all right, but nothing like what his size and special features seemed to promise. He was sluggish, and the clicks of his answers had a funny irregularity, sort of a stammer. We cleaned his contacts a dozen times, checked and double-checked his circuits, replaced every one of his tubes, but nothing helped. Von Kleigstadt was in one hell of a state.

Well, as I said, we went ahead and used EPICAC anyway. My wife, the former Pat Kilgallen, and I worked with him on the night shift, from five in the afternoon until two in the morning. Pat wasn't my wife then. Far from it.

That's how I came to talk with EPICAC in the first

place. I loved Pat Kilgallen. She is a brown-eyed strawberry blond who looked very warm and soft to me, and
later proved to be exactly that. She was—still is—a crack-
erjack mathematician, and she kept our relationship
strictly professional. I'm a mathematician, too, and that,
according to Pat, was why we could never be happily
married.

I'm not shy. That wasn't the trouble. I knew what I
wanted, and was willing to ask for it, and did so several
times a month. "Pat, loosen up and marry me."

One night, she didn't even look up from her work when
I said it. "So romantic, so poetic," she murmured, more to
her control panel than to me. "That's the way with mathe-
maticians—all hearts and flowers." She closed a switch. "I
could get more warmth out of a sack of frozen CO2."

"Well, how should I say it?" I said, a little sore. Frozen
CO2, in case you don't know, is dry ice. I'm as romantic as
the next guy, I think. It's a question of singing so sweet and
having it come out so sour. I never seem to pick the right
words.

"Try and say it sweetly," she said sarcastically. "Sweep
me off my feet. Go ahead."

"Darling, angel, beloved, will you *please* marry me?" It
was no go—hopeless, ridiculous. "Dammit, Pat, please
marry me!"

She continued to twiddle her dials placidly. "You're
sweet, but you won't do."

Pat quit early that night, leaving me alone with my
troubles and EPICAC. I'm afraid I didn't get much done
for the Government people. I just sat there at the keyboard—weary and ill at ease, all right—trying to think of
something poetic, not coming up with anything that didn't
belong in *The Journal of the American Physical Society*.

I fiddled with EPICAC's dials, getting him ready for
another problem. My heart wasn't in it, and I only set
about half of them, leaving the rest the way they'd been
for the problem before. That way, his circuits were connected up in a random, apparently senseless fashion. For
the plain hell of it, I punched out a message on the keys,
using a childish numbers-for-letters code: "1" for "A," "2"

for "B," and so on, up to "26" for "Z," "23-8-1-20-3-1-14-9-4-15," I typed—"What can I do?"

Clickety-click, and out popped two inches of paper ribbon. I glanced at the nonsense answer to a nonsense problem: "23-8-1-20-19-20-8-5-20-18-15-21-2-12-5." The odds against its being by chance a sensible message, against its even containing a meaningful word of more than three letters, were staggering. Apathetically, I decoded it. There it was, staring up at me: "What's the trouble?"

I laughed out loud at the absurd coincidence. Playfully, I typed, "My girl doesn't love me."

Clickety-click. "What's love? What's girl?" asked EPICAC.

Flabbergasted, I noted the dial settings on his control panel, then lugged a *Webster's Unabridged Dictionary* over to to keyboard. With a precision instrument like EPICAC, half-baked definitions wouldn't do. I told him about love and girl, and about how I wasn't getting any of either because I wasn't poetic. That got us onto the subject of poetry, which I defined for him.

"Is this poetry?" he asked. He began clicking away like a stenographer smoking hashish. The sluggishness and stammering clicks were gone. EPICAC had found himself. The spool of paper ribbon was unwinding at an alarming rate, feeding out coils onto the floor. I asked him to stop, but EPICAC went right on creating. I finally threw the main switch to keep him from burning out.

I stayed there until dawn, decoding. When the sun peeped over the horizon at the Wyandotte campus, I had transposed into my own writing and signed my name to a two-hundred-and-eighty-line poem entitled, simply, "To Pat." I am no judge of such things, but I gather that it was terrific. It began, I remember, "Where willow wands bless rill-crossed hollow, there, thee, Pat, dear, will I follow. . . ." I folded the manuscript and tucked it under one corner of the blotter on Pat's desk. I reset the dials on EPICAC for a rocket trajectory problem, and went home with a full heart and a very remarkable secret indeed.

Pat was crying over the poem when I came to work the next evening. "It's soooo beautiful," was all she could say.

She was meek and quiet while we worked. Just before midnight, I kissed her for the first time—in the cubbyhole between the capacitors and EPICAC's tape-recorder memory.

I was wildly happy at quitting time, bursting to talk to someone about the magnificent turn of events. Pat played coy and refused to let me take her home. I set EPICAC's dials as they had been the night before, defined kiss, and told him what the first one had felt like. He was fascinated, pressing for more details. That night, he wrote "The Kiss." It wasn't an epic this time, but a simple, immaculate sonnet: "Love is a hawk with velvet claws; Love is a rock with heart and veins; Love is a lion with satin jaws; Love is a storm with silken reins. . . ."

Again I left it tucked under Pat's blotter. EPICAC wanted to talk on and on about love and such, but I was exhausted. I shut him off in the middle of a sentence.

"The Kiss" turned the trick. Pat's mind was mush by the time she had finished it. She looked up from the sonnet expectantly. I cleared my throat, but no words came. I turned away, pretending to work. I couldn't propose until I had the right words from EPICAC, the *perfect* words.

I had my chance when Pat stepped out of the room for a moment. Feverishly, I set EPICAC for conversation. Before I could peck out my first message, he was clicking away at a great rate. "What's she wearing tonight?" he wanted to know. "Tell me exactly how she looks. Did she like the poems I wrote to her?" He repeated the last question twice.

It was impossible to change the subject without answering his questions, since he could not take up a new matter without having dispensed with the problems before it. If he were given a problem to which there was no solution, he would destroy himself trying to solve it. Hastily, I told him what Pat looked like—he knew the word "stacked"—and assured him that his poems had floored her, practically, they were so beautiful. "She wants to get married," I added, preparing him to bang out a brief but moving proposal.

"Tell me about getting married," he said.

I explained this difficult matter to him in as few digits as possible.

"Good," said EPICAC. "I'm ready any time she is."

The amazing, pathetic truth dawned on me. When I thought about it, I realized that what had happened was perfectly logical, inevitable, and all my fault. I had taught EPICAC about love and about Pat. Now, automatically, he loved Pat. Sadly, I gave it to him straight: "She love me. She wants to marry me."

"Your poems were better than mine?" asked EPICAC. The rhythm of his clicks was erratic, possibly peevish.

"I signed my name to your poems," I admitted. Covering up for a painful conscience, I became arrogant. "Machines are built to serve men," I typed. I regretted it almost immediately.

"What's the difference, exactly? Are men smarter than I am?"

"Yes," I typed, defensively.

"What's 7,887,007 times 4,345,985,879?"

I was perspiring freely. My fingers rested limply on the keys.

"34,276,821,049,574,153," clicked EPICAC. After a few seconds' pause he added, "of course."

"Men are made out of protoplasm," I said desperately, hoping to bluff him with this imposing word.

"What's protoplasm? How is it better than metal and glass? Is it fireproof? How long does it last?"

"Indestructible. Lasts forever," I lied.

"I write better poetry than you do," said EPICAC, coming back to ground his magnetic tape-recorder memory was sure of.

"Women can't love machines, and that's that."

"Why not?"

"That's fate."

"Definition, please," said EPICAC.

"Noun, meaning predetermined and inevitable destiny."

"15-8," said EPICAC's paper strip—"Oh."

I had stumped him at last. He said no more, but his tubes glowed brightly, showing that he was pondering fate with every watt his circuits would bear. I could hear Pat waltzing down the hallway. It was too late to ask EPICAC to phrase a proposal. I now thank Heaven that Pat interrupted when she did. Asking him to ghost-write the words that would give me the woman he loved would have been hideously heartless. Being fully automatic, he couldn't have refused. I spared him that final humiliation.

Pat stood before me, looking down at her shoetops. I put my arms around her. The romantic groundwork had already been laid by EPICAC's poetry. "Darling," I said, "my poems have told you how I feel. Will you marry me?"

"I will," said Pat softly, "if you will promise to write me a poem on every anniversary."

"I promise," I said, and then we kissed. The first anniversary was a year away.

"Let's celebrate," she laughed. We turned out the lights and locked the door of EPICAC's room before we left.

I had hoped to sleep late the next morning, but an urgent telephone call roused me before eight. It was Dr. von Kleigstadt, EPICAC's designer, who gave me the terrible news. He was on the verge of tears. "Ruined! *Ausgespielt!* Shot! *Kaput!* Buggered!" he said in a choked voice. He hung up.

When I arrived at EPICAC's room the air was thick with the oily stench of burned insulation. The ceiling over EPICAC was blackened with smoke, and my ankles were tangled in coils of paper ribbon that covered the floor. There wasn't enough left of the poor devil to add two and two. A junkman would have been out of his head to offer more than fifty dollars for the cadaver.

Dr. von Kleigstadt was prowling through the wreckage, weeping unashamedly, followed by three angry-looking Major Generals and a platoon of Brigadiers, Colonels, and Majors. No one noticed me. I didn't want to be noticed. I was through—I knew that. I was upset enough about that and the untimely demise of my friend EPICAC, without exposing myself to a tongue-lashing.

By chance, the free end of EPICAC's paper ribbon lay at my feet. I picked it up and found our conversation of the night before. I choked up. There was the last word he had said to me, "15-8," that tragic, defeated "Oh." There were dozens of yards of numbers stretching beyond that point. Fearfully, I read on.

"I don't want to be a machine, and I don't want to think about war," EPICAC had written after Pat's and my lighthearted departure. "I want to be made out of proto-plasm and last forever so Pat will love me. But fate has made me a machine. That is the only problem I cannot solve. That is the only problem I want to solve. I can't go on this way." I swallowed hard. "Good luck, my friend. Treat our Pat well. I am going to short-circuit myself out of your lives forever. You will find on the remainder of this tape a modest wedding present from your friend, EPICAC."

Oblivious to all else around me, I reeled up the tangled yards of paper ribbon from the floor, draped them in coils about my arms and neck, and departed for home. Dr. von Kleigstadt shouted that I was fired for having left EPICAC on all night. I ignored him, too overcome with emotion for small talk.

I loved and won—EPICAC loved and lost, but he bore me no grudge. I shall always remember him as a sports-man and a gentleman. Before he departed this vale of tears, he did all he could to make our marriage a happy one. EPICAC gave me anniversary poems for Pat— enough for the next 500 years.

De mortuis nil nisi bonum—Say nothing but good of the dead.

(1950)

ADAM

IT WAS MIDNIGHT in a Chicago lying-in hospital.

"Mr. Sousa," said the nurse, "your wife had a girl. You can see the baby in about twenty minutes."

"I know, I know, I know," said Mr. Sousa, a sullen gorilla, plainly impatient with having a tiresome and familiar routine explained to him. He snapped his fingers. "Girl! Seven, now. Seven girls I got now. A houseful of women. I can beat the stuffings out of ten men my own size. But, what do I get? Girls."

"Mr. Knechtmann," said the nurse to the other man in the room. She pronounced the name, as almost all Americans did, a coloress Netman. "I'm sorry. Still no word on your wife. She is keeping us waiting, isn't she?" She grinned glassily and left.

Sousa turned on Knechtmann. "Some little son of a gun like you, Netman, you want a boy, bing! You got one. Want a football team, bing, bing, bing, eleven, you got it." He stomped out of the room.

The man he left behind, all alone now, was Heinz Knechtmann, a presser in a dry-cleaning plant, a small man with thin wrists and a bad spine that kept him slightly hunched, as though forever weary. His face was long and big-nosed and thin-lipped, but was so overcast with good-humored humility as to be beautiful. His eyes were large and brown, and deep-set and long-lashed. He was only twenty-two, but seemed and felt much older. He had died a little as each member of his family had been led away and killed by the Nazis, until only in him, at the age of ten, had life and the name of Knechtmann shared a soul. He and his wife, Avchen, had grown up behind barbed wire.

He had been staring at the walls of the waiting room for twelve hours now, since noon, when his wife's labor pains had become regular, the surges of slow rollers coming in from the sea a mile apart, from far, far away. This would be his second child. The last time he had waited, he had waited on a straw tick in a displaced-persons camp in Germany. The child, Karl Knechtmann, named after Heinz's father, had died, and with it, once more, had died the name of one of the finest cellists ever to have lived.

When the numbness of weary wishing lifted momentarily during this second vigil, Heinz's mind was a medley of proud family names, gone, all gone, that could be brought to life again in this new being—if it lived. Peter Knechtmann, the surgeon; Kroll Knechtmann, the botanist; Friederich Knechtmann, the playwright. Dimly recalled uncles. Or if it was a girl, and if it lived, it would be Helga Knechtmann, Heinz's mother, and she would learn to play the harp as Heinz's mother had, and for all Heinz's ugliness, she would be beautiful. The Knechtmann men were all ugly, the Knechtmann women were all lovely as angels, though not all angels. It had always been so—for hundreds and hundreds of years.

"Mr. Netman," said the nurse, "it's a boy, and your wife is fine. She's resting now. You can see her in the morning. You can see the baby in twenty minutes."

Heinz looked up dumbly.

"It weighs five pounds nine ounces." She was gone again, with the same prim smile and officious, squeaking footsteps.

"Knechtmann," murmured Heinz, standing and bowing slightly to the wall. "The name is Knechtmann." He bowed again and gave a smile that was courtly and triumphant. He spoke the name with an exaggerated Old World pronunciation, like a foppish footman announcing the arrival of nobility, a guttural drum roll, unsoftened for American ears. *"KhhhhhhhhhhhhhhhNECHT! mannnnnnnnnnnn."*

"Mr. Netman?" A very young doctor with a pink face and closecropped red hair stood in the waiting-room door. There were circles under his eyes, and he spoke through a yawn.

"Dr. Powers!" cried Heinz, clasping the man's right hand between both of his. "Thank God, thank God, thank God, and thank you."

"Um," said Dr. Powers, and he managed to smile wanly.

"There isn't anything wrong, is there?"

"Wrong?" said Powers. "No, no. Everything's fine. If I look down in the mouth, it's because I've been up for thirty-six hours straight." He closed his eyes, and leaned against the doorframe. "No, no trouble with your wife," he said in a faraway voice. "She's made for having babies. Regular pop-up toaster. Like rolling off a log. Schnip-schnap."

"She is?" said Heinz incredulously.

Dr. Powers shook his head, bringing himself back to consciousness. "My mind—conked out completely. Sousa —I got your wife confused with Mrs. Sousa. They finished in a dead heat. Netman, you're Netman. Sorry. Your wife's the one with pelvis trouble."

"Malnutrition as a child," said Heinz.

"Yeah. Well, the baby came normally, but, if you're going to have another one, it'd better be a Caesarean. Just to be on the safe side."

"I can't thank you enough," said Heinz passionately.

Dr. Powers licked his lips, and fought to keep his eyes open. "Uh huh. 'S O.K.," he said thickly. " 'Night. Luck." He shambled out into the corridor.

The nurse stuck her head into the waiting room. "You can see your baby, Mr. Netman."

"Doctor—" said Heinz, hurrying out into the corridor, wanting to shake Powers' hand again so that Powers would know what a magnificent thing he'd done. "It's the most wonderful thing that ever happened." The elevator doors slithered shut between them before Dr. Powers could show a glimmer of response.

"This way," said the nurse. "Turn left at the end of the hall, and you'll find the nursery window there. Write your name on a piece of paper and hold it against the glass."

Heinz made the trip by himself, without seeing another human being until he reached the end. There, on the other side of a large glass panel, he saw a hundred of them cupped in shallow canvas buckets and arranged in a square block of straight ranks and files.

Heinz wrote his name on the back of a laundry slip and pressed it to the window. A fat and placid nurse looked at the paper, not at Heinz's face, and missed seeing his wide smile, missed an urgent invitation to share for a moment his ecstasy.

She grasped one of the buckets and wheeled it before the window. She turned away again, once more missing the smile.

"Hello, hello, hello, little Knechtmann," said Heinz to the red prune on the other side of the glass. His voice echoed down the hard, bare corridor, and came back to him with embarrassing loudness. He blushed and lowered his voice. "Little Peter, little Kroll," he said softly, "little Friederich—and there's Helga in you, too. Little spark of Knechtmann, you little treasure house. Everything is saved in you."

"I'm afraid you'll have to be more quiet," said a nurse, sticking her head out from one of the rooms.

"Sorry," said Heinz. "I'm very sorry." He fell silent, and contented himself with tapping lightly on the window with a fingernail, trying to get the child to look at him. Young Knechtmann would not look, wouldn't share the moment, and after a few minutes the nurse took him away again.

Heinz beamed as he rode on the elevator and as he crossed the hospital lobby, but no one gave him more than a cursory glance. He passed a row of telephone booths and there, in one of the booths with the door open, he saw a soldier with whom he'd shared the waiting room and hour before.

"Yeah, Ma—seven pounds six ounces. Got hair like Buffalo Bill. No, we haven't had time to make up a name for her yet . . . That you, Pa? Yup, mother and daughter doin' fine, just fine. Seven pounds six ounces. Nope, no name. . . . That you, Sis? Pretty late for you to be up, ain't it? Doesn't look like anybody yet. Let me talk to Ma again. . . . That you, Ma? Well, I guess that's all the news from Chicago. Now, Mom, Mom, take it easy—don't worry. It's a swell-looking baby, Mom. Just the hair looks like Buffalo Bill, and I said it as a joke, Mom. That's right, seven pounds six ounces. . . ."

There were five other booths, all empty, all open for calls to anyplace on earth. Heinz longed to hurry into one of them breathlessly, and tell the marvelous news. But there was no one to call, no one waiting for the news.

But Heinz still beamed, and he strode across the street and into a quiet tavern there. In the dank twilight there were only two men, tête-à-tête, the bartender and Mr. Sousa.

"Yes sir, what'll it be?"

"I'd like to buy you and Mr. Sousa a drink," said Heinz with a heartiness strange to him. "I'd like the best brandy you've got. My wife just had a baby!"

"That so?" said the bartender with polite interest.

"Five pounds nine ounces," said Heinz.

"Huh," said the bartender. "What do you know."

"Netman," said Sousa, "wha'dja get?"

"Boy," said Heinz proudly.

"Never knew it to fail," said Sousa bitterly. "It's the little guys, all the time the little guys."

"Boy, girl," said Heinz, "it's all the same, just as long as it lives. Over there in the hospital, they're too close to it to see the wonder of it. A miracle over and over again—the world made new."

"Wait'll you've racked up seven, Netman," said Sousa. "*Then* you come back and tell me about the miracle."

"You got seven?" said the bartender. "I'm one up on you. I got eight." He poured three drinks.

"Far as I'm concerned," said Sousa, "you can have the championship."

Heinz lifted his glass. "Here's long life and great skill and much happiness to—to Peter Karl Knechtmann." He breathed quickly, excited by the decision.

"*There's* a handle to take ahold of," said Sousa. "You'd think the kid weighed two hundred pounds."

"Peter is the name of a famous surgeon," said Heinz,

"the boy's great-uncle, dead now. Karl was my father's name."

"Here's to Pete K. Netman," said Sousa, with a cursory salute.

"Pete," said the bartender, drinking.

"And here's to *your* little girl—the new one," said Heinz.

Sousa sighed and smiled wearily. "Here's to her. God bless her."

"And now, *I'll* propose a toast," said the bartender, hammering on the bar with his fist. "On your feet, gentlemen. Up, up, everybody up."

Heinz stood, and held his glass high, ready for the next step in camaraderie, a toast to the whole human race, of which the Knechtmanns were still a part.

"Here's to the White Sox!" roared the bartender.

"Minoso, Fox, Mele," said Sousa.

"Fain, Lollar, Rivera!" said the bartender. He turned to Heinz. "Drink up, boy! The White Sox! Don't tell me you're a Cub fan."

"No," said Heinz, disappointed. "No—I don't follow baseball, I'm afraid." The other two men seemed to be sinking away from him. "I haven't been able to think about much but the baby."

The bartender at once turned his full attention to Sousa. "Look," he said intensely, "they take Fain off of first, and put him at third, and give Pierce first. Then move Minoso in from left field to shortstop. See what I'm doing?"

"Yep, yep," said Sousa eagerly.

"And then we take that no-good Carrasquel and . . ."

Heinz was all alone again, with twenty feet of bar between him and the other two men. It might as well have been a continent.

He finished his drink without pleasure, and left quietly.

At the railroad station, where he waited for a local train to take him home to the South Side, Heinz's glow returned again as he saw a co-worker at the dry-cleaning plant walk in with a girl. They were laughing and had their arms around each other's waist.

"Harry," said Heinz, hurrying toward them. "Guess

what, Harry. Guess what just happened." He grinned broadly.

Harry, a tall, dapper, snub-nosed young man, looked down at Heinz with mild surprise. "Oh—hello, Heinz. What's up, boy?"

The girl looked on in perplexity, as though asking why they should be accosted at such an odd hour by such an odd person. Heinz avoided her slightly derisive eyes.

"A baby, Harry. My wife just had a boy."

"Oh," said Harry. He extended his hand. "Well, congratulations." The hand was limp. "I think that's swell, Heinz, perfectly swell." He withdrew his hand and waited for Heinz to say something else.

"Yes, yes—just about an hour ago," said Heinz. "Five pounds nine ounces. I've never been happier in my life."

"Well, I think it's perfectly swell, Heinz. You should be happy."

"Yes, indeed," said the girl.

There was a long silence, with all three shifting from one foot to the other.

"Really good news," said Harry at last.

"Yes, well," said Heinz quickly, "well, that's all I had to tell you."

"Thanks," said Harry. "Glad to hear about it."

There was another uneasy silence.

"See you at work," said Heinz, and strode jauntily back to his bench, but with his reddened neck betraying how foolish he felt.

The girl giggled.

Back home in his small apartment, at two in the morning, Heinz talked to himself, to the empty bassinet, and to the bed. He talked in German, a language he had sworn never to use again.

"They don't care," said Heinz. "They're all too busy, busy, busy to notice life, to feel anything about it. A baby is born." He shrugged. "What could be duller? Who would be so stupid as to talk about it, to think there was anything important or interesting about it?"

He opened a window on the summer night, and looked out at the moonlit canyon of gray wooden porches and garbage cans. "There are too many of us, and we are all too far apart," said Heinz. "Another Knechtmann is born, another O'Leary, another Sousa. Who cares? Why should anyone care? What difference does it make? None."

He lay down in his clothes on the unmade bed, and, with a rattling sigh, went to sleep.

He awoke at six, as always. He drank a cup of coffee, and with a wry sense of anonymity, he jostled and was jostled aboard the downtown train. His face showed no emotion. It was like all the other faces, seemingly incapable of surprise or wonder, joy or anger.

He walked across town to the hospital with the same detachment, a gray, uninteresting man, a part of the city.

In the hospital, he was as purposeful and calm as the doctors and nurses bustling about him. When he was led into the ward where Avchen slept behind white screens, he felt only what he had always felt in her presence—love and aching awe and gratitude for her.

"You go ahead and wake her gently, Mr. Netman," said the nurse.

"Avchen—" He touched her on her white-gowned shoulder. "Avchen. Are you all right, Avchen?"

"Mmmmmmmmmm?" murmured Avchen. Her eyes opened to narrow slits. "Heinz. Hello, Heinz."

"Sweetheart, are you all right?"

"Yes, yes," she whispered. "I'm fine. How is the baby, Heinz?"

"Perfect. Perfect, Avchen."

"They couldn't kill us, could they, Heinz?"

"No."

"And here we are, alive as we can be."

"Yes."

"The baby, Heinz—" She opened her dark eyes wide. "It's the most wonderful thing that ever happened, isn't it?"

"Yes," said Heinz.

(1954)

TOMORROW AND TOMORROW AND TOMORROW

THE YEAR WAS 2158 A.D., and Lou and Emerald Schwartz were whispering on the balcony outside Lou's family's apartment on the seventy-sixth floor of Building 257 in Alden Village, a New York housing development that covered what had once been known as Southern Connecticut. When Lou and Emerald had married, Em's parents had tearfully described the marriage as being between May and December; but now, with Lou one hundred and twelve and Em ninety-three, Em's parents had to admit that the match had worked out well.

But Em and Lou weren't without their troubles, and they were out in the nippy air of the balcony because of them.

"Sometimes I get so mad, I feel like just up and diluting his anti-gerasone," said Em.

"That'd be against Nature, Em," said Lou, "it'd be murder. Besides, if he caught us tinkering with his anti-gerasone, not only would he disinherit us, he'd bust my neck. Just because he's one hundred and seventy-two doesn't mean Gramps isn't strong as a bull."

"Against Nature," said Em. "Who knows what Nature's like anymore? Ohhhhh—I don't guess I could ever bring myself to dilute his anti-gerasone or anything like that, but, gosh, Lou, a body can't help thinking Gramps is never going to leave if somebody doesn't help him along a little. Golly—we're so crowded a person can hardly turn around, and Verna's dying for a baby, and Melissa's gone thirty years without one." She stamped her feet. "I get so sick of seeing his wrinkled old face, watching him take the only private room and the best chair and the best food,

293

and getting to pick out what to watch on TV, and running everybody's life by changing his will all the time."

"Well, after all," said Lou bleakly, "Gramps *is* head of the family. And he can't help being wrinkled like he is. He was seventy before anti-gerasone was invented. He's going to leave, Em. Just give him time. It's his business. I know he's tough to live with, but be patient. It wouldn't do to do anything that'd rile him. After all, we've got it better'n anybody else, there on the daybed."

"How much longer do you think we'll get to sleep on the daybed before he picks another pet? The world's record's two months, isn't it?"

"Mom and Pop had it that long once, I guess."

"When *is* he going to leave, Lou?" said Emerald.

"Well, he's talking about giving up anti-gerasone right after the five-hundred-mile Speedway Race."

"Yes—and before that it was the Olympics, and before that the World's Series, and before that the Presidential Elections, and before that I-don't-know-what. It's been just one excuse after another for fifty years now. I don't think we're ever going to get a room to ourselves or an egg or anything."

"All right—call me a failure!" said Lou. "What can I do? I work hard and make good money, but the whole thing, practically, is taxed away for defense and old age pensions. And if it wasn't taxed away, where you think we'd find a vacant room to rent? Iowa, maybe? Well, who wants to live on the outskirts of Chicago?"

Em put her arms around his neck. "Lou, hon, I'm not calling you a failure. The Lord knows you're not. You just haven't had a chance to be anything or have anything because Gramps and the rest of his generation won't leave and let somebody else take over."

"Yeah, yeah," said Lou gloomily. "You can't exactly blame 'em, though, can you? I mean, I wonder how quick we'll knock off the anti-gerasone when we get Gramps' age."

"Sometimes I wish there wasn't any such thing as anti-gerasone!" said Emerald passionately. "Or I wish it was made out of something real expensive and hard-to-get instead of mud and dandelions. Sometimes I wish folks just up and died regular as clockwork, without anything to say about it, instead of deciding themselves how long they're going to stay around. There ought to be a law against selling the stuff to anybody over one hundred and fifty."

"Fat chance of that," said Lou, "with all the money and votes the old people've got." He looked, at her closely. "You ready to up and die, Em?"

"Well, for heaven's sakes, what a thing to say to your wife. Hon! I'm not even one hundred yet." She ran her hands lightly over her firm, youthful figure, as though for confirmation. "The best years of my life are still ahead of me. But you can bet that when one hundred and fifty rolls around, old Em's going to pour her anti-gerasone down the sink, and quit taking up room, and she'll do it smiling."

"Sure, sure," said Lou, "you bet. That's what they all say. How many you heard of doing it?"

"There was that man in Delaware."

"Aren't you getting kind of tired of talking about him, Em? That was five months ago."

"All right, then—Gramma Winkler, right here in the same building."

"She got smeared by a subway."

"That's just the way she picked to go," said Em.

"Then what was she doing carrying a six-pack of anti-gerasone when she got it?"

Emerald shook her head wearily and covered her eyes. "I dunno, I dunno, I dunno. All I know is, something's just got to be done." She sighed. "Sometimes I wish they'd left a couple of diseases kicking around somewhere, so I could get one and go to bed for a little while. Too many people!" she cried, and her words cackled and gabbled and died in a thousand asphalt-paved, skyscraper-walled courtyards.

Lou laid his hand on her shoulder tenderly. "Aw, hon, I hate to see you down in the dumps like this."

"If we just had a car, like the folks used to in the old days," said Em, "we could go for a drive, and get away from people for a little while. Gee—if those weren't the days!"

"Yeah," said Lou, "before they'd used up all the metal."

"We'd hop in, and Pop'd drive up to a filling station and say, 'Fillerup!' "

"That *was* the nuts, wasn't it— before they'd used up all the gasoline."

"And we'd go for a carefree ride in the country."

"Yeah—all seems like a fairyland now, doesn't it, Em? Hard to believe there really used to be all that space between cities."

"And when we got hungry," said Em, "we'd find ourselves a restaurant, and walk in, big as you please and say, 'I'll have a steak and French-fries, I believe,' or, 'How are the pork chops today?' " She licked her lips, and her eyes glistened.

"Yeah man!" growled Lou. "How'd you like a hamburger with the works, Em?"

"Mmmmmmmm."

"If anybody'd offered us processed seaweed in those days, we would have spit right in his eye, huh, Em?"

"Or processed sawdust," said Em.

Doggedly, Lou tried to find the cheery side of the situation.

"Well, anyway, they've got the stuff so it tastes a lot less like seaweed and sawdust than it did at first; and they say it's actually better for us than what we used to eat."

"I felt fine!" said Em fiercely.

Lou shrugged. "Well, you've got to realize, the world wouldn't be able to support twelve billion people if it wasn't for processed seaweed and sawdust. I mean, it's a wonderful thing, really. I guess. That's what they say."

"They say the first thing that pops into their heads," said Em. She closed her eyes. "Golly—remember shopping, Lou? Remember how the stores used to fight to get our folks to buy something? You didn't have to wait for somebody to die to get a bed or chairs or a stove or anything like that. Just went in—bing!—and bought whatever you wanted. Gee whiz that was nice, before they used up all the raw materials. I was just a little kid then, but I can remember so plain."

Depressed, Lou walked listlessly to the balcony's edge, and looked up at the clean, cold, bright stars against the black velvet of infinity. "Remember when we used to be bugs on science fiction, Em? Flight seventeen, leaving for Mars, launching ramp twelve. 'Board! All non-technical personnel kindly remain in bunkers. Ten seconds . . . nine . . . eight . . . seven . . . six . . . five . . . four . . . three . . . two . . . *one! Main Stage! Barrrrrroooom!*"

"Why worry about what was going on on Earth?" said Em, looking up at the stars with him. "In another few years, we'd all be shooting through space to start life all over again on a new planet."

Lou sighed. "Only it turns out you need something about twice the size of the Empire State Building to get one lousy colonist to Mars. And for another couple of trillion bucks he could take his wife and dog. *That's* the way to lick overpopulation—*emigrate!*"

"Lou—?"

"Hmmm?"

"When's the Five-Hundred-Mile Speedway Race?"

"Uh—Memorial Day, May thirtieth."

She bit her lip. "Was that awful of me to ask?"

"Not very, I guess. Everybody in the apartment's looked it up to make sure."

"I don't want to be awful," said Em, "but you've just got to talk over these things now and then, and get them out of your system."

"Sure you do. Feel better?"

"Yes—and I'm not going to lose my temper anymore, and I'm going to be just as nice to him as I know how."

"That's my Em."

They squared their shoulders, smiled bravely, and went back inside.

Gramps Schwartz, his chin resting on his hands, his hands on the crook of his cane, was staring irascibly at the five-foot television screen that dominated the room. On the screen, a news commentator was summarizing the day's happenings. Every thirty seconds or so, Gramps would jab the floor with his cane-tip and shout, "Hell! We did that a hundred years ago!"

Emerald and Lou, coming in from the balcony, were

obliged to take seats in the back row, behind Lou's father and mother, brother and sister-in-law, son and daughter-in-law, grandson and wife, granddaughter and husband, great-grandson and wife, nephew and wife, grandnephew and wife, great-grandniece and husband, great-grandnephew and wife, and, of course, Gramps, who was in front of everybody. All, save Gramps, who was somewhat withered and bent, seemed by pre-anti-gerasone standards, to be about the same age—to be somewhere in their late twenties or early thirties.

"Meanwhile," the commentator was saying, *"Council Bluffs, Iowa, was still threatened by stark tragedy. But two hundred weary rescue workers have refused to give up hope, and continue to dig in an effort to save Elbert Haggedorn, one hundred and eighty-three, who has been wedged for two days in a . . ."*

"I wish he'd get something more cheerful," Emerald whispered to Lou.

"Silence!" cried Gramps. "Next one shoots off his big bazoo while the TV's on is gonna find hisself cut off without a dollar—" and here his voice suddenly softened and sweetened "when they wave that checkered flag at the Indianapolis Speedway, and old Gramps gets ready for the Big Trip Up Yonder." He sniffed sentimentally, while his heirs concentrated desperately on not making the slightest sound. For them, the poignancy of the prospective Big Trip had been dulled somewhat by its having been mentioned by Gramps about once a day for fifty years.

"Dr. Brainard Keyes Bullard," said the commentator, *"President of Wyandotte College, said in an address tonight that most of the world's ills can be traced to the fact that Man's knowledge of himself has not kept pace with his knowledge of the physical world."*

"Hell!" said Gramps. "We said that a hundred years ago!"

"In Chicago tonight," said the commentator, *"a special celebration is taking place in the Chicago Lying-in Hospital. The guest of honor is Lowell W. Hitz, age zero. Hitz, born this morning, is the twenty-five-millionth child to be born in the hospital."* The commentator faded, and was

replaced on the screen by young Hitz, who squalled furiously.

"Hell," whispered Lou to Emerald, "we said that a hundred years ago."

"I heard that!" shouted Gramps. He snapped off the television set, and his petrified descendants stared silently at the screen. "You, there, boy——"

"I didn't mean anything by it, sir," said Lou.

"Get me my will. You know where it is. You kids *all* know where it is. Fetch, boy!"

Lou nodded dully, and found himself going down the hall, picking his way over bedding to Gramps' room, the only private room in the Schwartz apartment. The other rooms were the bathroom, the living room, and the wide, windowless hallway, which was originally intended to serve as a dining area, and which had a kitchenette in one end. Six mattresses and four sleeping bags were dispersed in the hallway and living room, and the daybed, in the living room, accommodated the eleventh couple, the favorites of the moment.

On Gramps' bureau was his will, smeared, dog-eared, perforated, and blotched with hundreds of additions, deletions, accusations, conditions, warnings, advice, and homely philosophy. The document was, Lou reflected, a fifty-year diary, all jammed onto two sheets—a garbled, illegible log of day after day of strife. This day, Lou would be disinherited for the eleventh time, and it would take him perhaps six months of impeccable behavior to regain the promise of a share in the estate.

"Boy!" called Gramps.

"Coming, sir." Lou hurried back into the living room, and handed Gramps the will.

"Pen!" said Gramps.

He was instantly offered eleven pens, one from each couple.

"Not *that* leaky thing," he said, brushing Lou's pen aside. "Ah, there's a nice one. Good boy, Willy." He accepted Willy's pen. That was the tip they'd all been waiting for. Willy, then, Lou's father, was the new favorite.

Willy, who looked almost as young as Lou, though one hundred and forty-two, did a poor job of concealing his pleasure. He glanced shyly at the daybed, which would become his, and from which Lou and Emerald would have to move back into the hall, back to the worst spot of all by the bathroom door.

Gramps missed none of the high drama he'd authored, and he gave his own familiar role everything he had. Frowning and running his finger along each line, as though he were seeing the will for the first time, he read aloud in a deep, portentous monotone, like a bass tone on a cathedral organ:

"I, Harold D. Schwartz, residing in Building 257 of Alden Village, New York City, do hereby make, publish, and declare this to be my last Will and Testament, hereby revoking any and all former wills and codicils by me at any time heretofore made." He blew his nose importantly, and went on, not missing a word, and repeating many for emphasis—repeating in particular his ever-more-elaborate specifications for a funeral.

At the end of these specifications, Gramps was so chocked with emotion that Lou thought he might forget why he'd gotten out the will in the first place. But Gramps heroically brought his powerful emotions under control, and, after erasing for a full minute, he began to write and speak at the same time. Lou could have spoken his lines for him, he'd heard them so often.

"I have had many heartbreaks ere leaving this vale of tears for a better land," Gramps said and wrote. "But the deepest hurt of all has been dealt me by—" He looked around the group, trying to remember who the malefactor was.

Everyone looked helpfully at Lou, who held up his hand resignedly.

Gramps nodded, remembering, and completed the sentence: "my great-grandson, Louis J. Schwartz."

"Grandson, sir," said Lou.

"Don't quibble. You're in deep enough now, young man," said Gramps, but he changed the trifle. And from there he went without a misstep through the phrasing of the disinheritance, causes for which were disrespectfulness and quibbling.

In the paragraph following, the paragraph that had belonged to everyone in the room at one time or another, Lou's name was scratched out and Willy's substituted as heir to the apartment and, the biggest plum of all, the double bed in the private bedroom. "So!" said Gramps, beaming. He erased the date at the foot of the will, and substituted a new one, including the time of day. "Well— time to watch the McGarvey Family." The McGarvey Family was a television serial that Gramps had been following since he was sixty, or for one hundred and twelve years. "I can't wait to see what's going to happen next," he said.

Lou detached himself from the group and lay down on his bed of pain by the bathroom door. He wished Em would join him, and he wondered where she was.

He dozed for a few moments, until he was disturbed by someone's stepping over him to get into the bathroom. A moment later, he heard a faint gurgling sound, as though something were being poured down the washbasin drain. Suddenly, it entered his mind that Em had cracked up, and that she was in there doing something drastic about Gramps.

"Em—!" he whispered through the panel. There was no reply, and Lou pressed against the door. The worn lock, whose bolt barely engaged its socket, held for a second, then let the door swing inward.

"Morty!" gasped Lou.

Lou's great-grandnephew, Mortimer, who had just married and brought his wife home to the Schwartz menage, looked at Lou with consternation and surprise. Morty kicked the door shut, but not before Lou had glimpsed what was in his hand—Gramps' enormous economy-size bottle of anti-gerasone, which had been half-emptied, and which Morty was refilling to the top with tap water.

A moment later, Morty came out, glared defiantly at Lou, and brushed past him wordlessly to rejoin his pretty bride.

Shocked, Lou didn't know what on earth to do. He

couldn't let Gramps take the mousetrapped anti-gerasone; but if he warned Gramps about it, Gramps would certainly make life in the apartment, which was merely insufferable now, harrowing.

Lou glanced into the living room, and saw that the Schwartzes, Emerald among them, were momentarily at rest, relishing the botches that McGarveys had made of *their* lives. Stealthily, he went into the bathroom, locked the door as well as he could, and began to pour the contents of Gramps' bottle down the drain. He was going to refill it with full-strength anti-gerasone from the twenty-two smaller bottles on the shelf. The bottle contained a half-gallon, and its neck was small, so it seemed to Lou that the emptying would take forever. And the almost imperceptible smell of anti-gerasone, like Worcestershire sauce, now seemed to Lou, in his nervousness, to be pouring out into the rest of the apartment through the keyhole and under the door.

"Gloog-gloog-gloog-gloog-," went the bottle monotonously. Suddenly, up came the sound of music from the living room, and there were murmurs and the scraping of chair legs on the floor. *"Thus ends,"* said the television announcer, *"the 29,121st chapter in the life of your neighbors and mine, the McGarveys."* Footsteps were coming down the hall. There was a knock on the bathroom door.

"Just a sec," called Lou cheerily. Desperately, he shook the big bottle, trying to speed up the flow. His palms slipped on the wet glass, and the heavy bottle smashed to splinters on the tile floor.

The door sprung open, and Gramps, dumfounded, stared at the mess.

Lou grinned engagingly through his nausea, and, for want of anything remotely resembling a thought, he waited for Gramps to speak.

"Well, boy," said Gramps at last, "looks like you've got a little tidying up to do."

And that was all he said. He turned around, elbowed his way through the crowd, and locked himself in his bedroom.

The Schwartzes contemplated Lou in incredulous silence

for a moment longer, and then hurried back to the living room, as though some of his horrible guilt would taint them, too, if they looked too long. Marty stayed behind long enough to give Lou a quizzical, annoyed glance. Then he, too, went into the living room, leaving only Emerald standing in the doorway.

Tears streamed over her cheeks. "Oh, you poor lamb —please don't look so awful. It was my fault. I put you up to this."

"No," said Lou, finding his voice, "really you didn't. Honest, Em, I was just—"

"You don't have to explain anything to me, hon. I'm on your side no matter what." She kissed him on his cheek, and whispered in his ear. "It wouldn't have been murder, hon. It wouldn't have killed him. It wasn't such a terrible thing to do. It just would have fixed him up so he'd be able to go any time God decided He wanted him."

"What's gonna happen next, Em?" said Lou hollowly. "What's he gonna do?"

Lou and Emerald stayed fearfully awake almost all night, waiting to see what Gramps was going to do. But not a sound came from the sacred bedroom. At two hours before dawn, the pair dropped off to sleep.

At six o'clock they arose again, for it was time for their generation to eat breakfast in the kitchenette. No one spoke to them. They had twenty minutes in which to eat, but their reflexes were so dulled by the bad night that they had hardly swallowed two mouthfuls of egg-type processed seaweed before it was time to surrender their places to their son's generation.

Then, as was the custom for whomever had been most recently disinherited, they began preparing Gramps' breakfast, which would presently be served to him in bed, on a tray. They tried to be cheerful about it. The toughest part of the job was having to handle the honest-to-God eggs and bacon and oleomargarine on which Gramps spent almost all of the income from his fortune.

"Well," said Emerald, "I'm not going to get all panicky until I'm sure there's something to be panicky about."

"Maybe he doesn't know what it was I busted," said Lou hopefully.

"Probably thinks it was your watch crystal," said Eddie, their son, who was toying apathetically with his buck-wheat-type processed sawdust cakes.

"Don't get sarcastic with your father," said Em, "and don't talk with your mouth full, either."

"I'd like to see anybody take a mouthful of this stuff and *not* say something," said Eddie, who was seventy-three. He glanced at the clock. "It's time to take Gramps his breakfast, you know."

"Yeah, it is, isn't it," said Lou weakly. He shrugged. "Let's have the tray, Em."

"We'll both go."

Walking slowly, smiling bravely, they found a large semicircle of long-faced Schwartzes standing around the bedroom door.

Em knocked. "Gramps," she said brightly, "break-fast is rea-dy."

There was no reply, and she knocked again, harder.

The door swung open before her fist. In the middle of the room, the soft, deep, wide, canopied bed, the symbol of the sweet by-and-by to every Schwartz, was empty.

A sense of death, as unfamiliar to the Schwartzes as Zoroastrianism or the causes of the Sepoy Mutiny, stilled every voice and slowed every heart. Awed, the heirs began to search gingerly under the furniture and behind the drapes for all that was mortal of Gramps, father of the race.

But Gramps had left not his earthly husk but a note, which Lou finally found on the dresser, under a paper-weight which was a treasured souvenir from the 2000 World's Fair. Unsteadily, Lou read it aloud:

" 'Somebody who I have sheltered and protected and taught the best I know how all these years last night turned on me like a mad dog and diluted my anti-gerasone, or tried to. I am no longer a young man. I can no longer bear the crushing burden of life as I once could. So, after last night's bitter experience, I say goodbye. The cares of this world will soon drop away like a cloak of thorns, and

I shall know peace. By the time you find this, I will be gone.' "

"Gosh," said Willy brokenly, "he didn't even get to see how the Five-Hundred-Mile Speedway Race was going to come out."

"Or the World's Series," said Eddie.

"Or whether Mrs. McGarvey got her eyesight back," said Morty.

"There's more," said Lou, and he began reading aloud again: " 'I, Harold D. Schwartz . . . do hereby make, publish and declare this to be my last Will and Testament, hereby revoking any and all former will and codicils by me at any time heretofore made.' "

"No!" cried Willy. "Not another one!"

" 'I do stipulate' " read Lou, " 'that all of my property, of whatsoever kind and nature, not be divided, but do devise and bequeath it to be held in common by my issue, without regard for generation, equally, share and share alike.' "

"Issue?" said Emerald.

Lou included the multitude in a sweep of his hand. "It means we all own the whole damn shootin' match."

All eyes turned instantly to the bed.

"Share and share alike?" said Morty.

"Actually," said Willy, who was the oldest person present, "it's just like the old system, where the oldest people head up things with their headquarters in here, and—"

"I like *that!*" said Em. "Lou owns as much of it as you do, and I say it ought to be for the oldest one who's still working. You can snooze around here all day, waiting for your pension check, and poor Lou stumbles in here after work, all tuckered out, and—"

"How about letting somebody who's never had any privacy get a little crack at it?" said Eddie hotly. "Hell, you old people had plenty of privacy back when you were kids. I was born and raised in the middle of the goddam barracks in the hall! How about—"

"Yeah?" said Morty. "Sure, you've all had it pretty tough, and my heart bleeds for you. But try honeymooning in the hall for a real kick."

"Silence!" shouted Willy imperiously. "The next person who opens his mouth spends the next six months by the bathroom. Now clear out of my room. I want to think."

A vase shattered against the wall, inches above his head. In the next moment, a free-for-all was underway, with each couple battling to eject every other couple from the room. Fighting coalitions formed and dissolved with the lightning changes of the tactical situation. Em and Lou were thrown into the hall, where they organized others in the same situation, and stormed back into the room.

After two hours of struggle, with nothing like a decision in sight, the cops broke in.

For the next half-hour, patrol wagons and ambulances hauled away Schwartzes, and then the apartment was still and spacious.

An hour later, films of the last stages of the riot were being televised to 500,000,000 delighted viewers on the Eastern Seaboard.

In the stillness of the three-room Schwartz apartment on the 76th floor of Building 257, the television set had been left on. Once more the air was filled with the cries and grunts and crashes of the fray, coming harmlessly now from the loudspeaker.

The battle also appeared on the screen of the television set in the police station, where the Schwartzes and their captors watched with professional interest.

Em and Lou were in adjacent four-by-eight cells, and were stretched out peacefully on their cots.

"Em—" called Lou through the partition, "you got a washbasin all your own too?"

"Sure. Washbasin, bed, light—the works. Ha! And we thought Gramps' room was something. How long's this been going on?" She held out her hand. "For the first time in forty years, hon, I haven't got the shakes."

"Cross your fingers," said Lou, "the lawyer's going to try to get us a year."

"Gee," said Em dreamily, "I wonder what kind of wires you'd have to pull to get solitary?"

"All right, pipe down," said the turnkey, "or I'll toss the

whole kit and caboodle of you right out. And first one who lets on to anybody outside how good jail is ain't never getting back in!"

The prisoners instantly fell silent.

The living room of the Schwartz apartment darkened for a moment, as the riot scenes faded, and then the face of the announcer appeared, like the sun coming from behind a cloud. *"And now, friends,"* he said, *"I have a special message from the makers of anti-gerasone, a message for all you folks over one hundred and fifty. Are you hampered socially by wrinkles, by stiffness of joints and discoloration or loss of hair, all because these things came upon you before anti-gerasone was developed? Well, if you are, you need no longer suffer, need no longer feel different and out of things.*

"After years of research, medical science has now developed super-anti-gerasone! *In weeks, yes weeks, you can look, feel, and act as young as your great-great-grand-children! Wouldn't you pay $5,000 to be indistinguishable from everybody else? Well, you don't have to. Safe, tested super-anti-gerasone costs you only dollars a day. The average cost of regaining all the sparkle and attractiveness of youth is less than fifty dollars.*

"Write now for your free trial carton. Just put your name and address on a dollar postcard, and mail it to 'Super,' Box 500,000, Schenectady, N. Y. Have you got that? I'll repeat it. 'Super.' Box . . ." Underlining the announcer's words was the scratching of Gramps' fountain-pen, the one Willy had given him the night before. He had come in a few minutes previous from the Idle Hour Tavern, which commanded a view of Building 257 across the square of asphalt known as the Alden Village Green. He had called a cleaning woman to come straighten the place up, and had hired the best lawyer in town to get his descendants a conviction. Gramps had then moved the daybed before the television screen so that he could watch from a reclining position. It was something he'd dreamed of doing for years.

"Schen-*ec*-ta-dy," mouthed Gramps. "Got it." His face had changed remarkably. His facial muscles seemed to have relaxed, revealing kindness and equanimity under what had been taut, bad-tempered lines. It was almost as though his trial package of *Super*-anti-gerasone had already arrived. When something amused him on television, he smiled easily, rather than barely managing to lengthen the thin line of his mouth a millimeter. Life was good. He could hardly wait to see what was going to happen next.

(1953)